•• Second edition

D0243691

CAMBRIDGE

Objective

PET

Louise Hashemi
Barbara Thomas

Teacher's Book

CAMBRIDGE LEARNER CORPUS

REAL ENGLISH GUARANTEE

CAMBRIDGE
UNIVERSITY PRESS

CAMBRIDGE UNIVERSITY PRESS
Cambridge, New York, Melbourne, Madrid, Cape Town,
Singapore, São Paulo, Delhi, Mexico city

Cambridge University Press
The Edinburgh Building, Cambridge CB2 8RU, UK

www.cambridge.org
Information on this title: www.cambridge.org/9780521732697

First published 2003
Second edition published 2010
4th printing 2013

Printed and bound in the United Kingdom by the MPG Books Group

A catalogue record for this publication is available from the British Library

ISBN 978-0-521-732680 Student's Book without answers with CD-ROM
ISBN 978-0-521-732666 Student's Book with answers with CD-ROM
ISBN 978-0-521-732697 Teacher's Book
ISBN 978-0-521-732741 Audio CDs (3)
ISBN 978-0-521-732703 Workbook without answers
ISBN 978-0-521-732710 Workbook with answers
ISBN 978-0-521-732727 Self-study pack
ISBN 978-0-521-168274 For Schools Pack without answers
ISBN 978-0-521-15724-7 Classware

Cover concept by Dale Tomlinson and design by David Lawton

Produced by Kamae Design, Oxford

Contents

Photocopiable recording scripts are on the CD-ROM included with *Objective PET Second edition Student's Book* and are available on the website at www.cambridge.org/elt/objectivepet

Map of Objective PET Student's Book

TOPIC	GRAMMAR	FUNCTIONS AND VOCABULARY	PRONUNCIATION	REVISION
Unit 1 **A question of sport** 10–13 Sports and hobbies	Present simple / *to be* + frequency adverbs	Definitions and explanations; *a kind of* + *-ing*/noun; sports; hobbies; expressing attitude	/aɪ/ as in *like* /iː/ as in *steep* /ɪ/ as in *big*	Present simple; the alphabet; *like* + *-ing*
Exam folder 1 14–15 Reading Part 1 Speaking Part 1				
Unit 2 **I'm a friendly person** 16–19 People	*like/enjoy* + *-ing; want / would like* + *to; to be* + *a(n)* + occupation	Describing people: appearance, personality, interests; inviting and responding to invitations	/ɒ/ as in *pop* /ʌ/ as in *fun* /juː/ as in *university*	*have got*
Exam folder 2 20–21 Listening Part 3 **Writing Parts 1, 2 and 3**				
Unit 3 **What's your job?** 22–25 Work	Present simple vs. present continuous (for present actions); state verbs; short answers	Saying what people are doing; jobs	/æ/ as in *cat* /ɑː/ as in *cart* /ʌ/ as in *cut*	Present simple (Unit 1)
Exam folder 3 26–27 Speaking Part 3 Reading Part 5				
Unit 4 **Let's go out** 28–31 Entertainment	Prepositions of time; present continuous for future plans	Entertainment; making appointments; dates	Saying days and months	*would you like* + *to?* (Unit 2); present continuous for present actions (Unit 3)
Exam folder 4 32–33 Listening Part 1 **Writing Part 2**				
Unit 5 **Wheels and wings** 34–37 Transport	*need*; countable and uncountable nouns; expressions of quantity	Transport; airport language; compound nouns	Unstressed *a, of, to* and *some*	Frequency adverbs and present simple (Unit 1); compound nouns from Units 1–4
Exam folder 5 38–39 Reading Part 2				
Unit 6 **What did you do at school today?** 40–43 Education and history	Past simple; short answers; adjectives ending in *-ing* and *-ed*	School life; school subjects; describing feelings and opinions; dates (years and decades)	Final sound of regular verbs in past tense: /t/, /d/ and /ɪd/	Expressing opinions
Exam folder 6 44–45 Listening Part 2 **Writing Part 3**				
Units 1–6 Revision 46–47				
Unit 7 **Around town** 48–51 Towns and buildings	Prepositions of place and movement; comparative adjectives; commands	Places/buildings in towns; directions; polite questions; saying you don't understand	/aʊ/ as in *out* /ɔː/ as in *or*	Adjectives from earlier units; spelling rules
Exam folder 7 52–53 Reading Part 3				
Unit 8 **Let's celebrate** 54–57 Special days	Present perfect simple; *just, already, yet*	Describing experiences and recent activities; celebrations, festivals and parties; giving good wishes	Dates	Dates (Unit 4); talking about pictures (Unit 3); present tenses

MAP OF OBJECTIVE PET STUDENT'S BOOK   5

TOPIC	GRAMMAR	FUNCTIONS AND VOCABULARY	PRONUNCIATION	REVISION
Exam folder 16 108–109 Listening Part 2 **Writing Part 1**				
Unit 17 **Next week's episode** 110–113 Predictions	*will* future; *will* vs. *going to*; *everyone, no one, someone, anyone*	Saying what will happen; TV and radio	/ɑː/ as in *car* /ɔː/ as in *sore* /ɜː/ as in *third*	*need* (Unit 5); telling a story; present continuous for present actions (Unit 3)
Exam folder 17 114–115 Reading Part 4				
Unit 18 **Shooting a film** 116–119 Films	Past perfect; past perfect vs. past simple	Talking about the order of past events; films; telling a story	/ə/ at the end of words	Past simple (Unit 6); giving opinions (Units 2 and 6)
Exam folder 18 120–121 Listening Part 3 **Writing Part 2**				
Units 13–18 Revision 122–123				
Unit 19 **Happy families** 124–127 Family life	Verbs and expressions followed by *to* and *-ing*; *make* and *let*	Families; agreeing and disagreeing; giving opinions	/ð/ as in *their* /θ/ as in *thirsty*	Advice (Unit 9)
Exam folder 19 128–129 Reading Part 5				
Unit 20 **So you think you've got talent?** 130–133 Music	Comparison of adverbs; *so* and *such*; connectives	Music, musical instruments; congratulating; saying what you like and prefer; jobs	Homophones	Comparative adjectives (Unit 7); superlative adjectives (Unit 11)
Exam folder 20 134–135 Listening Part 1 **Writing Part 3**				
Unit 21 **Keep in touch!** 136–139 Communicating	*Have something done*; reported commands and requests; possessive pronouns and adjectives	Making phone calls	Telephone numbers	Present simple (Unit 1); commands (Unit 7); plans (Unit 16)
Exam folder 21 140–141 Reading Part 3				
Unit 22 **Strange but true?** 142–145 The unexplained	Reported speech	Saying what you (don't) believe; reporting verbs; science fiction	Silent consonants	modals: *it could/might/must/ can't be* (Unit 13); present and past tenses; giving opinions, agreeing and disagreeing
Exam folder 22 146–147 Listening Part 4 **Writing Part 1**				
Unit 23 **Best friends?** 148–151 Friendship	Relative clauses; adjectives + prepositions	Friendship; introducing people	Linking words ending in a consonant	Personality adjectives (Units 2 and 6)
Exam folder 23 152–153 Reading Part 1 Speaking Part 2				
Unit 24 **I've got an idea** 154–157 Inventions	Past simple passive; future passive	Describing objects; talking about things you don't know the name of; guessing vocabulary	Linking words ending in *r* and *re*	modals: *it could/might/must/ can't be* (Unit 13); *a kind of* (Unit 1); present simple passive (Unit 11); dates (years) (Units 6 and 14)

TOPIC	GRAMMAR	FUNCTIONS AND VOCABULARY	PRONUNCIATION	REVISION
Exam folder 24 158–159 Listening Part 3 **Writing Part 3**				
Units 19–24 Revision 160–161				
Unit 25 **Shop till you drop** 162–165 Shopping	Reported questions; *too much, too many, not enough*; verbs with two objects	Shops and shopping; asking for things; trying on clothes	Stress: correcting what people say	Reported speech (Unit 22); clothes (Unit 14)
Exam folder 25 166–167 Reading Part 3				
Unit 26 **Persuading people** 168–171 Advertising and persuasion	First conditional; *unless; if* and *when*	Understanding writer or speaker purpose; advertising; reporting verbs	Stress in common short phrases	Making plans (Unit 16); telling a story (Unit 12)
Exam folder 26 172–173 Speaking Parts 1 and 2 **Writing Part 3**				
Unit 27 **Travellers' tales** 174–177 Travel experiences	Adverbs at the beginning of a sentence; reflexive pronouns: *myself, yourself,* etc; *every, each, all*; using the passive	Saying why people do things; travel; word building	/eə/ as in *chair* /ɪə/ as in *here*	Guessing unknown words; present and past simple passive (Units 11 and 24); giving advice (Units 9 and 19)
Exam folder 27 178–179 Reading Part 2				
Unit 28 **What would you do?** 180–183 Celebrities	Second conditional	Jobs; expressions with prepositions	Auxiliaries	Modals: *it could/might/ must/can't be* (Units 13 and 24); agreeing and disagreeing, opinions (Unit 19); *if* and *when* and first conditional (Unit 26)
Exam folder 28 184–185 Listening Part 2 **Writing Part 1**				
Unit 29 **What's on the menu?** 186–189 Food and restaurants	*So do I, Neither/Nor do I*; polite question forms	Asking politely; food; restaurants; apologising	Unstressed words	Reported questions (Unit 25)
Exam folder 29 190–191 Reading Part 4 **Speaking Parts 3 and 4**				
Unit 30 **Blue for a boy, pink for a girl?** 192–195 Boys and girls	*hardly; before/after + -ing*	Informal language; saying goodbye	Revision of /ʌ/, /æ/, /ɒ/, /ɑː/, /aʊ/, /ɔː/, /e/, /eɪ/, /ɪ/, /iː/, /ʊ/, /uː/, /ɜː/, /aɪ/, /eə/	Tenses and vocabulary from previous units
Exam folder 30 196–197 Listening Part 4 Speaking Parts 3 and 4 **Writing Parts 1, 2 and 3**				
Units 25–30 Revision 198–199				

Introduction

Second edition

This new edition of Objective PET is the result of extensive updating and revision in consultation with teachers around the world who have been using the book with their classes.

⊙ For the second edition, the authors have also taken the opportunity to refer frequently to the Cambridge Learner Corpus (CLC), an electronic collection of Cambridge ESOL candidates' scripts from all over the world. Currently containing more than 27 million words of data, around 3 million words of recent candidate writing are added to the CLC each year. This unique resource has given the authors a more accurate and fully up-to-date picture of the strengths and weaknesses of PET candidates. When you see the above icon in the Student's Book, it means that this language area has been identified in the Cambridge Learner Corpus as an area in which learners often need extra practice, and the exercises are based on actual examples taken from the corpus.

Preliminary English Test

Objective PET provides a course for Lower Intermediate students and preparation for the Preliminary English Test (PET), which is administered by the University of Cambridge ESOL Examinations. Its level is based on the Council of Europe Threshold Level and is between the Key English Test (KET) and the First Certificate in English (FCE).

The PET examination consists of three papers – Paper 1 Reading and Writing, Paper 2 Listening and Paper 3 Speaking. There are four grades: Pass with Merit (85% of the total marks); Pass (70%–84%), Narrow Fail (65%–69%), Fail (64% and below). The results slip gives an overall score out of 100 as well as information about how the candidate performed in each paper. For more information about the content of the PET examination, see pages 8–9 of the Student's Book.

Objective PET covers the language required for PET. The main units are designed to provide students with a good general grounding in English at the level and are not exclusively exam-oriented, whereas the Exam folders and Writing folders build on language learnt in the unit to focus on exam skills. Where material in the main units is particularly relevant to PET skills, this is indicated in the Teacher's Book.

Unit structure

Each unit consists of four elements:
Introduction, Reading or Listening, Language Focus (including activities and pronunciation practice) and Exam Folder (with a Writing Folder in alternate units).

- The **Introduction** offers stimulating exercises encouraging students to use and add to language they already know and preparing them for the language and ideas in the rest of the unit.
- The second part of the unit consists alternately of a **Reading** or a **Listening** task with comprehension exercises. These tasks introduce target language in context.
- The third and longest part of the unit is the **Language focus**, which practises the target language in a progression of exercises and activities.
  New features of the second edition include:
  Corpus spots – exercises focusing on typical student errors, with examples from the CLC (see above).
  Grammar spots – interactive summaries of important grammar points which provide a reference for revision as well as a practical teaching aid.
- There is a **Pronunciation** exercise in each unit, focusing on one area which students at this level may find useful to practise. These exercises are offered as a way of raising awareness as well as to practise speaking. PET students are not expected to speak without a foreign accent, but they should be comprehensible to a reasonably patient listener.
- **Exam folders** after each unit progressively develop students' understanding of the reading, listening and speaking tasks in PET. Each folder focuses on one or more parts of the exam, each part being dealt with three times in all, the third time giving students a chance to try an exam-level task.

- There are **Writing folders** after alternate Exam folders covering the three parts of the Writing paper. The exercises practise the skills needed for each task type, progressing to exam level later in the book. Photocopiable sample answers are provided at the back of the Teacher's Book.
- **Revision units** contain a variety of exercises related to the previous six units.
- The **Grammar folder** is a new feature which provides a reference at the back of the book and is cross-referenced in each unit. Contracted forms of verbs are used here and throughout the Student's Book, except in texts where they would be inappropriate. Students should be encouraged to use contracted forms in their speaking and writing for PET.

Suggested lesson timings for each unit:
Introduction: 20 minutes   Main part of the unit: 2 hours   Exam and Writing folders: 40 minutes

Teacher's Book

Answers are provided for all exercises. **Suggested answers** are given where wording or content may vary.

The symbol ◄ appears where the teacher will need to replay the CD track.

There are five photocopiable **Progress tests** which can be used during and at the end of the course to diagnose any language areas requiring further attention.

Photocopiable materials which accompany activities appear at the back of the book. Where materials need photocopying for an activity, there is a reminder at the beginning of the teacher's notes for that unit under **Preparation**.

Photocopiable recording scripts are available for some of the Listening tasks and can be found on both the CD-ROM and the website (see below). The teacher's notes suggest how these can be used in the lesson.

Group work is often suggested in lesson plans. It is occasionally essential (e.g. in some competitive activities). However, in very small or large classes, regular group work may be impractical and whole-class or pair work can be used instead. Suggestions are given where appropriate. The objective is to offer a chance for students to speak and listen as often as possible and the class should be organised to allow this in whichever ways are most suitable.

Workbook

This has been revised and offers further practice in the grammar, vocabulary, pronunciation and exam skills covered in each unit. Some of the new exercises are based on the Cambridge Learner Corpus.

CD-Rom

With the second edition there is a new CD-Rom, which comes with the Student's Book. On the CD-ROM there are 90 exercises, six for each pair of units, giving extra practice in vocabulary, grammar, reading, listening, writing and pronunciation, and there is a new PET Practice Test. There is also an interactive word game and additional resources for both teachers and students, such as wordlists and teaching tips for using these, and photocopiable recording scripts for some of the Listening tasks in the Student's Book. The CD-ROM also contains a number of exercises and illustrations from the Student's Book which can be projected onto a screen for whole class work. The Teacher's Book notes suggest how to use these.

Website

The second edition has a dedicated website: www.cambridge.org/elt/objectivepet. On this website you will find an additional free photocopiable PET Practice Test with audio (different from the test on the CD-ROM), and you will also find the additional resources for teachers and students which are on the CD-ROM: photocopiable wordlists and teaching tips, as well as photocopiable recording scripts for classroom use and a number of exercises and illustrations from the Student's Book, which can be projected onto a screen for whole class work. The website includes a further interactive game (Vocabulary Trainer) to practise vocabulary.

1 A question of sport

In this unit:

Grammar	Present simple and *to be* + frequency adverbs
Functions and vocabulary	Definitions and explanations with *a kind of* + *-ing* or noun; expressing attitude; sports, sports equipment
Pronunciation	/aɪ/ as in *like*; /iː/ as in *steep*; /ɪ/ as in *big*
PET skills	Talking about personal interests (Speaking Part 1); listening for detailed understanding (Listening Part 1); talking about things you don't know the name of (Speaking Part 3); guessing unknown words
Revision	present simple; the alphabet; *like* + *-ing*; spelling aloud (Speaking Part 1)
Exam folder	Reading Part 1; Speaking Part 1

Preparation

Vocabulary spot If you prefer not to draw on the board in class, use the blank vocabulary tree available on the CD-ROM or webpage and project it onto the whiteboard, or use an OHT.

Activity *Free time* Plan which sport or hobby you will use when demonstrating the activity.

SB pages 10–13

Introduction

PET Speaking Part 1

1   Ask students to look at pictures a–o. Invite them to identify some of the sports pictured.

Check that they understand what an anagram is, using the example. Ask them to do the others as quickly as they can and match them to the pictures.

When several students have finished, stop the exercise and ask students to take turns to come up and write the answers on the board. Ask students to say the words aloud when they have written them on the board and make sure their pronunciation is correct.

Point out that the names of sports are not preceded by *the* in English.

You could also use this exercise as an opportunity to check how well students know the alphabet in English.

Correct major errors and draw their attention to the importance of the alphabet – it is a life skill and is tested in Speaking Part 1 and sometimes in Listening Part 3.

Answers
a cycling   b horse riding   c skiing   d basketball
e sailing   f table tennis   g volleyball   h tennis
i gymnastics   j surfing   k windsurfing   l hockey
m football   n rugby   o athletics

2   Ask students to work alone, ticking the statements that are true for them, then invite them to give their opinions, using *like* + *-ing*. Elicit/supply the names of sports or other activities they like doing.

⤵ Corpus spot

Answers
play for ball games (*football, basketball, hockey, rugby, table tennis, tennis, volleyball*)
do for sports which are individual skills (*athletics, gymnastics*)
go for sports ending in *-ing*, which involve travelling from one point to another (*swimming, cycling, horse riding, sailing, skiing, surfing, windsurfing*)

a play   b go   c play   d go   e do

3   Ask students to work in pairs. If they do not have English–English dictionaries, recommend that they get them if possible, for example the *Cambridge Learner's Dictionary*. Where dictionaries are not available, offer definitions yourself when necessary as they do this exercise.

Go through the exercise by saying each word in turn as you write it on the board and asking students to supply the names of the sport(s).

Suggested answers

bike – cycling	bat – table tennis
boat – sailing	board – surfing, windsurfing
net – football (part of goal), hockey, table tennis, tennis, volleyball	helmet – cycling* racket – tennis skis – skiing
sail – sailing, windsurfing	
stick – hockey (**not** skiing – skiers use *poles*)	

*(Note: students may suggest horse riding. If they do, tell them that the term for this is *hard hat*, not *helmet*.)

Listening

1   This task practises guessing unknown words.

Check the answers round the class.

Ask students how they guessed. There are linguistic clues in the names of three of the sports. *Curling* can then be guessed by elimination. Point out that it is often possible to guess the meaning of words and phrases even without pictures to help, because there can be words you already recognise within them.

2   **1 02** This task practises listening for gist.

Ask students to look at the photographs in Exercise 1 and explain that they have to match what they hear to the photographs. Tell them not to worry if they do not understand every word, but just to try and match the speakers and photographs.

Play the four initial statements and check the answers. Discuss what helped them. (See the underlined words for suggestions.) ◀ If they found it difficult, play the recording again, stopping as necessary.

Answers
a speaker 2   b speaker 1   c speaker 4   d speaker 3

Recording script

1   We always wear <u>shorts</u>. We sometimes wear shoes, but I usually have <u>bare feet</u>.
2   We have a board <u>like the board we use for snowboarding</u>, and we use <u>a kind of sail</u>.
3   We use special <u>stones</u> and <u>brushes</u> and we play on <u>ice</u>.
4   You can go up to 45 kph <u>indoors</u>, so you wear a <u>helmet</u>, but it's not very dangerous – really!

PET Listening Part 1

3   **1 03** This task practises listening for details of factual information.

Tell students they are going to hear some more from the same speakers. Ask them to read through the questions and think about the information they need to answer them. They can write their answers during or after listening. They need not write full sentences.

Play the four statements and check the answers.

Recording script

1   We always wear shorts. We sometimes wear shoes, but I usually have bare feet. It's called bossaball. It's a new sport. It's like a kind of volleyball with trampolines. It's fun in the sun and we usually play <u>in the summer</u>.
2   We use <u>special stones and brushes</u> and we play on ice. It's called curling. It's a very old sport. People sometimes say <u>it's a kind of chess on ice</u>. It's exciting and it's quite skilful. We sometimes wear special shoes.
3   <u>You can go up to 45 kph indoors</u>, so you wear a helmet, but it's not very dangerous – really! It's called karting. We use <u>a kind of small racing car</u>. It's got a real engine. Champion racing drivers often begin in them.
4   The weather's very cold and windy in Canada in winter and there's always <u>ice and snow on the lakes and fields</u>. It's called snowfering. <u>We have a board like the board we use for snowboarding, and we use a kind of sail</u>. It's a kind of windsurfing <u>on the snow</u>. It's wonderful.

Elicit the explanation of *a kind of* (*like / one type of*). If necessary, briefly drill the pronunciation of *a kind of*, drawing attention to the weak stress of *a* and *of*.

4   **1 03** This task practises listening for detail in expressions of attitude. Ask students how the speakers feel about their sports. Do they enjoy them?

◀ Ask them to listen again for the adjectives which describe these feelings. Play the four statements and check the answers.

Elicit other words they could use, e.g. *great, pleasant, enjoyable*, and perhaps some negative ones, e.g. *boring, silly, difficult*.

Language focus
a kind of

Language presentation

Discuss the example with the class. *A kind of + -ing*/noun is language which can be used strategically in explanations and definitions to compensate for the necessarily restricted vocabulary of students at this level. It is especially valuable in the Speaking test in PET, and such discourse strategies will be awarded marks when used appropriately.

Point out that we can use a noun or the *-ing* form.

Do the exercise round the class. This could be homework, if time is short.

Answers
b It's a kind of bat.
c It's a kind of surfing on water.
d It's a kind of tennis.
e It's a kind of team game.
f It's a kind of car.
g It's a kind of windsurfing on the snow.

Present simple + frequency adverbs

Direct students to the tables.
Check that they understand the grammatical terms.

Grammar spot   Frequency adverbs

Discuss the answers to the Grammar spot.

Answer
Frequency adverbs go <u>before</u> a main verb but <u>after</u> an auxiliary verb and *to be*.

1 Ask students to write their answers to the exercise individually.

   When they have finished, ask students to read each answer. Let others say whether the adverb is in the correct position and then comment on the choice of adverb (which is a matter of opinion).

Suggested answers
b Cyclists sometimes go very fast.
c Footballers are often very rich.
d Surfers always get wet.
e Gymnasts never wear helmets.
f There are usually two people in a tennis match.
g Good athletes never smoke.

2 Remind students of the rule in the Grammar spot. Practise the examples briefly with the class if necessary. Ask students to work through the exercise orally in pairs.

Corpus spot   Word order

Let the students do the exercise, then discuss the correct versions of the sentences with reference to the tables in their books. Draw particular attention to the negative sentences.

Answers
a She <u>often comes</u> to my house.
b I <u>sometimes meet</u> them in my free time.
c At weddings people <u>are usually</u> happy and have fun together.
d I don't <u>often go</u> to the countryside.
e He <u>doesn't usually</u> make jokes.
f We have a basketball team and we <u>often play</u> against other teams.

3 Ask students to write their answers to the exercise and remind them to make some of the sentences negative.

4 This could be done for homework.

❮❮Pronunciation❯❯

This practises making and distinguishing between the sounds /aɪ/, /iː/ and /ɪ/.
Note: Producing the sound /iː/ is unlikely to cause difficulties, but understanding the ways it can be spelt in English is important, especially as so many languages use *i* to represent the sound. In English, this is normally only the case in words originally from other languages (e.g. visa /viːzə/). There are very few of these at PET level.

1 Write on the board *like*. Elicit the pronunciation. Write /aɪ/ on the board. Model the sound and ask students to repeat it. Tell students about phonetic symbols and, if appropriate, explain that they don't have to know them – they are just an accurate way of showing sounds on paper.

   Write on the board *big*. Elicit the pronunciation. Write /ɪ/ on the board. Model the sound and ask students to repeat it. Remind students that the letter *i* is usually pronounced /aɪ/ or /ɪ/ in English.

   Write on the board *wheel* and *please*. Elicit the pronunciation. Point out that in English different letters can (and often do) sound the same in different words. This sound is /iː/.

2 Ask students to complete the table in their books.

3 **1 04** Play the recording for them to check their answers. Check answers by getting individual students to read out a word, and make a list on the board according to what they say. The class can correct any errors as you do this.

Answers

/aɪ/	/iː/	/ɪ/
quite	*steep*	*hill*
like	field	little
kind	knee	stick
ice	people	big
line	street	rich
ride	wheel	
bike	team	

Recording script

steep quite hill field like knee kind people ice little stick line big street ride rich wheel bike team

4 Elicit the four different spellings of /iː/: *ee ie eo ea*. Ask students to note them. When they see new words with these spellings, remind them to think about the pronunciation.

«Activity» Free time

1 This exercise is preparation for a game in the next exercise (Exercise 2). If your students are not used to this sort of activity, you may like to do a demonstration with three students to show them what to do (see Preparation).

If you think your students will tend to choose the same sports (or hobbies), you can allocate different ones to each pair. To add a more competitive element, you can say that the winners will be the pair whose sport requires the largest number of questions to be asked before it is guessed. To demonstrate this, think of a sport or hobby yourself and get students to ask you questions about it.

Tell students to make sure no one but their partner knows what they are writing about. Ask them to write as many facts as they can in a given time (e.g. four minutes).

2 Ask students to work with another pair. If some pairs have chosen hobbies rather than sports, they must tell the other pair before they begin. They should answer *Yes* or *No* or give the facts they are asked for, but no other clues. If they cannot answer a question, they should say *We don't know*.

When a sport or hobby has been guessed, the pairs change roles, so that the other pair asks questions.

When they have finished, students should look at the facts each pair wrote in Exercise 1 to see if they are about the same things as the questions they asked.

Vocabulary spot   Word tree

See Preparation. This task is useful consolidation of the Activity above.

If students have not met vocabulary trees before, point out how the words are grouped on the example and explain that this can help you to remember words because you can make a picture of the tree in your head and visualise the words in position.

Using the board, an OHT or a large piece of paper, demonstrate filling in a blank tree with the class. Then ask them to work out their own tree for a sport or hobby they are interested in, so that they have a record of important words that they need to talk about it. This could be homework, if time is short. Alternatively, students could work in small groups producing shared trees to display round the class.

«Activity» Make a poster

This exercise (or the preparation for it) could be homework, if time is short. If appropriate, the posters can be displayed in the classroom. Where accessible, websites, magazines, etc. could be used for pictures and information. Insist that all the wording the students use is their own.

Exam folder 1

SB pages 14–15

Reading Part 1

This Exam folder is at a lower level than the exam but gives students an introduction to the type of task they will find in the exam.

1   Ask the class to look at the texts, but not to read them just yet.

 If necessary, explain the vocabulary *email*, *text message*, *Post-it note*, *telephone message* and *notice*, and ask students to guess which is which. Do not indicate whether they are correct at this stage.

2   Ask students to read the five texts and decide whether their guesses were correct. Check their answers and ask what clues the texts contained. Draw attention to the Exam Advice box.

Answers
1   email (the typeface and layout suggest an email)
2   notice (the style shows that this is a notice and the words suggest it is for anyone to read)
3   text message (the typeface and layout suggest a text message)
4   telephone message (the word *phone*)
5   Post-it note (*Here's ...* means the note is stuck to something, e.g. a leaflet)

3   Check that students understand what they have to do.

 Go through the question and elicit the words about Maria and her friends in the email in Exercise 1 (*my friends and I eat in the park*). Does *the park* mean the same as *outdoors*?

 Elicit the words about the café (*always crowded*) and the changing room (*small and dirty*) and check that they understand that these words do not mean that Maria likes the café or the changing room.

4   Ask students to find the answers to the questions for the other texts. Suggest that underlining the words which help them is a good idea. Go through the answers, asking which words contain the information.

Answers
2   B   3   A   4   C   5   A

Speaking Part 1

1   Ask students to make some questions to ask Pablo and Cristina, using the prompts provided. Supply/elicit suitable questions, e.g.
 Where do you come from?
 Where do you live? How old are you?
 What do you like doing?
 Practise briefly with the class as necessary.

2   Read the texts with the class and teach any vocabulary as necessary. Get them to find the answers to the questions they prepared in Exercise 1.

3   Ask students to work in pairs, asking and answering as Pablo and Cristina.

 Note: In the PET Speaking test, students will be asked these kinds of question by the examiner, not the other student. It is important that students understand the questions, and saying them reinforces this.

4   Draw students' attention to the Exam Advice box. Ask them to think about the answers they need to give for themselves. Teach any necessary language, e.g. their nationality in English.

5   Students practise answering as themselves.

6   Ask students to write a short text about themselves which answers the questions they practised in Exercises 1 and 3.

 Draw students' attention to the two uses of the word *text* current in English – i.e. short for *text message* (SMS) or meaning a piece of written language.

2 I'm a friendly person

TOPIC: Meeting and describing people

In this unit:	
Grammar	*like/enjoy* + *-ing*; *want / would like* + *to* infinitive; *to be* + *a(n) ...*
Functions and vocabulary	Describing people: appearance, personality, interests; inviting and responding to simple invitations
Pronunciation	/ɒ/ as in *pop*; /ʌ/ as in *fun*; /juː/ as in *university*
PET skills	Introduction to multiple-choice format; talking about your interests (Speaking Parts 1 and 2)
Revision	*have got*
Exam folder	Listening Part 3
Writing folder	Writing Parts 1, 2 and 3

Preparation

Introduction, Exercise 4 If appropriate, bring blank pieces of paper to class so that students' work cannot be identified by the paper it is written on.

Exam folder 2 Make copies of the recording scripts (from CD-ROM or webpage) for students.

Writing folder Make OHTs of Exercises 1, 3 and 4, or project them from the CD-ROM or webpage, so that the answers can be marked on them when you go through the exercises with the class. Have coloured markers available, if possible.

SB pages 16–19

Introduction

1 This task practises describing people's appearance and area of study.

Language presentation

Read the instructions and talk about the people on the website. Elicit the structures *to be* for age (*He's 17*) and *to be* + *a(n)* for occupation (*She's a business student*).

Remind students how we ask about appearance (*What does X look like?*) and practise briefly. Elicit some of the vocabulary underlined in the recording script in preparation for Exercise 2.

2 **1 05** Play the recording and check answers with students.

Answers
a Stefan **b** Mike **c** Mandana **d** Julia
e Kurt (not heard) **f** Anastasia (not heard)

Recording script

Stefan: Hello, Mandana?
Mandana: Yes. Is that Stefan?
Stefan: Yes, I'm meeting you this afternoon. What do you look like?
Mandana: Oh, well, I've got short dark hair and dark eyes. I'm average height. What about you?
Stefan: Right, er, I'm not very tall, but I'm broad-shouldered and I've got blue eyes. My hair is fair and it's quite short and curly.

Julia: Hi Mike, this is Julia. I'm meeting you at the coach station tomorrow.
Mike: Oh, right. What do you look like?
Julia: Well, I'm slim, and I've got fair hair. It's wavy and shoulder-length. I've got green eyes. And you?
Mike: Er, I'm tall, with short dark hair and I've got a moustache.
Julia: OK. See you tomorrow.

Language presentation

Go through the table of basic structures used in describing people (*to be* + *tall, slim,* etc., *to have (got)* + *dark hair / blue eyes,* etc. or *with* + *dark hair / blue eyes,* etc.).

3 Practise briefly round the class, then students practise in pairs.

4 If you have prepared them, hand out blank pieces of paper to students. Invite students to check with you if they need specific vocabulary (e.g. *red hair*) as they work, and list all the extra words on the board so that the class can note them after they have guessed who each description applies to. With a large class, divide students into two or three groups. Alternatively, students could complete the notes for homework and you could then use the guessing game as a revision exercise next lesson.

⬇ Corpus spot   Describing people

Confirm the correct answers with the class.

Answers
a She is tall and slim.
b He's got short fair hair.

Reading

These exercises are about describing people's personality and interests.

1   Check that students understand the meaning of the words *Travel*, *Contacts* and *Accommodation*. Ask them to read the notices as quickly as possible and label them.

Check the answers with the class, discussing which parts of the texts gave them clues.

> **Answers**
> 2 Travel   3 Accommodation   4 Contacts
> 5 Travel   6 Accommodation

2   Complete the answers for question **a** with the class, then let them work alone or in pairs. Explain new language as you go through the answers.

Answers

Who	Elena	Adrian	Carola	Henry	Sandra	Maggie
a knows what job he/she wants in the future?	✓				✓	
b has a part-time job now?	✓					
c offers to pay for something?	✓		✓			
d wants to go to another part of the world?		✓				
e wants to find somewhere to live?			✓			
f enjoys sport?		✓		✓		
g likes quiet hobbies?						✓

3   Encourage a short class discussion so that students can practise the language in the texts by using it to justify their answers.

Language focus

Personality

1   Direct students to the question at the top of the quiz: *What kind of person are you?* Elicit the meaning of *kind of* (see Unit 1). This is an opportunity to introduce students to multiple-choice questions if they have not encountered them before and point out that PET Reading Parts 1, 4 and 5 and Listening Parts 1 and 2 use multiple-choice questions.

Ask students to work in pairs, noting their partner's answers. Elicit/supply definitions of new vocabulary as necessary. When they have finished, direct them to the results on page 19.

> **Language presentation**
> The meaning of *want* and *would like* is the same, but *would like* sounds less certain and is therefore more polite. *Would like* is extremely widely used in English. Suggest that if in doubt, students should use *would like*. If necessary, also remind students that *would* is usually contracted in positive statements.

If students know each other well enough, ask them to read out the result for their partner to the rest of the class and let the class enjoy commenting on its accuracy or otherwise. If students don't know each other, let them comment on their own results. Reassure students, if necessary, that this is not a serious psychological test!

like, enjoy, want, would like and *have got*

> **⊗ Grammar spot**
> Tell students that the structures are exemplified in the quiz.
>
> > **Answers**
> > **a** going   **b** going   **c** to go   **d** to go
> >
> > Note that *like* can of course be followed by the *to* infinitive in certain contexts which students will meet at a more advanced level.

1   This could be homework. Ask students to write their answers and go through them with the class.

> **Answers**
> **b** Would   like   likes
> **c** have   got   haven't got
> **d** Does   like   's/has got
> **e** do   like   like
> **f** Would   like   don't like
> **g** 'd/would like   likes
> **h** 'd/would like   have   got   haven't got

2   It may be useful to do a sample with the whole class first, eliciting suggestions to demonstrate how they can use phrases from the texts on page 17 to write their own notice.

If appropriate, ask students to write their notices out on pieces of paper and display them on a noticeboard in the classroom. You could ask them to choose a notice to write a response to for homework.

«Pronunciation»

This practises making and distinguishing between the sounds /ɒ/, /ʌ/ and /juː/.

1 Elicit/supply the three sounds /ɒ/, /ʌ/ and /juː/ exemplified by the sentence *Stop studying, students!* and practise them briefly with the class.

2 Students could do this exercise in pairs or small groups. You may need to point out that some words contain sounds other than /ɒ/, /ʌ/ and /juː/.

3 **1 06** Play the recording for them to check their answers before going through them on the board.

Answers		
/juː/	/ʌ/	/ɒ/
university music Tuesday you future	*fun* become some other club above discuss	*pop* long doctor want cost

Recording script

university fun pop music become some Tuesday other club long you above doctor discuss want cost future

4 **1 07** Ask students to underline the targèt sounds before playing the recording for them to listen and repeat.

Answers
/juː/ is heard in *university, students, music*
/ʌ/ is heard in *become, some, fun, run, club, above, other, brother*
/ɒ/ is heard in *want, doctor, lot, shop, got, long*

Recording script

I <u>want</u> to <u>become</u> a <u>doctor</u>.
<u>Some</u> university students have a <u>lot</u> of <u>fun</u>.
I <u>run</u> a <u>music club above</u> a <u>shop</u>.
His <u>other brother</u>'s <u>got long</u> hair.

PET Speaking Parts 1 and 2

«Activity» Invitations and replies

1 Remind students of the sports or hobbies they talked about in Unit 1 and of any other free-time activities mentioned in this unit. If necessary, revise the use of the noun or *-ing* form after *I like*.

2 Briefly practise the target language with the class.

If possible, let students walk around talking to each other; otherwise let them talk to the five or six students sitting nearest them.

At the end, ask who has found someone to spend some free time with at the weekend. An extension of this language will be practised in Unit 16.

«Activity» What kind of person?

Students can work in pairs or threes. Make sure they choose a character, not an actor. Remind them of the descriptions in the Quiz results and that they are to write about personality, not appearance.

If appropriate, choose a character known to all and write a model description together.

Students can write their descriptions for homework and compare in class.

Exam folder 2

SB pages 20–21

Listening Part 3

This Exam folder gives students an introduction to the task. Students practise listening for specific information and should not worry that they cannot understand everything.

1 Tell students they are going to hear a student called Dan talking about how he usually spends his day. Ask them to look at the pictures and tell you what Dan does every day. Make sure they use the present simple for routines.

Elicit/supply vocabulary from the listening (see recording script), e.g. *gym, lectures, canteen* and *match*.

2 **1 08** This listening task gives students a chance to practise looking at notes on the page and listening to something slightly different which means the same.

Direct students to the second picture and say *Dan goes to the gym every day*. Indicate the picture of Dan cycling. Ask *How does he get there?* Elicit and write on the board the two ways of saying this: *He cycles to the gym. He goes to the gym by bike (or bicycle)*. Remind students that there is often more than one way of saying the same thing.

Tell students to do the exercise while they listen. Play the recording. ◀ Replay as necessary.

Answers
b I have a huge breakfast at about <u>half past eight</u>.
c <u>I'm studying</u> geography.
d I usually study in my room <u>in the afternoon</u>.
e I <u>enjoy</u> spending time with my friends.
f I <u>would like</u> to travel round the world.

Recording script

Dan: My name is Dan Jones and I'm a third-year student at Southgate University. My days are really busy because my hobby is tennis and I play in national matches, so I have to practise a lot.

My day begins at 6 am. I get up and go straight to the gym before breakfast. <u>I always go there by bicycle</u> because the fresh air wakes me up. After an hour or so I come back to the university and then <u>I have a huge breakfast at about eight thirty</u>. Oh, I always have a shower of course before breakfast or nobody would sit next to me! From 9.30 until 1.00, I go to lectures. <u>My subject is geography</u>.

Then all the students have lunch together in the canteen at 1 o'clock. <u>I usually study in my room after lunch</u> – that is, except for one afternoon a week, when we play matches, sometimes against another university. They're always on Wednesday afternoons. In the evenings <u>I like spending time with my friends</u> – we sometimes go to the cinema or to a disco. When I leave university next year, <u>I want to travel round the world</u>.

3 ▸1 08 ◀ Give out the photocopied recording scripts (see Preparation) and play the recording again while students follow. Ask some comprehension questions and check vocabulary, but remind students that they do not need to understand everything.

4 Do the first one together: *go there by bicycle*.

Students do the others, then check their answers (see underlining in the recording script).

Answers
b eight thirty   c My subject is   d after lunch
e like   f want

5 Look at the pictures together and talk about what Katy does every day. Some things are the same as Dan and some are different. Ask *How does Katy get to the gym?* and elicit *on foot / she walks*. Ask *Do you think she studies geography like Dan?* and elicit the names of some science subjects and the word *laboratory*. Establish that her sport is football.

6 ▸1 09 Tell students to listen and fill in the spaces. Don't go through the answers yet.

Play the recording. ◀ Replay as necessary.

Recording script

Katy: My name is Katy Williamson and I'm a student at Southgate University. I'm the captain of the university women's football team. Women's football is becoming more and more popular and the team is really busy playing matches all over the country.

I get up at 6 am and at 6.30 I go to the <u>gym</u>. I always walk. I usually spend about an hour there and I walk back to the university and have a huge breakfast in the student canteen at <u>about a quarter past eight</u>. I meet all my friends there, so breakfast sometimes takes a long time. Lectures are from 10 o'clock until about 1. I'm studying <u>biology</u>, so I spend quite a lot of time in the laboratories.

I usually have lunch in the canteen but I sometimes go to a café over the road. After lunch I usually study in the <u>library</u>. There's sometimes football practice between 5 and 6, so I have to work hard to finish all my work before then. We play matches against other university women's teams on <u>Friday</u> afternoons, so I have to make sure I'm always free then. Then I have my evening meal – usually in the canteen because it's cheaper there. In the evenings I like <u>watching TV</u> – I'm usually too tired to do anything else. And I go to bed really early, about 10.

When I leave university next year, I want to be a <u>nurse</u>, but I'll continue playing football as a hobby because I love it.

7 ▸1 09 Give out the photocopied recording scripts (see Preparation). ◀ Play the recording again and check the answers. Discuss any other vocabulary. Remind students that they do not need to understand everything in order to answer the questions.

Answers
1 gym   2 8.15 / (a) quarter past eight   3 biology
4 library   5 Friday   6 watching TV   7 nurse

Look at the Exam Advice box together. In Listening Part 3, the words in the notes are not usually exactly the same as the words on the recording. Students must be able to recognise the prompt, even if they don't hear the actual words, so they are ready to write down the missing word(s).

Writing folder

Writing Parts 1, 2 and 3

1   Ask students to work through the exercise in pairs, then project or use the OHT or poster (see Preparation) to go through it together. Draw attention to the Exam Advice.

Only go into detail on questions **f** and **g** if your students are already used to English punctuation.

> **Answers**
> **a** There are ten. We use them at the beginning of sentences, for someone's name and for the pronoun '*I*'. They are also used for place names, days of the week and months.
> **b** To show the beginning and end of each piece of spoken language. These could also be double (" ").
> **c** There are four. Three replace missing letters. (In speech and informal written English, these forms are correct. PET students can use them throughout the exam as they are not expected to use formal written English, but they should understand which letters they replace, for grammatical reasons.) One is used to show possession. There is no letter missing.
> **d** With a full stop.
> **e** At the end of a question.
> **f** Between the two halves of a sentence, especially before words like *but* and *so*, but not usually before *and* or *that*; between items in lists, until the last item which is preceded by *and*; in addresses and at the beginning and end of letters (although in the PET exam students would not lose marks for omitting these). Commas are mentioned in later units when they are important (e.g. conditional sentences in Unit 26).
> **g** The only other punctuation mark PET students may want to use is the exclamation mark. Make sure that they understand that in English it is always at the end of a sentence. It normally denotes surprise or humour or excitement and loses force if overused.
> Students may meet colons, semicolons and dashes in printed texts, dialogues, lists, etc. but they do not need to use them.

2   Teach/revise the position of the apostrophe, which depends on the number of possessors, not the number of things possessed, e.g. *my sister's books*, *the student's car* (singular possessor); *my sisters' books*, *the students' car* (plural possessor). Teach/revise also the irregular plural possessives *people's houses* and *children's room*.

3   This exercise focuses on apostrophes and capital letters. Let students do this exercise individually, then go through it with the class, projecting it if possible. When going through the answers, point out that *Dad*, *Uncle Ian* and *National Gallery* are names and start with capital letters, but *my uncle*, *my father* and *a museum* are not.

> **Answers**
> **a** My brother and I usually watch football matches at my grandparents' flat because their television's very big.
> **b** On Thursday I'm going to the match between Italy and Scotland with Dad and Uncle Ian.
> **c** We're travelling in my uncle's car to Edinburgh and after the match, we're staying at the Norton Hotel.
> **d** Then on Friday morning my uncle and I are visiting Edinburgh Castle and my father's going to the National Gallery and a museum.

4   Let students make corrections individually (this could be homework, if time is short) and then go through it with the class, if possible projecting it and correcting it together.

Draw students' attention to the commas after *Pia* and *With love*.

An exclamation mark can be used to emphasise that Andy is excited about the new club.

> Dear Pia,
> How are you? I must tell you about a new club in my town./! It's in Oxford Road and I think you'd love it. We can play tennis and go swimming and there's a small gym. I made a new friend there last Sunday. Her name's Jessica. She's from Canada and she's got blonde hair and she makes me laugh. She's a good dancer too. I hope you can come here soon and meet her.
> With love,
> Andy

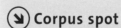 **Corpus spot**   Irregular plurals

Revise irregular plurals.
Persons exists, but is only used in formal written contexts, so not relevant to PET students.
If there is time, you could ask students if they can think of any other words like these, e.g. *man/men*; *tax/taxes*; *mouse/mice*; *wife/wives* and mention *sheep/sheep*, which does not change.

> **Answers**
> **a** In my country, all the <u>women</u> wear new clothes at weddings.
> **b** I like the London streets with their red telephone <u>boxes</u>.
> **c** There are a lot of friendly <u>people</u> at the club.
> **d** I look after the <u>children</u> when their parents are working.
> **e** During the break we talk about our <u>lives</u> and our friends.

3 What's your job?

TOPIC: Work

In this unit:

Grammar	Present simple versus present continuous; state verbs; short answers
Functions and vocabulary	Saying what people are doing; jobs
Pronunciation	/æ/ as in *cat*; /ɑː/ as in *cart*; /ʌ/ as in *cut*
PET skills	Talking about a picture (Speaking Part 3); talking about the job you do / would like (Speaking Part 1)
Revision	Present simple (Unit 1)
Exam folder	Speaking Part 3; Reading Part 5

Preparation

Listening If possible, project the image from the CD-ROM or webpage or make an OHT or enlarged photocopy of the picture to display and point to, rather than having to hold up the book.

Activity *Spot the difference* You can project the CD-ROM or webpage image and also the image from the Listening above.

SB pages 22–25

Introduction

1 **1 10** This exercise practises present simple for habitual actions.

Ask students to look at the photographs and think about the people's jobs. Say that they are going to hear the people talking about things they do in their jobs and ask them to match the speakers to the photographs.

Play the recording.

Language presentation

Ask if the photographs show the activities that the people spoke about. Elicit/supply that the speakers were talking generally about what they do in their jobs (present simple), not what they are doing in the photographs (present continuous).

Write a few examples on the board, e.g. *He cuts people's hair. He sells cars and vans.* (Add any that they found difficult to understand.) Leave the examples on the board for Exercise 3.

Students should have met this basic distinction between present simple and continuous before, although they may not always get it right.

Answers
a speaker 3   b speaker 1   c speaker 6   d speaker 5
e speaker 7   f speaker 4   g speaker 2

Recording script

1 I look after the passengers on an aeroplane.
2 I design roads and bridges.
3 I help people in a fashion shop.
4 I cut people's hair.
5 I mend engines and change tyres.
6 I sell cars and vans.
7 I design websites.

2 This exercise practises present simple for occupations. Elicit/supply the names of the occupations shown.

Briefly practise the forms *What does he/she do? What do you do?* making sure that students understand that this is how you ask what someone's occupation is in English.

Remind them to use *a/an* before the name of the job.

Answers
a shop assistant   b flight attendant   c (car) salesperson
d mechanic   e website designer   f hairdresser
g engineer

3 This exercise practises present continuous for present actions.

Ask students to look at the photographs again. Ask what the people are doing in the photographs. Direct students to the table to help them form the present continuous correctly.

Write some of the students' suggestions in present continuous sentences next to the examples you wrote on the board for Exercise 1, e.g. *The hairdresser's showing a woman her new haircut. The salesperson is working at his computer.*

Suggested answers
a The shop assistant's tidying some clothes.
b The flight attendant is bringing the pilot some food.
c The salesperson's working at his computer.
d The mechanic's having a break.
e The website designer's plugging in her computer.
f The hairdresser's holding a mirror.
g The engineer's looking at a plan.

4   Invite students to discuss which jobs they would like or not like to do and encourage them to say why, as far as they can.

Listening

1   See Preparation. This exercise practises present continuous for present actions.

Elicit from the class what all the people are doing, by pointing to the individuals in the picture as you ask *What's he doing?* (for example, pointing to journalist) *He's writing in a notebook*, etc.

Invite the class to guess the occupations of the people (e.g. *She's a model*). Do not say whether or not they are correct, as this comes up in the listening (see below).

2   **1 11** This exercise practises listening for gist.

Ask students to listen to the recording and answer the questions. Tell them not to worry about anything they do not understand.

Answers
He is a security officer in a shopping mall.
He's talking to a police officer.

Recording script

Security officer: Grand City Mall. Security.

Police officer: Hello, Security? This the police. We have a report that there's a thief in the shopping mall.

Security officer: Oh, yeah? What kind of a thief?

PO: A shoplifter. Someone who steals clothes and things from shops. Can you see anyone? Does anyone look like a thief?

SO: I can see … oh, about six people on the security cameras. And you.

PO: Oh. Well, one of the others is a criminal. Does one of them look like a criminal? Is one of them carrying a big bag?

SO: Er, no. I can tell you what they're doing.

PO: OK. Go ahead.

SO: Well, first, there's a woman. She's painting a picture of a child. She's got a box.

PO: A big box?

SO: No, no. A box of paints. She's an <u>artist</u>. She paints pictures of the children and sells them to their parents. I know her. Then, there's a young woman. She's standing near the fountain. A man is taking a photograph of her. He's got a case.

PO: Is it a big case?

SO: Yeah, but the case has got different cameras in it. He's a fashion <u>photographer</u> and she's a <u>model</u>. He takes photos all the time and sells them to magazines.

PO: OK. So – anyone else?

SO: There's another man. He's standing outside a shop. He's holding a notebook. He's looking up and down the mall and he's writing something in his notebook.

PO: Does he look like a thief?

SO: No, he's not a thief. He's a <u>journalist</u>. He often walks round to see what news he can find. He always writes everything in his notebook.

PO: Is that all you can see?

SO: There's the <u>bank guard</u>. He's standing near the door of the bank.

PO: He's not a thief!

SO: Probably not. I know him. He's too lazy. He never does anything.

PO: Isn't there anyone else?

SO: The only other person I can see now is a woman with short grey hair. I don't know her but she doesn't look like a thief.

PO: Short grey hair? Aha! What's she doing?

SO: She's walking through the mall.

PO: Is she carrying a big bag?

SO: No, she isn't *carrying* a big bag.

PO: Oh.

SO: But she's pulling a shopping bag on wheels. It's quite big.

PO: That's her! She looks like a housewife. She steals things and puts them in the bag. Everyone thinks she's got shopping in it. OK, watch her carefully. I'm coming to arrest her.

---

3   This exercise practises listening for detail.

1 11 ◄ Play the recording again. Check students' answers and discuss any comprehension problems. *Thief* is not one of the jobs, nor is *housewife*.

Answers
1 artist   2 photographer   3 model
4 journalist   5 bank guard

Language focus

Present simple and present continuous

Language presentation

Ask questions about the people in the picture, using the forms *What does he/she do?* and *What is he/she doing?*

Draw attention to the contrast between *She paints pictures* (it's her job, or it's something she often does, but not necessarily now) and *She's painting a picture* (she's doing it now).

Ask students to write their answers and check them round the class.

Answers
b is standing   **c** sells   **d** is pulling   **e** steals
f isn't looking   **g** does   **h** is taking   **i** sells
j isn't stealing   **k** is writing

 Grammar spot

Present simple and present continuous
Revise the rules with the class.

Answers
We use the *present simple* to talk about what we usually do.
We use the *present continuous* to talk about what we're doing now.

2   This exercise introduces present simple for habit versus present continuous for a temporary situation.

Language presentation

Say *Sonia is a schoolgirl. What does Sonia usually do or not do?* Elicit/Supply answers using the relevant prompts: *She cycles to school. She does lessons all day.*

Point out that Sonia is doing some things this week which she doesn't usually do. Ask *What is Sonia doing or not doing this week?* Elicit/Supply answers using the relevant prompts: *She isn't going to school*, etc. (You may wish to explain that this is a different use of the present continuous from that practised in the Introduction and Listening because she isn't doing these things *right now*, but *now*, i.e. *this week*, in contrast to *usually*.)

Ask students to write the rest of the answers.

Answers
usually
She does lessons all day.
She studies at home in the evening.
She plays volleyball after school.
She doesn't wear her best skirt every day.

this week only
She isn't doing any homework.
She's working in a hotel.
She's having meals with her colleagues.
She's speaking French with hotel guests.

3   **1 12** This exercise practises present tenses and state verbs. Students could work in pairs.

Answers
b 'm doing   **c** 'm working   **d** aren't/'re not working
e 'm helping   **f** like   **g** prefer   **h** are staying
i understand   **j** get up   **k** 'm starting
l 'm looking forward to

Play the recording for students to check their answers. Draw attention to the state verbs. Explain or remind students that certain verbs such as *like, prefer, understand* cannot be used in the present continuous.

Recording script

Sonia: Hi, Granny. How are you?
Granny: Oh, not bad. How's school?
Sonia: I'm not going to school this week.
Granny: Why not? Are you ill?
Sonia: No, I'm doing work experience. I'm working in a hotel.
Granny: I hope you're not working in the kitchen. You're not good at cooking!
Sonia: No, I'm not in the kitchen. I'm helping the receptionist and the manager.
Granny: Is that nice?
Sonia: Yes. Well, I like working with the manager, she's really friendly. But I prefer helping the receptionist because I can talk to the guests. I can practise my French because some French people are staying in the hotel. I understand almost everything they say. Isn't that great?
Granny: Yes, that's very good.
Sonia: Yes. But I am tired. When I go to school, I get up at half past seven, but this week I'm starting work at seven o'clock.
Granny: Oh, well, you can have a good rest at the weekend.
Sonia: Oh, yes. I'm looking forward to it.

Students do the Grammar spot as consolidation.

Grammar spot   State verbs

Work through the Grammar spot with the class.

> **Answers**
> **b** Are those jeans new? <u>I like</u> them very much.
> **c** <u>We think</u> this CD is very expensive.
> **d** <u>Do you want</u> some coffee?
> **e** I can't phone you because <u>I don't know</u> your number.
> **f** The teacher is speaking quickly and <u>I don't understand</u> what she's saying.
> **g** My friends are watching a pop programme on TV but <u>I don't like</u> it, so I'm listening to my MP3 player.

4 Initiate a brief class or group discussion.

Short answers

> ## Language presentation
>
> Refer to the picture on page 23. Ask *Is the police officer talking to the security officer?* and *Is the thief standing by the fountain?* Elicit/Supply the answers *Yes, he is* and *No, she isn't*. Write the questions and answers on the board.
>
> Repeat with further questions as necessary.
>
> Revise/Teach other third person short answer forms by asking questions round the class and eliciting/supplying answers, such as:
> *Are the photographer and the model working? Yes, they are.*
> *Do the artist and the photographer sell their work? Yes, they do.*
>
> Practise first and second person forms in a similar way, by asking students questions about themselves and yourself, e.g.
> *Are you studying English? Yes, I am.*
> *Do I live near the school? No, you don't.*
>
> Let students do the matching exercise and correct it with the class.

1

> **Answers**
> **b** 1   **c** 5   **d** 7   **e** 2   **f** 8   **g** 6   **h** 4

2 Students work in threes. They take turns so that two ask and answer questions and the third student in the group checks they are grammatically correct.

《Pronunciation》

This practises making and distinguishing between the sounds /æ/, /ɑː/ and /ʌ/.

1   **1 13** Ask students to look at the words and think about the way they sound. Make sure they understand that they must mark them in the order they hear them.

Play the recording.

> **Answers**
> **a** cat 3 cart 2 cut 1   **b** bag 1 bug 2
> **c** carry 2 curry 1   **d** match 1 March 3 much 2

> ## Recording script
>
> **a** I've got a <u>cut</u> on my knee.
> Can you move the <u>cart</u>?
> Where is the <u>cat</u> exactly?
> **b** There's a <u>bag</u> on the table.
> I can see a <u>bug</u> under your chair.
> **c** Would you like some <u>curry</u>?
> Please <u>carry</u> that for her.
> **d** We can meet at the <u>match</u>.
> There isn't <u>much</u> here.
> They often stay here in <u>March</u>.

Elicit/Supply the three sounds /æ/, /ɑː/ and /ʌ/ and practise them briefly with the class.

2   **1 13** ◀ Play the recording again for students to repeat.

3   **1 14** Play the recording and elicit which of the words have the same sounds as cat /æ/, cart /ɑː/ and cut /ʌ/.

> **Answers**
> Same sound as cat /æ/:   can
> Same sound as cart /ɑː/:   can't are aren't
> Same sound as cut /ʌ/:   does doesn't must mustn't

> ## Recording script
>
> does doesn't can can't must mustn't are aren't

《Activity》 Spot the difference

This activity practises present continuous forms and can be used later for revision, if preferred.

When you go through the answers you can project the pictures on SB pages 23 and 25 from the CD-ROM or webpage if you wish.

«Activity» What's my job?

This activity practises question forms and short answers in present simple and present continuous.

If necessary, briefly revise the question forms, short answers and meanings of the two tenses with the whole class before they begin. Explain that *mime* means *act silently*.

Note: This can be played as a competitive team game, with a member of one team miming the activity while the other team ask the questions to find out what the job is. A count is kept of the number of questions needed each time and the team who asked fewer questions overall wins the game.

Exam folder 3

SB pages 26–27

Speaking Part 3

This Exam folder gives students an introduction to the task and supplies a basic framework to help them think what to talk about when confronted by a photograph and asked to describe it.

1   Direct students to the picture and ask them to match the questions and answers.

Answers
a 6   b 7   c 5   d 3   e 1   f 4   g 2

2   Ask students to work with a partner, asking and answering the questions.

Suggested answers
a   She's in an office.
b   She's slim and she's got long, wavy hair.
c   She's wearing a green dress.
d   She's hard-working/untidy.
e   She's reading an email and eating a sandwich.
f   I wouldn't like to do this.
g   Because I don't like office work. It's boring.

Point out that the answers to these questions give a description of the picture and an opinion. Tell students to look at the Exam Advice.

Students will be given a photograph to comment on in the Speaking test. The photograph almost always shows a person or people engaged in some activity, so this framework of seven questions and answers is worth learning, as it will offer useful support if students are struggling to think of things to say. The examiner doesn't ask any questions but you can reassure students that if they do run out of ideas, the examiner will help them.

3   See how many of the questions students can remember.

4   Suggest that students look at the seven questions and think about their photograph, then cover the questions up before they start to speak.

Reading Part 5

This gives a very brief introduction to the cloze test which appears in Part 5. It gives students a chance to practise choosing one word out of four to complete a sentence.

1   Look at question 1 together and talk about why B, C and D are wrong. Ask students to do the other questions, then discuss their answers.

Draw their attention to the Exam Advice.

Answers
2 C   3 B

2   Ask students to do the questions, then discuss how they chose their answers.

Answers
1 B   2 A   3 D

4 Let's go out

TOPIC: Entertainment

In this unit:

Grammar	Prepositions of time; present continuous for future plans
Functions and vocabulary	Entertainment; making appointments; dates
Pronunciation	Saying days and months
PET skills	Reading for gist (Reading Part 4); scanning for specific information (Reading Part 2); listening for specific detail (Listening Part 3); understanding and writing days and months (Listening Part 3); making plans (Speaking Part 2)
Revision	*would you like to?* (Unit 2); present continuous for present actions; present simple (Unit 3)
Exam folder	Listening Part 1
Writing folder	Writing Part 2

Preparation

Language Focus, Exercise 3 Make an OHT of the table if you wish or project the table from the CD-ROM or webpage. **Activity** *Time expressions* Photocopy the board (on page 174) – enough for groups of either three or six students. Each group needs three circles – one of each (*at*, *on* and *in*). Each group needs a dice and each student needs a counter.

SB pages 28–31

Introduction

1 15 Begin with books shut. Play the recording, which contains six extracts of music from different kinds of shows or entertainment. Ask students to think about when they might hear each piece.

1 Students look at the photographs. Elicit/Supply the words to go with the kinds of entertainment pictured, so students can write them down.

> **Answers**
> **b** ballet   **c** magic show   **d** music festival
> **e** musical   **f** film

2 **1** 15 ◀ Play the recording again and ask students to match the pieces of music with the photographs.

Go through the answers – variations are possible. Students can compare them with the guesses they made earlier when they had their books shut.

> **Suggested answers**
> **a** 1   **b** 4   **c** 6   **d** 3   **e** 5   **f** 2

3 Revise present continuous for present actions by asking students to tell you what is happening in each photograph. Encourage them to use *a kind of* if they don't know a word.

4 You could do a hand count to see which shows are popular/unpopular.

EXTRA
Students might like to talk about other kinds of entertainment that have not been mentioned.

Reading

PET Reading Part 4

1 Look at the entertainment sections in the website together and check that students understand the word *event*.

Tell students you are going to time them while they decide which entertainment section each paragraph belongs to. The time limit will encourage them to read for gist rather than detail. You could do this as a competition to see who finishes first.

> **Answers**
> **B** Children   **C** Music   **D** Clubbing   **E** Dance shows
> **F** Music

PET Reading Part 2

2 This time students scan the texts for specific information. Time them again while they find the answers to the questions without worrying about words they don't understand.

> **Answers**
> **b** B* and F   **c** A   **d** C and E   **e** A   **f** B and F
> *The expression Big Top is mainly used for the big tent used by circuses, although it is sometimes borrowed for other entertainments taking place in an outsize tent. So the circus is outdoors but inside a tent.

⤵ Vocabulary spot

When you have checked the answers, point out that students managed to answer in spite of not knowing all the words in the text.

Answers
1 a   2 b   3 c

Ask students to reread the paragraphs silently, underlining any other words they do not know. Discuss meanings with the whole class or put them in groups.

⤵ Corpus spot   *Fun* and *funny*

Look at *fun* and *funny* in context in the Reading texts and then do the exercise.

(Text A: the funny story; Text F: a weekend of rock music and fun)

Answers
If something or someone is *funny*, it/he/she makes you laugh.
If something is *fun*, you enjoy doing it.
a fun
b funny
c fun

Language focus

Prepositions of time

1   ▶1 16 Play the recording. Students listen for gist.

Answers
1 the circus   2 the cinema   3 a nightclub

Recording script and answers for Exercise 2

Conversation 1

Sara: I know. It sounds good. I'd like to go.

Ed: I'm taking my little brother. Would you like to come too?

Sara: That would be great. I love the noise, the music and all the excitement. The last time I went was in 2005 when I was ten.

Ed: Oh, really? Well, I like the clowns best. Are you free today or tomorrow? The afternoon show is best for my brother.

Sara: Sorry, I'm busy then. I'm going to the cinema this afternoon – I've got the tickets, so I can't change it – and I'm playing tennis tomorrow afternoon.

Ed: Oh, well ... can you go at the weekend? It finishes on 29 August. That's Saturday.

Sara: I'm free on Saturday afternoon.

Ed: Good. I'm free then, too. It only comes once a year, so we mustn't miss it.

Conversation 2

Sam: Hi, Juliet, it's Sam here. Have you got the tickets yet?

Juliet: Yeah, for tonight.

Sam: What time does it start?

Juliet: Just a minute. I'll look. Er, it starts at a quarter to eight.

Sam: Oh, you know I work in a shop on Wednesdays? In the city centre. Well, there's a sale this week, so I'm working late. I have to tidy the shop at the end of the day, so I'm working till seven thirty this evening. I usually finish at seven o'clock, which is better.

Juliet: Don't worry. There are lots of adverts before the film actually starts.

Sam: OK. See you later then. Outside?

Juliet: See you there. Bye.

Conversation 3

Max: It's so boring here in August, Rachel. There's nothing to do.

Rachel: There are lots of good things on at the moment. What are you doing next weekend? My mum's going to see a dance show on Sunday afternoon. We can go with her.

Max: Oh, boring. And I don't like going to things like that in the afternoon.

Rachel: Well, there's the rock festival in the park. That looks good. I like listening to music outside in the summer. But it's very expensive.

Max: Mm. I've only got £10.

Rachel: Well, would you like to go to the new nightclub? I went there last week on my birthday. It's only £8 before eleven. We can go on Saturday.

Max: I'd really like to go to the rock festival, but OK then. Shall we meet at your house?

Rachel: Yeah. About nine?

Max: See you then.

PET Listening Part 3

2   ▶1 16 ◀ Students listen again for specific details and fill in the spaces. You may need to pause the recording. Go over any vocabulary they don't understand.

Answers
b today　**c** this afternoon　**d** tomorrow afternoon
e at the weekend　**f** on 29 August
g on Saturday afternoon　**h** at a quarter to eight
i on Wednesdays　**j** this week
k at the end of the day　**l** at 7 o'clock
m in August　**n** at the moment　**o** next weekend
p on Sunday afternoon　**q** in the afternoon
r in the summer　**s** on my birthday　**t** on Saturday

3 Project (see Preparation) or copy the table onto the board and complete it together using the answers to Exercise 2.

Answers

on	at
29 August	the weekend
Saturday afternoon	a quarter to eight
Wednesdays	the end of the day
Sunday afternoon	7 o'clock
my birthday	the moment
Saturday	
in	**no preposition**
2005	*today*
August	this afternoon
the afternoon	tomorrow afternoon
the summer	this week
	next weekend

↘ Grammar spot　Prepositions of time

This gives some general rules for the use of prepositions of time. Students use their answers from the previous exercises to complete them.

Answers
We use *on* before days of the week and dates.
We use *at* before times, *the weekend, the end of the day, the moment.*
We use *in* before months, seasons and years.
We use *no preposition* before *today, tomorrow (morning), this/next (afternoon, week).*

Point out that we say *on Monday,* but when we say *this/next/ last Monday* we omit the preposition; we say *in the morning* but *on Monday morning;* we say *in August* but *on 29 August.*

4 Ask students to work in pairs. Go through the answers with the whole class, referring to the table in Exercise 3 as necessary.

Answers
b on　**c** –　**d** on　**e** at　**f** in　**g** in
h on　**i** in　**j** at　**k** –　**l** at

This practises saying days, months and dates.

1 Check the number of syllables in *Sunday* and ask students to decide for the other days.

2 🔘1 17 Play the recording. Students repeat and check their answers. (Only *Saturday* has three syllables, the others all have two.)

This exercise will help them to pronounce *Wednesday* /wenzdeɪ/. Point out that *Sunday* and *Monday* have the same sound /ʌ/, although they are spelt differently. Check that they are pronouncing *Tuesday* and *Thursday* correctly as these two days can be easily confused. It may be useful to point out that mispronouncing the days of the week could lead to problems in real life (e.g. missed planes).

Talk about word stress – the days of the week are all stressed on the first syllable. English words with more than one syllable always have unequal stress.

Recording script

Sunday　Monday　Tuesday　Wednesday　Thursday
Friday　Saturday

3 Ask students to mark the stressed syllables in the names of the months. Do the first two together.

4 🔘1 18 Play the recording. If necessary, point out that we do not hear the /r/ on the end of *September,* etc.

Check they are saying *February* correctly; /febrʊri/ or /febrʊ[e]ri/ are both acceptable.

Answers and recording script
January　February　March　April　May　June　July
August　September　October　November　December

Students often have to write the day, the month or the date in Listening Part 3.

5, 6 🔘1 19 Discuss how we say these dates and then play the recording.

Recording script

the twenty-eighth of April　the fifteenth of August
the third of February

7 There is revision / further practice of this in Unit 8.

Answer
We *write* 15th January or 15 January but we *say* the fifteenth of January or January the fifteenth.

⟪Activity⟫ Time expressions

Divide the class into groups of three (or groups of six, composed of three pairs). Give each group a game board and dice (see Preparation). Give each of the three students (or pairs) in a group one of the preposition circles (either IN, AT or ON) and a counter.

Students take turns to roll the dice and move to a different square around the board according to the number on the dice. They can go in any direction on a throw. The aim is for a student to land on a square where the time phrase can be used with the preposition in their circle. So a student with the AT circle would try to land on squares such as *four o'clock*, *the weekend*, etc. When a student lands on such a square, they should say that they wish to write the expression in one of the six segments of their circle.

Example:

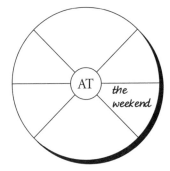

If, however, the student wishes to write a word in their circle that neither of the other players thinks fits, that student misses a throw next time. You can act as referee. If a student lands on a square they cannot use, the turn moves to the next student. The winner is the first one to complete their circle with time phrases. Note: this activity is adapted from an idea in *The Grammar Activity Book* by Bob Obee, Cambridge University Press.

Answers
ON: my birthday, Sunday, Friday, Tuesdays, Monday morning, Thursday evening, 24th April, 5th June
AT: four o'clock, the end of the week, night, 2.30, midnight, lunchtime, the moment, the weekend
IN: the winter, June, 2014, 1999, the morning, the spring, August, the evening

Present continuous for future plans

Language presentation

Check students remember the difference between: *I'm sitting at my desk* (= now) and *I come to school every day* (= a habit).

Point out that the present continuous can have different meanings. Ask what the difference is between:

I can' talk to you now – I'm watching a film. (= now) and *I can't see you on Friday because I'm playing football.* (= future plans)

Write some sentences from the conversations on page 30 on the board and check the meaning: *I'm working late on Wednesday. I'm going to the cinema this afternoon.*

If necessary, ask questions around the class to check, for example *What do you do on Saturdays? What are you doing next Saturday? Is it raining? Where are you going after school?*

Grammar spot

Present continuous for future plans
Use this to summarise.

Answers
We use the *present simple* to talk about what we usually do.
We use the *present continuous* to talk about future plans.

1   Look at picture **a**. Students write sentences for the other pictures.

Possible answers
b He's/is going (horse) riding next Monday.
c He's/is having lunch with a friend on Thursday.
d He's/is playing basketball tomorrow afternoon.
e He's/is going camping on 15th January.
f He's/is going to a party at the weekend.

Check students remember how to form the negative by making some of the sentences negative.

⟪Activity⟫ Diary   PET Speaking Part 2

Tell students to work in pairs. One is A and the other is B.

They complete all the blank spaces in their diaries on pages 200 and 202 in the Student's Book using the ideas in the Reading section and their own ideas. If they are stuck, get students to call out ideas and write suggestions on the board, e.g. *go to hairdresser, visit grandmother*, etc.

Tell them not to look at each other's diaries. Ask them to arrange a time when they are both free to meet next week by asking questions like *What are you doing on Friday morning / Saturday afternoon?* using present continuous for future plans.

Answer
You are both free on Saturday evening.

Exam folder 4

SB pages 32–33

Listening Part 1

This Exam folder is at a lower level than the exam, but gives students an introduction to the task.

1   Explain that students are going to hear a conversation between a boy and a girl. Ask about what sports are happening in the pictures (tennis, hockey and cycling). Ask students what they think Greg and Sophia are talking about.

2   **1 20** Look at the question together. Check students have noticed the tick under C.

Play the recording for question 1, which will be heard twice.

Go through the answers to the questions with the class.

Answers
a   No. Sophia is not very good at tennis.
b   No. They can't play hockey with two people.
c   Yes. Greg says *We could go out on our bikes. Let's cycle ...*
d   Yes. *Great idea* tells you that they agree.

Recording script

1
What do they decide to do tomorrow?
Greg: This weekend is so boring. Let's go out and do something tomorrow. I'd like to do some sport. Would you like to play tennis with me?
Sophia: I'm not very good at tennis. My best sport is hockey. I'd like to have a game tomorrow.
Greg: Don't be silly. We can't play hockey with just two people. We could go out on our bikes. Let's cycle to the lake and take a picnic.
Sophia: Great idea.

3   Ask students to work in pairs and look at questions 2–5 and the pictures. They should try to decide what the conversations are about.

Discuss the conclusions they reach briefly with the whole class.

4   **1 21** Play the recordings for 2–5, which will each be heard twice. Discuss students' answers after each conversation.

Explain any problem language, then look at the Exam Advice box together.

Answers
2 B   3 C   4 A   5 A

Recording script

2
Which shop are they going to first?
Woman: I want some shampoo to take on holiday. The chemist is at the other end of the shopping centre. So let's go and look for your swimming costume first.
Girl: Oh, yes. There's a really nice one in the sports shop over there.
Woman: OK. And remind me to buy something to read on the plane. The bookshop is next to the chemist's.

3
When is Tim meeting his father?
Man: Have a good time, Tim. Don't forget we're meeting tomorrow morning outside the railway station at eleven.
Tim: Dad, that's much too early. I'm going out with Simon tonight. We're spending the evening at a nightclub. We're staying there till midnight. I can't meet you until the afternoon. Two o'clock is better.
Man: OK. But don't be late. And have a good evening.

4
Where are they going on Saturday evening?
Boy: I've got an invitation to a concert on Saturday evening. Euan is playing the violin and he says I can have two free tickets. Do you want to come?
Girl: Well, I've got two tickets for the rock band at the Town Hall on Saturday evening. It starts at eight o'clock but I can go with someone else.
Boy: Oh, I'm coming with you to that. Please?
Girl: OK. And don't forget we're taking your little brother to the cinema on Saturday afternoon.

5
When is Paula's birthday party?
Woman: You know Paula's sixteen soon?
Man: Surely not! Time passes so quickly. Now, let me see, when is her birthday? It's the fifteenth of May, isn't it?
Woman: That's right. It's on a Monday. So the party's two days before, on the thirteenth. That's a Saturday.

Writing folder

Writing Part 2

This checks students cover the three points and know how many words to write.

1   Read the question together.

2   Students work in pairs and decide which one answers the question.

> **Answers**
>
> Answer **b** answers the question because it covers all three points.
>
> Answer **a** says what she would like to do but omits two elements of the question – time of arrival and where to meet. This answer would not get a good mark even though the English is good.
>
> Answer **c** omits to arrange a meeting place.

3   Point out the length requirement in this question and ask students where they can add *outside the museum* to answer c (at the end). This is not a good answer because it is too short. Tell them it is better to write slightly too much rather than too little.

Divide the class into three and ask each third to take one answer and count the words. Only b is within the limits – it has 44 words. Answer a has 59 words and c has 23 words.

4   Ask students to think for a moment and then pool some ideas, checking prepositions of place in the question which asks students to think of different places to meet. Remind them about answer a, which went into too much detail – they do not need to say much about what to do.

5, 6   Students write their own answers and check that they have answered the three parts of the question. Draw attention to the Exam Advice box.

7   This gives students a chance to see what 35–45 words of their own writing looks like.

5 Wheels and wings

TOPIC: Transport

In this unit:

Grammar	*Need* + noun; *need* + verb; *needn't*; countable/uncountable nouns; expressions of quantity: *some/any*; *a lot / several*; *a few / a little*; *a couple of*
Functions and vocabulary	Means of transport; airport language; compound nouns
Pronunciation	Unstressed *a*, *of*, *to* and *some*
PET skills	Understanding short conversations (Listening Part 1)
Revision	Frequency adverbs and present simple (Unit 1); compound nouns from Units 1–4
Exam folder	Reading Part 2

Preparation

Introduction, Exercise 1 Make an OHT of the blank crossword or project it from the CD-ROM or webpage.
Language focus *Need*, Exercise 1 Make copies of the recording script for the Grammar spot (from CD-ROM or webpage).
Activity *What do I need?* Photocopy the cards (on page 175) and cut them up – one card for each student.
Activity *Compound nouns* Photocopy the cards (on page 175) and cut them up – one word from A and one from B for each student. If possible, photocopy card A onto different coloured paper from card B.

SB pages 34–37

Introduction

1 If possible project the blank crossword onto the board or OHP (see Preparation). Ask students to do as much of the crossword as they can, using the photographs to help them.

   Preteach the following vocabulary from the clues or leave students to guess and go over it with them afterwards: *rails, air, goods, fit, engine, carriages, roof, motorway*.

2 Put students into groups to compare crosswords and to help each other. Ask students to come up and write words in the crossword on the board or an OHT. Ask them what the unit title refers to (*wings* as in an aeroplane).

Answers

A crossword grid with the following answers:
- 1 across: BUS
- 3 down: CAR
- 4 down: F (FERRY)
- 5 across: TRAM / 5 down: TRAIN
- 6 down: MOTORWAY
- 7 across: HELICOPTER / 7 down: HORREER
- 2 down: SCOOTER
- 8 across: LORRY
- 9 across: BICYCLE
- 10 down: COACH
- 11 across: TAXI / 11 down: TAKE
- 12 across: PLANE / 12 down: PC
- 13 across: SHIP

↘ Corpus spot

This summarises the use of prepositions with forms of transport.

> **Answers**
> a We always go to the city centre <u>by</u> car.
> b We can go there <u>on</u> foot.
> We go *by* car, train, bicycle, plane, boat but we go *on* foot.

3 Ask students to count the different ways of travelling which they personally use. Check who has the largest number and ask them to list them, making sure they use the correct prepositions, as practised in the Corpus spot.

   Ask students to write three sentences using *usually*, *sometimes* and *often*. Check they remember to use the present simple and put the adverb in the correct place (see Unit 1).

4 Encourage students to record new vocabulary at the end of a lesson. They can use word trees or spider diagrams.

Answers

AIR	LAND		WATER
helicopter	coach	car	ferry
plane	lorry	bicycle	ship
	motorbike	scooter	
	bus	taxi	
	tram	train	

Vocabulary spot

Some students may be more familiar with the American words for some forms of transport.

Answers
truck = lorry   *cab* = taxi   *freeway* = motorway

EXTRA

If students are interested, you could talk about other differences between British and American English.

Listening

1 These are all signs in an airport. Ask some questions round the class about the places, e.g. *Where can you book a hotel room? What do you do at check-in? Where do you wait for your flight?*

PET Listening Part 1

2 **1 22** Play the first conversation. Students listen for gist. Check the answers, then play the rest.

Answers
1 c   2 d   3 a   4 g   5 b   6 h

Recording script
and answers to Grammar spot (*Need*)

1

Man: Hello, can you help me? <u>I need a hotel room for tonight</u>. Near the airport.

Woman: Certainly, sir. I can book you a room.

Man: And can you call a taxi to take me there?

Woman: Oh, <u>you don't need a taxi</u>. There's a free bus.

2

Man: Passport, please. How long are you staying in the United Kingdom?

Woman: Only two weeks. Why? <u>Do I need a visa?</u>

Man: <u>No, you don't</u>. Enjoy your stay.

3

Woman: Good morning, sir. How many cases have you got?

Man: Just this one.

Woman: Right. Here's your boarding pass.

Man: <u>Do I need to go to the departure lounge now?</u>

Woman: Yes please, sir.

Man: OK. Thank you.

4

Woman 1: <u>Do we need to buy anything else before we leave?</u>

Woman 2: I don't think so. Well, we haven't got any shampoo.

Woman 1: Oh, <u>we don't need to buy that. The hotel has got everything we need.</u>

Woman 2: Oh, fine.

5

Woman: I've got this camera and this watch. The camera was a thousand dollars and the watch was a hundred. <u>Do I need to pay any tax?</u>

Man: Well, <u>you needn't pay any tax on the watch. But you need to pay tax on the camera.</u>

Woman: Oh, OK.

6

Man: Good afternoon. I want to fly to Madrid as soon as possible. In business class, please.

Woman: I can put you on the five o'clock flight. Is that all right?

Man: Yes, that's great. <u>I need to come back on Saturday evening</u>.

Woman: No problem.

Man: <u>Do I need to reconfirm my return flight?</u>

Woman: <u>No, you needn't do that.</u> It's all arranged.

Man: Thank you very much.

Language focus

Need

1 **1 22** Play the conversations again, stopping after each one to check the answers (see below).

Language presentation

Use the recordings and the answers to end up with a grammatical summary of *need* on the board:

need + noun
He needs a hotel room.
He doesn't need a taxi.
She doesn't need a visa.

need + verb
He needs to go to the departure lounge.
They don't need to buy any shampoo.
She needn't pay any tax on the watch.

Conversation 1   Answers: a a hotel room   b a taxi

Check the students understand the verb *need*. Write on the board:

need + noun
He needs a hotel room.   *He doesn't need a taxi.*

Conversation 2 | Answer: c a visa |

Write *She doesn't need a visa* under *He doesn't need a taxi.*

Conversation 3 | Answer: d go to the departure lounge |

Write on the board:

need + verb

He needs to go to the departure lounge.

Conversation 4 | Answer: e nothing |

Write *They don't need to buy any shampoo.*

Conversation 5

| Answer: f yes – on the camera but not on the watch |

Ask students what *needn't* is equivalent to. Write: *She needn't pay any tax on the watch* under the sentence in Conversation 4. Point out that *needn't* isn't followed by *to* and means the same as *don't need to*. Ask them if you can use *needn't* with a noun (no). You can't say ~~He needn't a taxi.~~

Conversation 6 | Answers: g on Saturday evening   h no |

Ask students to make a sentence with *need* (*he needs to come back on Saturday evening*) and with *needn't / doesn't need to* (*he doesn't need to / he needn't reconfirm his return flight*).

⬎ Grammar spot   *Need*

Students complete the Grammar spot as a reference.

Answers

***Need* + noun**

| + | **I need** a taxi. He needs a taxi. | - | **I don't need** a visa. He doesn't need a visa. | ? | **Do I need** a boarding pass? Does he need a boarding pass? |

***Need* + verb**

| + | **I need to** buy some shampoo. He needs to buy some shampoo. | - | I don't need to pay / I **needn't** pay any tax. He **doesn't need to** pay / He **needn't** pay any tax. | ? | **Do I need to** reconfirm my flight? Does he need to reconfirm his flight? |

Needn't is only used before a **verb**, not a **noun**. *Needn't* isn't used in a question.

2

Answers
b Do you need   **c** Do we need to
d don't need to / needn't   **e** need to
f I need to   **g** doesn't need   **h** don't need to / needn't

---

Countable and uncountable nouns

1   Look at the pictures of things which Joe is taking to Brazil. Ask students to identify them, using dictionaries if necessary.

2   This revises countable and uncountable nouns and *some* and *any*.

Talk about the difference between the three columns. Students work in pairs to put the other objects from the picture into the correct columns. When they have finished, get students to call out the answers while you put them on the board.

Answers

Countable (singular)	**Countable (plural)**	**Uncountable**
a camera	*some magazines*	*some shampoo*
a coat	some photos	some money
an address book		some chocolate
a passport		some tea
a mobile phone		some sunscreen
a sleeping bag		
a toothbrush		
a backpack		

⬎ Grammar spot

Countable and uncountable nouns

Ask students to complete the rules about countable and uncountable nouns. Some words could go in two columns – *shampoo, chocolate, tea* and *sunscreen* go in the uncountable column but *a bottle of shampoo, a bar of chocolate, a packet of tea* and *a bottle of sunscreen* can go in the countable column because we can count bottles and packets, etc.

Remind students that although dollars, euros, etc. can be counted, *money* cannot, grammatically speaking!

Answers
Countable nouns can be singular or plural. **Uncountable** nouns cannot be plural. We use *a* or *an* before **countable** nouns. We use *some* before **uncountable** nouns and plural **countable** nouns.

a glass or a bottle of water
a packet of tea
a bar of chocolate
a loaf of bread

---

3   Ask students to look again at the things on Joe's bed. Ask *Does he need to take a passport? Does he need to take a coat?*

Ask students to work in groups to finish the lists by writing the things from the picture in two columns.

4   Ask students from each group in turn to come and write things on the board. The other groups can disagree. Make sure they all use *a*, *some* and *any* correctly. Check they know that *any* is used in questions and negatives with both uncountables and plural countables. Encourage them to make some sentences round the class using nouns and verbs and *needn't* as well as *doesn't need to* with a verb.

Suggested answers

Things Joe needs to take	Things Joe doesn't need to take
a passport	a coat (it's hot in Brazil)
a camera	any shampoo
some money	any chocolate
an address book (so he can send postcards)	any photos of his family
some magazines (to read on the journey)	a sleeping bag (he's staying with a family)
a mobile phone	any tea
	any sunscreen
	a toothbrush (he can buy a toothbrush, sunscreen and shampoo when he gets there)

5   Partners write down at least four things they need and four things they don't need to take for a week in Britain in January. Ask them to write full sentences. (If in Britain, give them another place.) They then go to another pair and read out their lists. The other students decide if they agree with the things, using *some* and *any* correctly.

Ask students to tell you what they disagreed with, encouraging them to use both a noun and a verb after *need*.

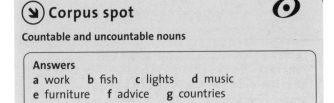

⊿ Corpus spot   ◉

Countable and uncountable nouns

> **Answers**
> **a** work   **b** fish   **c** lights   **d** music
> **e** furniture   **f** advice   **g** countries

Expressions of quantity

Language presentation

Look at the expressions of quantity in the Grammar spot. Ask what students notice about *a lot of* – it can be used with both countables and uncountables. Note that *lots of* is a common alternative. (*Too much, too many, enough* and *not enough* are practised in Unit 25.)

Check the meaning of *a few, several* and *a couple of*. Ask students what the difference is – *a couple* is two, *a few* and *several* are more than two but not usually more than six. Establish that these can only be used with countable nouns.

⊿ Grammar spot   Expressions of quantity

Get students to identify which column contains countable nouns and which column contains uncountable nouns.

> **Answers**
> Left-hand column: *countable nouns*
> Right-hand column: *uncountable nouns*

Look at the picture and talk about the names for the different objects the woman has – backpacks, suitcase, carrier bag, etc. Students choose the correct answers.

> **Answers**
> **b** much   **c** lots of   **d** several   **e** a few   **f** a lot of
> **g** a couple of   **h** much   **i** a little

«Pronunciation»

This practises unstressed *a, of, to* and *some*.

1   Students fill in the missing words.

> **Answers**
> **b** a of   **c** to   **d** a of   **e** to   **f** some

2   🔊**1 23** Play the recording and listen while students repeat the sentences. The words they filled in are unstressed and are normally pronounced with the sound /ə/ in connected speech – *a* /ə/, *of* /əv/, *to* /tə/ and *some* /səm/. This sound is very common in English and is vital for natural rhythm when speaking.

Recording script

a I need a visa.
b I've got a couple of suitcases.
c They need to take their passports.
d He's got a lot of luggage.
e Do we need to book a taxi?
f You need some money.

3   Students circle the unstressed words *a, of, to* and *some* in the sentences and practise saying them in pairs, correcting each other where they can.

Answers and recording script
a I need (a) hotel room.
b You need (to) pay tax.
c I want (some) shampoo.
d I'd like (to) go swimming.
e He's got (a) few magazines.
f I've got (a) new pair (of) shoes.

4   🔊**1 24** Students listen and repeat.

«Activity» What do I need?

This practises questions with *need*. Demonstrate the game with the class. Ask them to guess an activity you are thinking of by asking what you need for it. Use the answers *Yes*, *No*, *Sometimes* or *It doesn't matter*.

Put students in groups of four or five. Give out the cards (see Preparation). Remind them not to show each other their cards. Tell students to guess the activities on each others' cards, using *need* and answering as you did.

Faster groups can go on to make up their own activities for each other to guess.

«Activity» Compound nouns

Talk about compound nouns, e.g. *address book*, *riding hat*. Point out that they can be two words or have a hyphen or be one word, e.g. *volleyball*, *basketball*, *penfriend*. This activity concentrates on compounds which are two separate words. (See Unit 27 for compound nouns which are one word.)

The cards (see Preparation) show two halves of compound nouns which appear in Units 1–5. There are 20 pairs of words. Each student has one word from Card A and one word from Card B. The words on Card A come first in each compound. If using all 20 words, shuffle them first.

Students move around the room reading their words to other students. When they find a word which follows one of theirs, they take it, so everyone ends up holding a compound noun.

If you have fewer than 20 students, either do some of them together first or give some students four words (two from Card A and two from Card B). If you have more than 20 students, some can work in pairs. If your students cannot move around the room, give the cards out in groups according to the seating arrangements. For this reason, the cards can be divided into two halves (the top ten words on Card A match the top ten words on Card B).

Answers

Top half of cards	Bottom half of cards
boarding pass	flight attendant
sleeping bag	film star
departure lounge	night club
address book	carrier bag
adventure film	town hall
lorry driver	driving test
computer game	police officer
traffic lights	rock festival
mobile phone	business student
shop assistant	home town

Exam folder 5

SB pages 38–39

Reading Part 2

The format of the task in this Exam folder is the same as in the exam but the level is much lower so students get the opportunity to practise the exam skills without having to worry too much about the language.

Reading Part 2 is a matching task in which students have to read five texts about people and eight texts on a topic such as hotels or books, films, places to visit, etc. They have to match each person to the most suitable text. There are always eight texts, so three are not needed.

1 Students look at the pictures of people and suitcases and guess which suitcase belongs to each person by looking at the things in it. There are no set answers.

   Use the pictures to check the following vocabulary: *mobile phone*, *walking boots*, *paintbrushes*, *paints*, *paper*, *MP3 player/iPod*, *sunglasses*, *guidebook* and *camera*.

2 Read the information about the people with the class. Ask students to work in pairs and to try again to match the suitcases to the people.

Answers
1 d   2 a   3 e   4 b   5 f
Suitcase c does not belong to anyone.

Ask students which words helped them find the answer for Karen and underline them together.

Answers
1 Karen likes <u>pop music</u> and dancing in discos and she would like to find a hotel where she can <u>swim</u> every day. She also enjoys using a gym.

Ask students to underline important words for the other people. Go through this with the class.

Answers
2 Tom needs to find a quiet hotel in the country which has a good restaurant. He is taking some <u>work</u> on holiday with him and needs to hire a room for a business meeting in the hotel.
3 Maggie would like to relax in her hotel, <u>sunbathing</u>, swimming and <u>reading</u>. She wants to stay somewhere quiet with a good restaurant.

4 John wants to stay in the mountains. He likes <u>walking</u> and is interested in flowers and <u>birds</u>. He wants to stay in a family hotel.

5 Mike wants to spend his holiday <u>sightseeing</u> in the city. He likes taking <u>photographs</u> of the places he visits and wants a hotel which can organise trips. He would like a hotel with a swimming pool.

3 Ask students to read the hotel texts quickly and silently. Explain that they do not need to understand every word to do this task and persuade them not to ask about or look up any words they do not know for the moment. They should just have a general understanding of each text.

Ask a few students which hotel they would like to go to.

4 Look at the text about Karen on page 38 again together.

Read it aloud and together underline *dancing in discos* and *gym* (*pop music* and *swim* are already underlined).

5 Ask students to look quickly through the hotel texts and tick in the table those which have a disco – **C** and **E**.

Ask students if Karen can swim and use the gym at either of the hotels which have a disco. She can swim and use the disco at hotel **E**. Students put a tick under **E**, which is the best hotel for Karen.

Answers
Karen: E

Hotels	A	B	C	D	E	F	G	H
disco?			✓		✓			
swimming?					✓			
gym?					✓			

Point out that the students did not need to reread all the texts to find the answer to this question – they needed to learn to look for specific information and eliminate texts until they were left with only one. For example, once they have identified the hotels with a disco, they only need to read about those hotels again to see which has a swimming pool and a gym.

6 Read aloud the description of Tom and follow the same procedure. Underline *quiet hotel in the country, good restaurant* and *room for a business meeting*.

7 Students should tick **D, F** and **H** as being in the country. Hotel **F** has meeting rooms, but **D** and **H** don't. Hotel **F** also has a restaurant, and so this is the answer.

Answers
Tom: F

Hotels	A	B	C	D	E	F	G	H
in the country?				✓		✓		✓
good restaurant?						✓		
room for meeting?						✓		

8 Ask students to do Maggie, John and Mike on their own. They should start by underlining the important information about the people. Underline *swimming*, *quiet* and *good restaurant* for Maggie. Underline *mountains* and *family hotel* for John. Underline *city*, *organises trips* and *swimming pool* for Mike. Point out that there are three hotels (**C, D** and **G**) which do not suit anyone and that the correct hotel must offer all the things they underlined in the questions. Refer students to the Exam Advice box.

Answers
Maggie: B

Hotels	A	B	C	D	E	F	G	H
quiet?		✓		✓		✓		✓
swimming?		✓						
restaurant?		✓						

John: H

Hotels	A	B	C	D	E	F	G	H
family hotel?	✓				✓			✓
walking in the mountains?								✓
flowers and birds?								✓

Mike: A

Hotels	A	B	C	D	E	F	G	H
city?	✓		✓		✓		✓	
swimming pool?	✓				✓			
organises tours?	✓							

Check the answers round the class. Check which words students did not know in the hotel texts. Point out that although they needed to understand all the words in the questions, they did not need to understand all the words in the hotel texts in order to do the task.

6 What did you do at school today?

TOPIC: Education and history

In this unit:

Grammar	Past simple; short answers; adjectives ending in -ed and -ing
Functions and vocabulary	School life; school subjects; describing feelings; dates (years and decades)
Pronunciation	Final sound of regular verbs in past tenses: /t/, /d/ and /ɪd/
PET skills	Talking about photographs (Speaking Part 3); talking about feelings and experiences (Speaking Part 4); reading about opinions and attitudes (Reading Part 4); saying and writing years and decades (Listening Part 3)
Revision	Expressing opinions (Units 3 and 4)
Exam folder	Listening Part 2
Writing folder	Writing Part 3

Preparation

Vocabulary spot If applicable, note a few examples of 'false friends' in your students' language(s).

Language focus, Past simple, Exercise 1 If possible, make an OHT of the present stems of verbs from the texts to fill in as you go through the exercise, or project them from the CD-ROM or webpage.

Pronunciation Prepare enough cards (approx 10 × 8cms) for each student to have three. If appropriate, provide some marker pens in case students do not have them.

Activity *Past simple bingo* Photocopy the caller's cards (on page 176) and cut them up so that there is one set for each caller. Photocopy sufficient students' cards (on page 176) for each student or pair to have a different card, and cut them out. Have about ten plain 'counters' per student or pair.

Exam folder 6 Make copies of the recording scripts (from the CD-ROM or webpage) for students.

SB pages 40–43

Introduction
PET Speaking Parts 3 and 4

1 Using the photographs and questions, initiate a short discussion with the whole class about how students experience school/learning.

2 Divide the class into groups of three to discuss the statements.

Then go through the statements with the class, noting on the board how many people agree/disagree with each statement, so that you end with a rough analysis of the class's opinions.

3 Invite each group to offer an opinion and write this on the board.

↘ Vocabulary spot

Answers
I had a good education means *I went to a good school.*

Elicit/Supply examples of 'false friends' relevant to your students.

Reading
PET Reading Part 4

1 This exercise practises scanning for specific information. Briefly discuss with the class how old the three people are and let students speculate about their personalities, present jobs, etc., before asking them to read the texts.

Answers
A Mavis Carver (girls being addressed by their surnames is very old-fashioned)
B Neil Johnson (it was an 'all boys' school)
C Anita Green (computer rooms have only existed in the past twenty years)

PET Listening Part 3

2 Ask students to write in the names and suggested dates. Discuss the dates they come up with and the reasons for them (e.g. the age of people in the photographs). Elicit/Supply how to say years (e.g. 1930, 1973, 2001) and decades (the 50s, etc.). There is further practice in Units 14 and 24.

Suggested answers
a (about) 1935 / in the 1930s   b 1965 / in the 1960s
c 2005 / this century

Language focus
Adjectives describing feelings and opinions

1 Students underline adjectives which describe people's feelings.

2 Let students complete the lists. Invite them to extend the lists with other words they can think of (Units 2 and 3).

> **Answers**
> **Good feelings** important, interested, fun, friendly, happy, confident
> **Bad feelings** frightened, angry, miserable, terrible, difficult, tired

3 Have a brief discussion with the class.

-ing and -ed adjectives

1 Do the exercise with the class. Point out that the adjectives all end in -ed. Elicit/Supply that -ed adjectives describe the person who has the feeling.

> **Answers**
> **b** frightened **c** tired **d** amused **e** interested
> **f** worried

2 Do the exercise with the class. Point out that the adjectives all end in -ing.

> **Answers**
> **b** amusing **c** worrying **d** interesting **e** tiring
> **f** boring

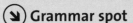 **Grammar spot** -ing and -ed adjectives

> **Answers**
> We use -ing adjectives to describe the thing (or person) that *causes* the feeling.
> We use -ed adjectives to describe the person who *has* the feeling.

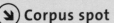 **Corpus spot** -ing and -ed adjectives

> **Answers**
> **a** bored   **f** boring
> **b** interesting **g** embarrassing
> **c** interested   **h** excited
> **d** relaxed   **i** surprising
> **e** surprised   **j** amazed

Past simple

1 Ask students to do the exercise as a race, then go through it, writing up the past forms (see Preparation).

> **Answers**
> **List A** arrived, asked, helped, looked, realised, showed, started, stopped, studied, used, walked, wanted
> **List B** was/were, became, began, could, felt, found, got, gave, went, made, met, took, told

2 Elicit/Supply the difference between the lists. The verbs in List A are regular verbs and those in List B are irregular. (**Note:** *can/could* here refers to ability. For speculative use of *could* see Unit 13.) If appropriate, refer students to spelling rules for regular verbs in the past simple, Grammar folder page 207.

> ### Language presentation
> Refer students to the table at the top of page 43 and discuss the past tense patterns. It may be helpful to draw parallels with the present simple. Draw attention to the pronunciation of *was*, *wasn't*, *were* and *weren't* and practise as necessary.

 Grammar spot

Negatives and questions in the past simple

> **Answers**
> **a** You use *was* and *were* in the same way as *is* and *are* in the present.
> **b** *did*

3 Do the exercise with the class.

> **Answers**
> **b** Were there any boys in the hall?
> **c** Did she walk to school alone?
> **d** Did the teacher give the girls any books?
> **e** Was Mavis's first lesson in the classroom?

4 Revise the principles of short answer forms by doing this exercise together. Point out that these work similarly to present simple short answers (Unit 3), but have only one form of the verb (*did*) except for *to be* (*was/were*).

> **Answers**
> **2** e   **3** b   **4** c   **5** d

5 Ask students to work in threes, writing and exchanging *Yes/No* questions and short answers about Neil and Anita. Do an example with the class, e.g. *Was Neil frightened? Did anyone help him?* Ask each student to write three questions and pass them to one of the others to write the answers. When they have written the answers, they should pass them to the third student to have them checked.

6 Introduce oral practice by asking questions round the class, e.g. *Did you go to the cinema yesterday, Pedro? Yes, I did. Did Pedro go to the cinema yesterday, Ernesto? Yes, he did.* When they are ready, let them ask and answer questions round the class or in small groups.

7 This exercise practises a variety of past simple forms. Briefly talk about the illustration with the class. Check that students understand the use of ordinal numbers with *century* (*nineteenth century* = 1801–1900). If the past simple is new to students, work through questions **a–e** with the whole class, then let them continue in pairs or alone (could be homework).

Answers
b were   **c** worked   **d** didn't learn   **e** Did go
f made   **g** became   **h** taught   **i** Did attend
j believed   **k** didn't / did not need   **l** had
m stayed

8 This exercise practises formation of questions in the past simple. If necessary, compose a few appropriate examples with the whole class first. Students could write questions for homework, hand them in to be checked for grammatical accuracy, then exchange them. If time allows, a class quiz could be organised.

≪Pronunciation≫

These exercises practise the final sounds (/t/, /d/ and /ɪd/) of regular verbs in past tenses.

1 Give out small blank cards (see Preparation). Ask students to write /t/ on one, /d/ on the second and /ɪd/ on the third.

2 **1 25** Tell students that they are going to hear some verbs in the past tense. They must listen carefully and decide on the sound at the end of each verb, then hold up the appropriate card.

Play the recording, stopping after the first verb. Help the class to arrive at a consensus about the sound at the end of the verb (/t/). Write the verb on the board. Continue with the recording, stopping each time for a show of cards, and allow the class to decide what the final sound was. Write each verb on the board but do not group them according to the final sound.

Recording script

checked   enjoyed   kissed   looked   mended   needed
prepared   realised   showed   stopped   studied
used   walked   wanted   wished

3 Ask students to say the verbs in the list to themselves and try to put them in the correct columns.

Answers
/d/   enjoyed prepared realised showed studied used
/t/   checked kissed looked stopped walked wished
/ɪd/   mended needed wanted

≪Activity≫ Past simple bingo

See Preparation.

In large classes, students can play in groups. Each student has a card, or two students can share one. There must be one 'caller' for every six students (or six pairs) so that each student (or pair) has a different student card. Thus the game can be played by the whole class (with the teacher as caller), or in groups (with students taking turns to be caller).

To play

The caller has the caller's cards in a shuffled pile face down, or in a bag. Each student, or pair, has one student's card, face up, and access to the counters.

The caller takes out one verb card at a time and reads it. Students check their cards and if they find the past form of that verb they cover it with a counter. The caller puts the verb cards aside in order. The winner is the first person to cover a horizontal row. The student reads out each past form and says the verb it belongs to while the caller checks that the verb was actually called by finding it in the pile of used verb cards. The caller's cards are then re-shuffled, the students exchange cards and the game is repeated as time allows.

≪Activity≫ Subjects to study

Divide the class into teams of about five. Tell them they must spell the subjects correctly and that they have three minutes. After three minutes, the team with the longest list writes it on the board, getting a point for each correctly spelt subject. At the end, other teams supply subjects they missed.

Exam folder 6

SB pages 44–45

Listening Part 2

This Exam folder is at a lower level than the exam but gives students an introduction to the task.

1 Discuss the picture together.

2 🔘 **1 26** Play the recording and ask students what is different from the picture.

Answers
In the recording, the taxi driver is male and the passenger is female; the passenger is worried; the bags are in the boot.

Recording script

Man: On my first day as a taxi driver, my first passenger was a woman who wanted to go to the airport. She was in a hurry because she needed to be at the airport at 10.30 to check in. She had lots of bags with her. Anyway, she got in the car and put the bags in the boot and we set off. I drove fast and we were lucky because there were no traffic jams. <u>We got to the airport at exactly 10.15</u>. Her flight was to New York where her sister lived and it left at 12.20.
She got out of the car and started to look for her purse. Then she looked across at the airport. She suddenly looked very annoyed. She took her ticket out of her bag and showed it to me. I realised the mistake. <u>She didn't tell me which airport to go to, so this was the International Airport. Her flight went from the City Airport</u> – about an hour away. She refused to pay me anything, so it wasn't a very good start for me.

3 🔘 **1 26** ◀ Play the recording again.

Answers
a to check in   b they arrived at the airport   c 12.20
d no   e no

4 These questions show the kind of skills students need to develop. The information is in Exercise 3.

Answers
1 A   2 C

5 🔘 **1 26** ◀ Give out the recording script (see Preparation) and play the recording again while students read. They should underline *We got to the airport at exactly 10.15* (this answers question 1) and *She suddenly looked very annoyed* (this cues question 2). Compare the questions with the script:

Question 1 says *arrive* and the script says *got to*.

Question 2 says *angry* and the script says *very annoyed*.

Look at the Exam Advice box together. For this task, it is important that students recognise the cue (the question) which tells them to listen for the answer.

6 Use the picture to elicit or teach key vocabulary.

7 🔘 **1 27** Ask students what they already know about the story from the instructions.

Play the recording. Talk about which words in the text give the correct answers.

◀ Give out the photocopied recording script (see Preparation) and play the recording again so students can read as they listen.

Answers
1 A   2 C   3 B

Recording script

Woman: When I was about 18, I started a new job in the kitchen of a restaurant. I liked cooking and I wanted to be a chef, so I was really pleased to have this job. In fact on the first morning I woke up very early and I went to the restaurant at about 7.30. <u>I just didn't want to wait any longer. I wanted to be in that kitchen!</u> Luckily, the restaurant was open. The chef met me and showed me what to do. But at about nine o'clock the chef felt ill and went home. <u>It was a terrible day. I was the only one in the kitchen</u> and the restaurant was very busy. The waiters came to the kitchen and ordered the food for the customers and I made it. The waiters helped me to find things. Twice I made a mistake and the customers got the wrong food. <u>But it wasn't a problem – in fact both of the customers ate the food and then came to the kitchen to say the food was really delicious.</u> And the waiters got a big tip.

Writing folder

Writing Part 3

1   Look at the question together.

2   In pairs, students decide which letter answers the question.

> **Answers**
> **C** answers the question. It says something about the school and says what the writer likes. **A** misinterprets the question and writes from the person who is coming to the school rather than the person who is already there. **B** gives only negative information about the school and spends too much time writing about the city.

3   Give students a few minutes to finish the list.

> **Answers**
> computers, sports, friends, size, timetable, laboratories, swimming pool, teachers

Write the list on the board, adding other suggestions.

4   Look at the example notes and ask students to make notes next to the other headings.

5   Students could do this for homework. They can use letter C as a model. They should aim to write between 90–110 words. Draw attention to the Exam Advice box.

6   This is an opportunity for students to see what an answer of the right length looks like in their handwriting.

Units 1–6 Revision

Speaking

1 Discuss the first sentence and the example answers with the whole class, then let them work through the others in pairs. If appropriate, have a brief whole class discussion of some of the other sentences at the end and revise any language problems which have arisen as they talked in pairs.

Exercises 2–7 could be set for homework and discussed afterwards in class.

Vocabulary

2

> **Answers**
> **b** engineer **c** slim **d** ferry **e** guest **f** century
> **g** joke **h** factory **i** performance

Reading

3

> **Answers**
> **b** No, he didn't. **c** Yes, he does. **d** Yes, they do.
> **e** No, there weren't. **f** Yes, he did. **g** Yes, there were.
> **h** No, he doesn't. **i** No, he didn't. **j** No, he wasn't.
> **k** No, they didn't. **l** Yes, they are. **m** Yes, he is.

Vocabulary

4

> **Answers**
> **b** became **c** finished **d** summer **e** job **f** excited
> **g** hard-working **h** tired **i** boring **j** exciting **k** take
> **l** describe **m** share **n** helped **o** design

Grammar

5

> **Answers**
> **2** B **3** A **4** C **5** A **6** A

6

> **Answers**
> **2** C **3** C **4** B **5** A **6** A

7

> **Answers**
> **b** I couldn't **c** Did you go **d** I went **e** Was it
> **f** it was **g** We saw **h** I don't usually like
> **i** I enjoyed **j** the concert began **k** it ended
> **l** we met **m** you had **n** I didn't do
> **o** Are you going **p** My cousin's giving
> **q** Do you want **r** He always has **s** he knows
> **t** I didn't realise

Progress Test 1 Key

1 A **2** C **3** C **4** B **5** A **6** B **7** B

8 C **9** U **10** C **11** C **12** U

13 C **14** C **15** U **16** U

17 it wasn't

18 she does

19 I am *or* we are

20 they do

21 I wasn't *or* we weren't

22 I did *or* we did

23 equipment

24 father's

25 nurse

26 laboratory

27 frightened

28 film's

29 receptionist

30 Thursday

Progress Test 1

Choose the correct answer, A, B or C.

1 .... to our party next Saturday?
   A Are you coming   **B** Come you   **C** Did you come

2 Mario .... rock music.
   A is like   **B** is liking   **C** likes

3 My sister is tall .... dark hair.
   A has   **B** and   **C** with

4 What time did the concert .... ?
   A beginning   **B** begin   **C** began

5 They've got .... money for shopping.
   A a little   **B** any   **C** several

6 You .... use a computer for this work.
   A need   **B** needn't   **C** don't need

7 What time .... the other team arrive at the sports ground?
   A were   **B** did   **C** is

Write C (countable) or U (uncountable) next to each word.

8 team	13 advertisement
9 money	14 website
10 meal	15 homework
11 journey	16 information
12 luggage	

Complete the short answer for each question.

17 Was the match exciting? No, ...

18 Does your sister go windsurfing? Yes, ...

19 Are you going swimming? Yes, ...

20 Do the boys know the time? Yes, ...

21 Were you late for the meeting? No, ...

22 Did you go to evening classes? Yes, ...

Find one spelling or punctuation mistake in each sentence. Write the correction in the space.

23 The theatre has lots of special equipement.
   ....

24 Sharon isn't coming with us because she's working in her fathers shop. ....

25 Did the nerse write something in her notebook?
   ....

26 These university students work in the science labratory.
   ....

27 I never felt frigtened at secondary school.
   ....

28 This films really boring and we're not learning anything. ....

29 The recepcionist confirmed our reservation.
   ....

30 I'd like to visit the city centre on thursday and go to the library. ....

7 Around town

In this unit:	
Grammar	Prepositions of place and movement; comparative adjectives; imperatives
Functions and vocabulary	Places/buildings in town; asking for and giving directions; polite questions; saying you don't understand; replying to thanks
Pronunciation	/aʊ/ as in *now* and /ɔː/ as in *four*
PET skills	Reading notes (Reading Part 1); understanding directions (Listening Part 1); saying when you don't understand (Speaking test); sentence transformation (Writing Part 1)
Revision	Adjectives from earlier units; spelling rules
Exam folder	Reading Part 3

Preparation

Activity *Comparatives Snap* Photocopy one set of the sheet of cards (on page 177) for each group. Cut up the words and suffixes to make two sets of cards. Shuffle each set thoroughly.
Activity *Mazes* Photocopy the mazes (on page 178) – enough for each student to have a copy of each maze.
Exam folder 7 If possible, make an OHT of the text or project it from the CD-ROM or webpage.

SB pages 48–51

Introduction
PET Reading Part 1

Look together at the map and the notes and talk about the dispatch rider and his job. Check understanding of the names of the places in the notes.

Language presentation

Check students' knowledge of prepositions of place by getting two students to the front and asking them to stand *opposite*, *behind*, *in front of* and *next to* each other, then you stand *between* them. Alternatively, you could do this after they have done Exercise 1, to check their understanding. If there is space, students could do this in pairs while you call out the prepositions. Other prepositions (and phrases) in this exercise are *outside*, *inside*, *in*, *in the corner of* and *by*.

Discuss which words are often missing in notes – articles and some verbs, e.g. (*the*) entrance (*is*) under (*the*) bridge. It is useful for students to get used to reading notes as preparation for Reading Part 1.

---

1 Students work in pairs to identify the places on the map using the notes. Some are interdependent.

Answers
2 car park (J) **3** nightclub (A) **4** museum (G)
5 library (H) **6** theatre (F) **7** bus station (B)
8 newspaper kiosk (C) **9** swimming pool (D)
10 petrol station (E)

EXTRA

Students can work in groups to think of which of the places shown on the map are in walking distance from their school. (You can change the distance to suit your circumstances.) If the school is not near any public buildings, pick a central point in the town. Give them a time limit and see which group has the most places.

2 This is an opportunity to add other important or relevant vocabulary such as *hospital*, *castle*, *cinema*, etc.

⟱ Grammar spot   Prepositions of place

This is a chance to summarise prepositions.

Answers
a opposite
b in front of; behind; next to / beside
c between

Listening
PET Listening Part 1

1 This practises understanding directions.

▶ 1 28 X, Y and Z are the starting points for the three conversations. Play the three conversations. Students follow the directions.

Answers
1 petrol station **2** shopping centre **3** skateboard park

Recording script

Conversation 1

Woman: OK. Turn right at the next roundabout and then take the second turning on the left. It's on your left on the corner opposite a supermarket.

Man: I'm sorry. Could you say that again, please?

Woman: Go down here. When you reach the roundabout, turn right. It's a one-way street. OK?

Man: Yes.

Woman: So, after the roundabout you don't take the first turning on the left, you take the second. You'll see it then. There's a supermarket on the other side of the road. All right?

Man: Yes. I see. Thank you very much for your help.

Woman: You're welcome.

Conversation 2

Man: It's near the market square, which is a pedestrian area. It's not far to walk from here.

Woman: Where can I leave my car?

Man: OK, well, at the next crossroads turn right, then turn right again. You'll see the entrance to the car park just on the right. Park your car there then you can walk across the road and you're there. There's a pedestrian crossing.

Woman: Thank you.

Conversation 3

Girl: Yes, of course. Are you on foot?

Boy: I'm sorry, I don't understand.

Girl: Are you walking?

Boy: Yes.

Girl: Good. That's easy then. Go straight down this road past the town hall. Then turn left at the traffic lights into Queen Street. Walk down there to the market square and walk across the square. Go straight on and it's at the next crossroads on the corner.

PET Speaking test

2   •1 **29** Ask students to write down suggestions.

Play the recording (this version has the questions too).

Tell students to keep a list of useful phrases for the Speaking test and learn them.

Answers

a Could you ... need to find
b could you tell me the way to
c can you tell me the way to
Could is more polite than *can*. We also use *please* a lot in English.

d sorry. Could you say that
e sorry
British people often say nothing in reply to *Thank you*, but *You're welcome* is a possible answer.

Language presentation

Talk about using the imperative for giving instructions – always the infinitive without *to*.

Recording script

Conversation 1

Man: <u>Could you help me, please? I need to find a petrol station.</u>

Woman: OK. Turn right at the next roundabout and then take the second turning on the left. It's on your left on the corner opposite a supermarket.

Man: <u>I'm sorry. Could you say that again, please?</u>

Woman: Go down here. When you reach the roundabout, turn right. It's a one-way street. OK?

Man: Yes.

Woman: So, after the roundabout you don't take the first turning on the left, you take the second. You'll see it then. There's a supermarket on the other side of the road. All right?

Man: Yes. I see. Thank you very much for your help.

Woman: You're welcome.

Conversation 2

Woman: <u>Excuse me, could you tell me the way to the shopping centre, please?</u>

Man: It's near the market square, which is a pedestrian area. It's not far to walk from here.

Woman: Where can I leave my car?

Man: OK, well, at the next crossroads turn right, then turn right again. You'll see the entrance to the car park just on the right. Park your car there, then you can walk across the road and you're there. There's a pedestrian crossing.

Woman: Thank you.

Conversation 3

Boy: <u>Excuse me, can you tell me the way to the skateboard park, please?</u>

Girl: Yes, of course. Are you on foot?

Boy: <u>I'm sorry, I don't understand.</u>

Girl: Are you walking?

Boy: Yes.

Girl: Good. That's easy then. Go straight down this road past the town hall. Then turn left at the traffic lights into Queen Street. Walk down there to the market square and walk across the square. Go straight on and it's at the next crossroads on the corner.

Language focus

Directions

1 Students complete the directions.

Answers
b second turning on
c straight on / straight down this road
d Turn left   crossroads   **e** Turn   into
f Turn right   roundabout   **g** corner

«Pronunciation»

This practises making and distinguishing between the sounds /aʊ/ and /ɔː/.

1 Demonstrate the two sounds using words students have come across in earlier units:

/aʊ/ as in *loud, clown*, /ɔː/ as in *short, four*

Students can work in pairs or groups to put the words into two columns.

2 **1 30** Play the recording so students can check their answers.

◄ Play the recording again so students can repeat the words. Remind students that English spelling sometimes does not give many clues to pronunciation, and identify the different ways of spelling /ɔː/ shown here.

Answers

/aʊ/	/ɔː/
out	or
round	sports
town	course
about	corner
down	hall
how	board
	walk

Recording script

out or round sports town course corner about hall board down how walk

3 Check students have underlined the words correctly in the sentences.

Answers
/aʊ/: down roundabout town outside
/ɔː/: *corner* walk course hall skateboard sports

4 **1 31** Play the recording and get students to repeat.

Recording script
a It's on the corner.
b Walk down the road.
c Of course.
d Turn right at the roundabout.
e Go past the town hall.
f Where's the skateboard park?
g It's outside the sports stadium.

«Activity» Directions

Establish where you are (i.e. the market square), then ask two or three individuals to give you directions. Ask them to repeat if they make errors which might lead to misunderstanding.

Students then give directions in pairs, asking each other for repetition where necessary. They can change pairs and repeat with different directions until they have had enough practice.

Prepositions of movement

1 Check students know what a skateboard and a mountain bike are. Give them a few minutes to choose the prepositions and then check round the class. Point out some useful vocabulary: *steps, tunnel, track*, etc.

Suggested answers
b along   **c** up   **d** through   **e** around
f across   **g** off   **h** over

Comparative adjectives

1 Look at **a** with the class and then ask students to underline the comparative adjective in each sentence.

Answers
b cheaper   **c** safer   **d** bigger   **e** more exciting
f more fashionable   **g** noisier   **h** more popular
i more common   **j** better

2 In groups, students discuss the sentences. When they disagree, they should say what they think, using the correct comparative structure. If some students are not interested in the topic, they could compare two other sports, pop groups, magazines, etc.

Grammar spot   **Comparative adjectives**

Pre-teach/Revise the terms *vowel, consonant* and *syllable*.
Students use sentences **a–j** in Exercise 1 to elicit the rules for
making comparative adjectives. Make sure students notice
the irregular ones – *good* → *better*; *bad* → *worse*.

The spelling rules for words ending in a vowel and a
consonant or ending in -*e* are the same as for the formation
of the present continuous (Unit 3) and the regular forms of
the past simple (Unit 6).

> **Answers**
>
> Most one-syllable adjectives (e.g. *light*) add *er*.
>
> One-syllable adjectives ending in *e* (e.g. *safe*) add *r*.
>
> Most adjectives ending in a **vowel** and a consonant
> (e.g. *big*) double the consonant and add *er*.
>
> Most adjectives with more than one **syllable** (e.g.
> *popular*) use *more* (e.g. *more popular*).
>
> Adjectives ending in *y* (e.g. *noisy*) usually change *y* to *i*
> and add *er*.
>
> *Good* and *bad* are irregular and become **better** and
> *worse*.

3   This gives further practice in the formation of
    comparative adjectives.

Answers

Add *er*	steeper stronger	older richer
Add *r*	nicer wider	
Double the last letter and add *er*	thinner wetter	
Use *more*	more famous more popular	more difficult more miserable
Change *y* to *i* and add *er*	friendlier lazier	busier tidier
Irregular	worse better	

PET Writing Part 1

4   This is useful practice for Writing Part 1.

Language presentation

Look back at sentence **a** in Exercise 1. Compare it with
sentence **a** in this exercise and elicit that they mean the
same. Tell students you can also say 'is not so light as'. Now
get students to help you rewrite the same sentence with *less
heavy*: *A skateboard is less heavy than a mountain bike*.

Do the same with sentence **b** so you end up with three
sentences with the same meaning:

A skateboard is cheaper than a mountain bike.

A mountain bike is not as/so cheap as a skateboard.

A skateboard is less expensive than a mountain bike.

Get students to do the exercise in pairs or do it together
if they are less confident. They should use the word in
brackets. Then use the Grammar spot to summarise.

> **Answers**
>
> **c** Skateboarding is not as/so safe as cycling.
> **d** A skateboard is not as/so big as a mountain bike.
> **e** Cycling is less exciting than skateboarding.
> **f** Skateboards are less fashionable than mountain bikes.
> **g** Mountain bikes are not as/so noisy as skateboards.
> **h** Mountain bikes are less popular than skateboards.
> **i** Mountain bikes are not as/so common as skateboards.
> **j** Skateboards are not as/so good as mountain bikes for
>   long journeys.

 Grammar spot   **Comparing two things**

> **Answers**
>
> Mountain bikes are more fashionable *than* skateboards.
> = Skateboards are not as/so fashionable *as* mountain
> bikes.
> = Skateboards are *less* fashionable *than* mountain bikes.

 Corpus spot   **Comparative adjectives**

> **Answers**
>
> **b** I would like to buy a new TV that is <u>bigger</u> than my
>   old one.
> **c** Hotels are <u>cheaper</u> here than in the city.
> **d** My parents are not <u>as/so</u> excited as I am about the
>   holiday.
> **e** Modern furniture is <u>easier</u> to clean than old
>   furniture.
> **f** This supermarket is <u>better</u> than the other one.
> **g** I think he is <u>taller</u> than I told you.
> **h** I'm not as good at tennis <u>as</u> you are.

5   This exercise practises *not as/so ... as* and *less ... than*.
    Students write the answers in class or for homework.

> **Answers**
>
> **b** Steve is hotter than John. / John isn't as/so hot as Steve.
> **c** Sue's homework is worse than Jack's (homework). /
>   Jack's homework isn't as/so bad as Sue's (homework).
> **d** The taxi is less slow than the school bus. / The taxi
>   isn't as/so slow as the school bus.
> **e** The Amazon is wider than the Thames. / The Thames
>   isn't as/so wide as the Amazon.
> **f** Jill is sadder than Liz. / Liz isn't as/so sad as Jill.
> **g** The ring is less expensive than the watch. / The ring
>   isn't as/so expensive as the watch.
> **h** The shorts are dirtier than the T-shirt. / The T-shirt isn't
>   as/so dirty as the shorts.

«Activity» Comparatives Snap

Work out how many groups of students there will be in your class (four students per group is best, but between two and six is fine). Organise the groups in circles.

Join one group to demonstrate while the others watch. Ask them to deal the cards (see Preparation) round the group, face down. They must not look at their cards.

In turn, each person in the group reveals the top card from his/her pile. If it matches another visible card, e.g. if the word is *busy* and the suffix is *ier*, the first player to say '*Snap – busier*' keeps that pair. As each player turns over a second card, they put it on top of the first one so that the first is no longer in play.

Anyone who says *Snap* when the cards do not match, or says the comparative form incorrectly, misses a turn.

When they get to the bottom of their piles of cards, they can shuffle them and start again. The game can continue until all the word cards are finished or a time limit (e.g. ten minutes) is reached. The winner is the person with the most pairs at the end of the game.

Monitor while they are playing that they are matching the cards correctly and correcting each other as necessary.

«Activity» Mazes

Photocopy the mazes (see Preparation). Half the class has one, the other half has the other.

Students work in pairs. Give each pair two copies of the same maze. They find their way through, marking the route on one copy.

They then join a pair from the other half of the class and give them the blank copy of their maze. They watch them trying to find the way and tell them when they are making a mistake (*no, turn right there*, etc.). They then do the other pair's maze in the same way.

Exam folder 7

SB pages 52–53

Reading Part 3

This Exam folder is at a lower level than the exam but gives students an introduction to the task. In the exam, there are ten questions in this part.

1. Ask students what they can guess about the text from the photograph, e.g. *It's about a city, it's old, it's got a cathedral and it's in Britain.*

2. Ask them to read the text quickly, without checking words they do not know, to see if their guesses are right.

3. Check the vocabulary as necessary in questions **a–f** and ask students to find the relevant parts of the text. In this task, there are parts of the text which are not tested at all.

   Project the text (see Preparation) and underline the relevant parts of the text with students. Supply the meaning of any unknown words within the marked sections of the text only at this stage.

Answers

The city of Lincoln is 2,000 years old and there are a lot of interesting buildings to see. <u>The cathedral is in the north of the city just outside the main city centre. You can walk to many of Lincoln's other attractions from the cathedral. It's not far from the castle.</u> There is a wonderful view of the city from there. <u>Behind the castle is The Lawn, an old hospital, which is now a museum with shops and a café. You can sit in the beautiful gardens to have lunch or a coffee.</u> There is a car park a few metres from the café. During the summer, walking tours leave from <u>the Tourist Information Centre, which is next to the castle.</u> They are not expensive, last about an hour and visit all the main attractions. There are some very interesting museums. The Toy Museum is near the Tourist Information Centre and has children's toys and games from the last century.

There are shops and a market in the old city centre. There are two shopping centres – one is the <u>Waterside Centre opposite the market</u> and the other is <u>St Mark's Shopping Centre. St Mark's is newer than the Waterside Centre</u> and is just south of the main city centre. Go straight down the High Street from the city centre and it is on the right.

<u>In the middle of the city centre, there are some beautiful spots away from the crowds.</u> For example, <u>you can walk by the river or take a boat trip. Trips leave from Bayford Pool.</u>

You can travel to Lincoln by train, bus or car. It is 216km from London. The bus station is beside the river and <u>the railway station is a few minutes' walk away from the bus station on the other side of St Mary's Street.</u>

4   Use this sentence to demonstrate that the text and the questions will not use the same words exactly.

Explain the system used in the exam – A is used for a correct sentence and B is used for an incorrect sentence. The answer sheets have A and B on them, not *correct/incorrect* or *true/false*.

Answer
1 A

5   Ask students to work in pairs, finding the parts of the text they need to check each sentence, and deciding if each one is correct or incorrect.

Go through the answers with the whole class. Explain any items of vocabulary not already covered. Draw students' attention to the Exam Advice box.

Answers
2 B   3 B   4 A   5 A   6 A

 Corpus spot   Prepositions

This picks up on some prepositions in the text. Students can find the following sentences to help them:

... just outside the main city centre (**a**)

It's not far from (**b**) the castle.

There is a wonderful view of the city from there. (**c**)

Behind the castle (**d**)

There is a car park a few metres from the café. (**e**)

... the Tourist Information Centre, which is next to the castle. (**f**)

The Toy Museum is near the Tourist Information Centre (**g**)

The bus station is beside the river (**h**)

... the railway station is a few minutes' walk away from the bus station (**i**)

Answers
a   We will meet 15 minutes before the film starts <u>outside</u> the cinema.
b   My flat isn't too far away <u>from</u> the town centre.
c   There is a lovely view of the sea <u>from</u> the window.
d   We saw a big tree and <u>behind it</u> was a lake.
e   The cinema is a few metres <u>from</u> the Underground station.
f   In my room there is a radio next <u>to</u> the TV.
g   I live in the south of France <u>near</u> Toulouse.
h   I am staying in a small town <u>beside</u> a large forest.
i   He works only one block away <u>from</u> where I am working.

8 Let's celebrate

In this unit:

Grammar	Present perfect simple; *just, already* and *yet*
Functions and vocabulary	Describing experiences and recent activities; celebrations, festivals and parties; giving good wishes
Pronunciation	Dates
PET skills	Talking about a photograph (Speaking Part 3); matching pictures to a recording (Listening Part 1); recognising collocations (Reading Part 5); talking about special occasions (Speaking Part 4)
Revision	Dates (Unit 4); talking about pictures (Unit 3); present tenses
Exam folder	Speaking Parts 3 and 4
Writing folder	Writing Part 2

Preparation

Writing folder If possible, put the three texts in Exercise 2 on an OHT, or project them from the CD-ROM or webpage. Photocopy the sample answers (on page 172).

SB pages 54–57

Introduction

PET Speaking Part 3

1 This exercise revises the present continuous for talking about pictures. Elicit descriptions of the photograph round the class, encouraging use of the present continuous. Teach *fireworks* and other vocabulary as necessary. The photograph shows New Year's Eve celebrations in Melbourne, Australia.

2 This exercise revises the present simple for customs, and also dates.

Have a brief discussion about when people celebrate with fireworks in different countries (or, for monocultural groups, their country). Encourage use of the present simple.

If necessary, revise present simple/continuous contrast (Unit 3). Revise dates (Unit 4).

3 This exercise introduces/revises ways of expressing good wishes. Encourage students to make guesses, but do not supply any language at this point.

PET Listening Part 1

4, 5 1 32 Play the recording, stopping it to allow students to write what they hear. Go through their answers, writing them on the board for them to check, and supplying the name of the occasion as well as the expression heard for each picture. Ask students if they thought of any other things people might be saying and add any appropriate ones.

Answers and recording script

a Congratulations! (They're getting married.)
b Good luck! (They're taking an exam.)
c Happy birthday! (It's the boy's birthday. Also possible: *Many happy returns*, or *Congratulations* for a special birthday, e.g. 18 or 60.)
d Have a good journey! (They're starting a journey. Also possible: *Enjoy your trip*.)
e Enjoy your meal! (They're having a meal.*)
f Well done! (He's won a race. Also possible: *Congratulations*.)
g Happy anniversary! (It's their wedding anniversary. Also possible: *Congratulations*.)
h Have a nice weekend! (The man is leaving work on Friday evening. Also possible: *See you on Monday*.)

* There is no set expression used by English speakers at the beginning of a meal. *Enjoy your meal* is normally said by the waiter, not a fellow diner.

Reading

1 Pre-teach *honeymoon*. Discuss the photographs with the class. Ask questions to elicit suggestions about the four couples, e.g. *Is the wedding happening in England? Is this a traditional wedding? Is this a rich couple?* Don't indicate yet whether students' ideas are likely to be correct.

Note: People from the UK can get married in a registry office, a church or other religious building, or at any other place licensed for weddings, which might be a hotel or historic building, etc. (At least a quarter of couples in the UK do not go through any form of marriage ceremony nowadays.)

Answers

Photo **a** shows a wedding ceremony at a traditional church wedding. With lots of guests, this will cost thousands of pounds and is traditionally paid for by the bride's father, though costs are often shared now.

Photo **b** shows an exotic location where a wedding can take place. The bride and groom fly out, get married and stay there for their honeymoon. This is an increasingly popular trend with couples who want a 'romantic' wedding and honeymoon, but cannot afford or do not wish to spend so much on the wedding and reception.

Photo **c** shows a registry office wedding (the most usual way to get married in the UK).

Photo **d** shows a wedding in a licensed wedding venue.

2 Ask students to do the matching exercise and go through it with the class, explaining any vocabulary as necessary.

Answers
a Nigel and Fiona   b Anna and Jay
c Dawn and Gary   d Lorne and Esmerelda

3 In this exercise students practise answering *Wh*-questions. Ask students to work in pairs. If appropriate, half of the class can work through **a–g**, and half through **h–n**.

Go through the answers with the class, focusing on the content rather than grammatical accuracy.

Answers
b A new bikini and some sunscreen.
c Their family and friends.
d When they come back.
e Because they're both very famous.
f The rings.
g Because no one can disturb them there on their honeymoon.
h All their friends and their parents and all their relations.
i Fiona's parents.
j (They've booked) a band.
k Because they're keeping that a secret until their wedding day.
l Because she doesn't know who's accepted and who's refused (their secretaries have organised everything).
m To a good restaurant. Back to work.
n Because they're too busy to go away (this year).

PET Reading Part 5

4 Ask students to match the words (they are all found in the newspaper articles). Recognising collocations can help with the Reading Part 5 cloze test.

Answers
b 9 keep a secret
c 2 book a band
d 3 organise a barbecue
e 7 refuse an invitation
f 1/8 make an appointment a mistake
g 6 rent a cottage
h 5 hire a car
i 8/1 make a mistake / an appointment

 Corpus spot   Verb + noun pairs

Encourage students to learn verb + noun pairs together.

Answers
a I often go there and <u>have</u> a barbecue with my friends.
b I had a rest and I <u>made</u> a plan for my holiday.
c My friend is leaving next week so we'd like to <u>have</u> a party.
d I will <u>make</u> some reservations because this is a busy time of year.
e I hope you don't <u>make</u> the same mistake as me.
f His name is John and we <u>are</u> the same age.

PET Speaking Part 4

5 Encourage students to give reasons for their answers. If appropriate, they might compare these wedding plans with weddings in their own country or community.

EXTRA

If they are interested, they can talk about their own ideas for a good wedding, or where they'd like to go for their honeymoon.

Language focus

Present perfect; *just*, *already* and *yet*

These exercises cover the formation and meaning of the present perfect tense.

1 Do the first two or three sentences with the whole class. Elicit the form of the present perfect (*has/have* + past participle). Ask students to complete the exercise, checking their own answers with the help of the newspaper article on page 55.

Answers (Contractions are acceptable.)
b have told   c have rented   d haven't planned
e haven't told   f have booked   g have sent
h has accepted; has refused   i has made

Language presentation

Look at the table with the students. Remind them that English has regular and irregular verbs (see Unit 6, past simple). Point out that some verbs use the same form for both the past simple and the participle in the present perfect. Suggest that they always check this when learning new verbs. Elicit the difference in form between the present perfect tense and the past simple (Unit 6) and work through the table together.

Use examples from the newspaper article to elicit or demonstrate the meaning of the present perfect, for example:

Anna is talking about a bikini which she *owns*. She's not telling us *when* she bought it, all we need to know is that it was before now.

Anna and Jay's families and friends *know* that they plan to marry soon. Anna and Jay are not saying *when* they told their families, because that is unimportant.

Lorne and Esmerelda *have* their rings. They're not telling us *when* they bought them, all we need to know is that it was before now.

↘ Grammar spot   Present perfect

Ask students to complete the Grammar spot.

Answers
Formation

verb	past simple	past participle
open	opened	*opened*
plan	*planned*	planned
organise	organised	*organised*
send	*sent*	sent
tell	told	*told*
make	*made*	made
take	*took*	taken
eat	ate	*eaten*
be	was/were	*been*
go	*went*	gone

Meaning
a past simple **b** present perfect

2   Ask students to do the exercise, using dictionaries to check participles if necessary. Go through the exercise with the class, writing the verbs up on the board so that they can check the spelling.

Suggested answers
b He's broken the chair.
c He's dropped his glass.
d They've lost the key.
e They've eaten all the food.
f She's spilt some orange juice.
g They've drunk all the fizzy drinks.
h They've made a terrible mess.

3   Draw students' attention to the question form. Refer to Jay's text on page 55 to elicit/supply the meaning of *just* (*very recently*). Do the exercise orally round the class before students write their answers. Invite students to write them on the board to check.

Answers
b Have you washed the glasses yet?
     Yes, I've just washed them.
c Have you tidied the living room yet?
     Yes, I've just tidied it.
d Have you found the key yet?
     Yes, I've just found it.
e Have you thrown away the rubbish yet?
     Yes, I've just thrown it away.
f Have you bought any food yet?
     Yes, I've just bought some.
g Have you mended the chair yet?
     Yes, I've just mended it.

Language presentation

Write *already* and *yet* on the board. Explain that these are often used with the present perfect. Ask students to look at Gary's part of the newspaper article on page 55 and find the examples there. If the meaning causes problems, give some true examples (e.g. *We haven't finished this unit yet, but we've already done lots of work. We've already done five exercises, but Pietro hasn't arrived yet.*)

Remind students of the meaning of *just*. Ask them to complete the sentences and check them together.

↘ Grammar spot

just, *already* and *yet* + present perfect

Answers
a just **b** already **c** yet **d** already **e** yet **f** yet

4   This can be homework. Check answers together.

Answers
b already **c** yet **d** yet **e** already **f** already

≪Pronunciation≫   PET Listening Part 3

This practises saying and understanding dates.

1   Ask students how to say the first date – we **say** *the third of July* (or *July the third*) but we **write** *3rd July* or just *3 July*. Refer to Unit 4 Pronunciation if necessary. Go round the class asking students to say the other dates, checking whether they need more practice. Check they know when to use the abbreviations *st*, *nd*, *rd* and *th*.

EXTRA

It may be appropriate to discuss how the date is spoken and written in American English – *July nineteen* in American English instead of *July the nineteenth* or *the nineteenth of July* in British English. This would be written 7/19 in American English and 19/7 in British English.

2 **1·33** Play the recording so students can repeat the dates. Stop after the first one to point out the weak form of *of* /əv/.

> ### Recording script
> the third of July
> the first of January
> the twenty-fifth of March
> the twenty-fourth of October
> the second of February

3 **1·34** Play the recording. Ask students to write down the dates they hear. They need to be able to write accurately the days of the week, months and dates which they hear in Listening Part 3.

> **Answers and recording script**
> (the) 11(th of) November   (the) 12(th of) June
> (the) 14(th of) December   (the) 20(th of) April
> (the) 21(st of) August   (the) 22(nd of) September

4 Students work in groups to think of important events on the dates given, e.g. *New Year's Day is on the first of January*. You may need to provide the names of some festivals. The first group to finish reports back to the others. You could make a rule that if they give a date such as *my brother's birthday*, someone else in another group should be able to vouch that this is true.

◀Activity▶ Planning a party

Brainstorm with students some of the things we do when preparing a party and write them on the board, eliciting or supplying vocabulary as needed, e.g. *buy drinks, plan the food, cook the food, choose where to have the party, decide who to invite, write invitations, organise the music*, etc. as appropriate to the class.

Divide the students into groups of between five and ten. Tell them that they are going to play a memory game. They are having a party tonight and everything is ready. They must tell their friends what they have done. Each student speaks in turn and adds one more thing to the list. You can begin by demonstrating with one group. The students may know a version of this game in their own language.

Example:

A: We've bought the drinks.
B: We've bought the drinks and we've organised the music.
C: We've bought the drinks, we've organised the music and we've written the invitations.
D: We've bought the drinks, we've organised the music, we've written the invitations and we've chosen where to have the party.

If a student misses an activity from the list, or gives them in the wrong order, or makes a grammatical error, the group must start again, beginning with the student who was due to take the following turn.

The group which can achieve the longest list is the winner.

Exam folder 8

SB pages 58–59

Speaking Part 3

1 Ask students to try to match the photographs with the festivals listed. Discuss briefly what the people are celebrating. Use some of the questions in Exam folder 3 (page 26) to get students to tell you more about the photographs.

> **Answers**
> 1 d   2 c   3 b   4 a

EXTRA

At Christmas time many people decorate real or artificial trees with sweets or tinsel.

On St Valentine's Day people traditionally send an anonymous card or present to the one they love or admire.

Eggs have pre-Christian associations with spring, but chocolate eggs are part of the Easter celebrations enjoyed by most UK children, whether their families are churchgoers or not.

Notting Hill is a very large public carnival which takes place in London. There are thousands of bands and dancers of many kinds, but especially from the Afro-Caribbean communities.

2 Ask students to turn to page 26 and briefly revise the questions and answers they practised there. Remind them that these can help them when they talk about photographs in the exam.

Reassure them that this is not a test of their general knowledge, but of their English. It does not matter if they do not know what festival their photograph shows. (Photograph **a** shows Holi Festival in India. Photograph **b** shows the Ice festival at Lake Shikotsu, Japan.)

3 Look at the Exam Advice box with the class. Ask students to work in pairs. In multinational classes, try to make sure they work with someone from a different country – this will be particularly helpful for Speaking Part 4, which follows. Before beginning to speak, they should spend a few moments thinking of answers to the questions from Exam folder 3. Tell them to listen carefully to check whether their partner answers the questions as they talk. They may be able to add one or two more questions.

Supply any important items of vocabulary when they have finished.

Speaking Part 4

Look at the question prompts with the class and practise making questions from them.

In multinational classes, give students a minute or two to think about festivals in their own country, then put them in pairs of different nationalities to ask each other questions.

In mononational classes, ask students for suggestions of festivals. Get them each to choose one to talk about, or, in a small class, allocate one festival to each student. Make sure pairs have not chosen the same festival. Tell them to take a minute or two to think, then to ask each other the questions. Ask some students to report back to the class.

Writing folder

Writing Part 2

This focuses on understanding some of the verbs commonly used in the instructions for Writing Part 2.

1 Give students a minute or so to read the questions and underline the three bulleted points. Look at the Exam Advice box together and check whether students know what the verbs mean.

2 Read letter **a** with the students and decide together who it is to (Matthew). Ask them to read **b** and **c** and decide which is to Catherine and which is to Ben.

Answers
b Ben   **c** Catherine

3 Do the rest of the underlining in letter **a** together. If possible, project the texts (see Preparation).

Answers
Dear *Matthew*,
I'm having a birthday party next Friday. <u>Would you like to come</u> (*these words invite Matthew to the party*)? <u>All our friends from school are coming and some of my family</u> (*these words tell him who is coming*). I live in the city centre. <u>Take a bus to the bus station, then you can walk from there</u> (*these words suggest how to get there*).

4 Ask students to do the same with letters **b** and **c**.

Answers
b
Dear *Ben*,
<u>Thank you very much for the book you sent me for my birthday</u> (*these words thank him for the present*). <u>I spent the day with my family and I went to a nightclub in the evening with my friends</u> (*these words describe what you did on your birthday*). <u>Can you tell me when your birthday is</u> (*these words ask him when his birthday is*)?
c
Dear *Catherine*,
<u>Thank you for inviting me to your birthday party next week</u> (*these words thank her*). <u>I'm sorry but I can't come</u> (*these words apologise*) <u>because my brother and his wife are visiting us with their new baby</u> (*these words explain why you can't go*). I hope you enjoy the party.

5 Students write answers to these two questions using letters **a**, **b** and **c** as models. See page 172 for photocopiable sample answers.

⬇ Corpus spot   *Come or go?*

Go through the exercise with the class. These verbs may give more problems to speakers of some languages than others. If students have a lot of difficulties, try using real movement to demonstrate, by directing a student to come to you (*Come here, Maria*), go to another student (*Maria, go to Nicola*), etc., then ask other students to give the orders.

Answers
a go   **b** come

9 How do you feel?

TOPIC: Health and fitness

In this unit:

Grammar	Short answers in the present perfect
Functions and vocabulary	Parts of the body; illnesses; giving advice; expressions with *at*
Pronunciation	/e/ as in *tell* and /eɪ/ as in *say*
PET skills	Speculating (Speaking Part 4); listening for specific information (Listening Part 1); coming to a consensus of opinion (Speaking Part 2)
Revision	Tenses already learnt (present simple, present continuous, past simple and present perfect tenses); short answers in the present simple (Unit 3) and past simple (Unit 6)
Exam folder	Reading Part 4 Speaking Part 2

Preparation

Language focus, Illnesses and advice Make copies of the recording script (from CD-ROM or webpage) for students.

Activity *Illnesses* Photocopy the cards (on page 179) and cut them up so each student has one.

Activity *Giving and receiving advice* Photocopy the cards (on page 179) and cut them up so each student has one. There are twelve different ones, so if you have more than twelve students, some can work in pairs or you can duplicate some of the cards.

Activity *How healthy are you?* Photocopy the board (on page 180) and, if you can, stick it onto card. Make one board and provide one dice or spinner per group of four students. Each student needs a counter or a coin to move round the board.

SB pages 60–63

Introduction

1 Talk together about the equipment and the people in the photographs.

Answers
They are lifting weights, exercising on a rowing machine, and exercising on an exercise bike. The weightlifter is exercising his arms, but also muscles all over his body – chest, shoulders, neck, back, legs, stomach. The rower is exercising her arms and legs and also other muscles, such as her stomach muscles. The cyclist is mainly exercising her legs.

2 Ask students to work individually to label the parts of the body. You could add some other words such as *bone, throat*.

Answers

a	finger	h	forehead	o	neck
b	thumb	i	lip	p	chin
c	shoulder	j	cheek	q	knee
d	wrist	k	brain	r	ankle
e	elbow	l	lung	s	toe
f	chest	m	heart		
g	eyebrow	n	stomach		

EXTRA

If you think students would be happy to play a game, you could play *Simon says*. You say *Simon says touch your nose* and everyone touches their nose, or *Simon says shut one eye* and everyone shuts one eye, etc. Students must only do the action if you say *Simon says*, i.e. they shouldn't do it if you just say *Touch your nose*. As you get faster, it is easy for them not to notice that you have omitted *Simon says*. Students can be 'out' if they make a mistake, so you end up with a winner who is really concentrating.

PET Speaking Part 4

3 Does anyone know how many calories we need per day? (The average adult needs about 2,200 per day (women and teenage girls) and 2,500 per day (men and teenage boys).)

Answers
The woman on the cycling machine would use about 450 calories in 30 minutes, the woman on the rowing machine about 300 and the man lifting weights about 110.

Talk about gyms and how students keep fit.

4 Get students to guess the answers and then discuss them.

Answers
washing the dishes – about 85 calories
playing the drums – about 150 calories
watching TV – about 35 calories
playing tennis – about 250 calories
running upstairs – about 550 calories
sweeping the floor – about 130 calories
playing the guitar – about 75 calories
swimming – about 330 calories

Listening

PET Listening Part 1

1 **1 35** Discuss the idea of a medical helpline and why people might ring it (to ask for advice over the phone and check whether they should go to the doctor or hospital).

Play the six conversations which introduce the vocabulary of illnesses. Stop after each one and discuss what the problem is. Point out the useful expression *I'm sorry to bother you* and ask when you would use it. Do not discuss any grammatical problems at the moment.

Answers
a His son has hurt his wrist.
b She has a cough and a sore throat.
c Her husband has a pain in his chest and he feels sick.
d The child has a stomach ache.
e The boy has sore eyes.
f The child has earache and a temperature.

Recording script

a
Nurse: Hello. Healthlink Phone Line. Can I help you?
Man: Oh, yes, thank you. My son fell over at school today. He was playing football. His arm hurts, well, his wrist really.
Nurse: Did he hit his head?
Man: No, he didn't.
Nurse: Can he move his fingers?
Man: No, he can't. He can't move them at all.
b
Nurse: Hello. Healthlink Phone Line. Can I help you?
Girl: Hello. I've got a cough and a sore throat. I cough all the time, especially at night. I can't stop and I can't sleep.
Nurse: Have you got a cold at the moment?
Girl: No, I haven't. I had one last week but it's gone. Now I've got this cough.
c
Nurse: Hello. Healthlink Phone Line. Can I help you?
Woman: Oh, yes. My husband isn't feeling well. He's got a pain in his chest. He's usually very healthy. I don't understand it.
Nurse: Does he feel sick?
Woman: Yes, he does.
d
Nurse: Hello. Healthlink Phone Line. Can I help you?
Man: Oh, hello. I'm sorry to bother you, but I'm looking after a friend's daughter and she has a terrible stomach ache.
Nurse: Does she have a headache?
Man: Yes, she does.

Nurse: Has she eaten a lot today?
Man: No, she hasn't. Well, let me see. She had a big breakfast. Then we went to the cinema and she had a burger and chips at lunchtime, oh, and some popcorn. Since then she's only had a bar of chocolate and a drink. Should I take her to the doctor's?
e
Nurse: Hello. Healthlink Phone Line. Can I help you?
Boy: Yes. Hello. I've got sore eyes. I can't open them very well.
Nurse: Have you spent a lot of time working at a computer this week? Are you very tired?
Boy: No, I'm not. I'm not working this week. I'm relaxing at home.
Nurse: Do you wear glasses or contact lenses?
Boy: No, I don't.
f
Nurse: Hello. Healthlink Phone Line. Can I help you?
Woman: Hello. My son's got earache. He cried all night. He's just stopped at last so I decided to phone. I don't want to ring the doctor at the weekend.
Nurse: Is he hot?
Woman: Yes, he is. He's got a temperature.
Nurse: Has he taken any aspirin or paracetamol?
Woman: Yes, he has. Just now.

2 **1 35** Students listen again and think about what the nurse's advice will be.

PET Speaking Part 2

3 Ask students to compare their answers in groups and try to come to a consensus.

4 **1 36** Tell students that they are going to compare their answers with what the nurse says.

Play the nurse's responses (this version contains all six conversations with the nurse's responses below at the end of each one).

Students compare their answers with the ones they heard and, where they are different, decide if they agree with the nurse or not.

Answers
a go to the hospital   b and d stay at home
c call an ambulance   e and f go to the doctor's

Recording script

a
Nurse: You should take him to the hospital. It's probably broken.
Man: OK. Thanks. We'll go now.

b

Nurse: People often have a cough for a few days after a cold. Why don't you take some cough mixture before you go to bed? Why don't you take a warm drink to bed with you too, and you should sleep with at least two pillows. Your cough will soon be better.

Girl: I hope so. Thank you.

c

Nurse: You should call an ambulance to take him to hospital. You'd better dial 999 at once. Can you do that now?

Woman: Yes, of course.

d

Nurse: You don't need to see a doctor. She shouldn't eat any more food today. But she should drink lots of water.

Man: OK. Thank you.

e

Nurse: Why don't you wash your eyes in warm water? And get an appointment with your doctor because you probably need some antibiotics.

Boy: Thanks for your help.

f

Nurse: Well, why don't you give him some more paracetamol after four hours? And you'd better phone the doctor. You can get an emergency appointment.

Woman: Thanks very much.

Language focus

Illnesses and advice

1 Ask students to do the exercise alone or in pairs. Photocopy the recording script (see Preparation) and either give it to students before they start the exercise so they can use it to help them or give it to them afterwards for checking.

> **Answers**
> **a** I've got a temperature. (= I've got a high temperature.)
> **b** I've got earache.
> **c** I've got a cough.
> **d** I've got a cold.
> **e** I've got a sore eye.
> **f** I've got a pain in my chest.
> **g** My arm hurts / is broken.
> **h** I feel sick.

Check students understand what *sore* means. We say *a headache, (a) backache, (a) stomach ache* and *(a) toothache* – we usually omit the article except before *headache. Stomach ache* is normally two words. Check the pronunciation of *ache* /eɪk/. Make sure students notice that we say *my/his*, etc. before parts of the body, not *the*.

You may like to teach *fever* as an alternative to *temperature* and the words *thermometer* and *sneeze*. In British English, *to feel sick* means you want to vomit, whereas in American English it has a more general meaning – to feel unwell.

2 **1** **37** Play the nurse's responses again and ask students to complete the sentences.

> **Answers**
> **b** don't you take   **c** should call   **d** shouldn't eat
> **e** don't you wash   **f** better phone

> **Recording script**
> **a** You should take him to the hospital.
> **b** Why don't you take some cough mixture?
> **c** You should call an ambulance.
> **d** She shouldn't eat any more food today.
> **e** Why don't you wash your eyes in warm water?
> **f** You'd better phone the doctor.

3 Elicit the word *medicine* and discuss the words and expressions. Add any others which might be useful. Go round the class asking students to give advice to people in the pictures, using the advice structures above.

Expressions with *at*

1 Ask students to do the exercise in pairs or individually. Students should learn any expressions they don't know.

> **Answers**
> **b** all   **c** night   **d** the moment   **e** lunchtime
> **f** home   **g** last   **h** the weekend   **i** least   **j** once

> ↘ **Corpus spot** Expressions with *at* and *in* ⊙
>
> **Answers**
> **a** The weather is cold <u>at</u> night.
> **b** I get bored staying <u>at</u> home doing nothing.
> **c** ✓
> **d** That's all I have to tell you <u>at</u> the moment.
> **e** We usually go to the beach <u>at</u> the weekend.
> **f** ✓

Short answers

1 Students have met short answers before (present simple in Unit 3 and past simple in Unit 6). This exercise revises those and introduces short answers in the present perfect.

Do the first two or three together, reminding students that the verb in the short answer always matches the auxiliary in the question.

Answers
b 9 c 8 d 2 e 7 f 3 g 6 h 5 i 1

↘ Grammar spot Short answers

Students use their answers to the exercise to complete the summary.

Answers

Question	Short answer
Present simple	*does, do* or *doesn't, don't*
Past simple	*did* or *didn't*
Present perfect	*has, have* or *hasn't, haven't*

Language presentation

Ask some quick questions around the class using a range of tenses, to practise and check the pronunciation of short answers (the auxiliary is stressed), e.g.

Has Pierre got black hair?

Do you like cheese?

Are you married?

Do Paola and Cristina live in the same street?

Is the school near the town centre?

Has Marina had lunch?

Did you go to the cinema yesterday?

Have you ever been in an aeroplane?

2 Ask students to do the exercise as fast as they can. Short answers need to become as automatic as possible. When they have finished, they can check each other's work.

Answers
b Yes, I do.   c Yes, he/she is.   d Yes, they are. / No, they aren't.   e Yes, I am.   f Yes, it is. / No, it isn't.
g No, I haven't.   h No, he/she hasn't.   i Yes, I/we do. / No, I/we don't.

«Activity» Illnesses

Give each student a card (see Preparation). Students work in teams. Each member of the team takes turns to mime what is wrong with them. The other team(s) say what the problem is. They must give the exact words on the card. Both teams get a mark if they get it correct. The guessing team gives advice and gets another mark if the advice they give is also grammatically correct.

«Activity» Giving and receiving advice

Give each student a card (see Preparation). There are twelve different ones, so if you have more than twelve students, some can work in pairs or you can duplicate some of the cards.

Students should read their cards and look up any words they don't know. They should then tear or cut their card in half so they have separated the problem and the advice. They move round the class reading their problem and listening to other people's problems. When they hear the problem which matches the advice they have, they should read the advice and then hand it over.

«Pronunciation»

This exercise practises the sounds /e/ and /eɪ/ and the different ways they are spelt.

1 Ask students to complete the words and then go through them.

Answers
b h<u>e</u>lp   c fri<u>e</u>nd t<u>a</u>kes tr<u>ai</u>n   d h<u>ea</u>lthy br<u>ea</u>kfast d<u>ay</u>   e h<u>ea</u>d p<u>ai</u>n   f br<u>ea</u>k   g gr<u>ea</u>t pl<u>ay</u> tod<u>ay</u>

2 Ask students to say the words aloud to themselves and try to choose between the two sounds – which rhyme with *tell* and which with *say*? Point out that the spelling won't always be helpful.

3 **1 38** Play the recording and have students repeat each one. Give them time to change their answers from Exercise 2 if necessary and then go through them.

Answers
/eɪ/: takes train day pain break great play today
/e/: fell help friend healthy breakfast head

Recording script

a My son fell over.
b Can I help you?
c My friend takes the train to college.
d I eat a healthy breakfast every day.
e I hit my head and now I've got a pain.
f Don't break that glass.
g I saw a great play today.

4

Answers
Spellings of /eɪ/: *a, ai, ay, ea*
Spellings of /e/: *e, ea, ie*

Point out that the usual spelling of the sound /eɪ/ is *ai* or *ay*; the letter *a* is normally pronounced /eɪ/ when the word ends in an *e*, as in *take* – other examples are *sale*, *make*, *ate*. The letters *ea* are almost always pronounced /e/ or /iː/ – *break* is an exception, and note that it is pronounced /e/ in *breakfast*.

The sound /e/ is usually spelt *e* or *ea*; *friend* is an exception.

«Activity» How healthy are you?

1   Ask students to answer the questions themselves.

2   Ideally students should work in groups of four. Give them one board and dice or spinner per group (see Preparation).

    Students play the board game. The aim is to get to the top of the board by throwing the dice and moving the correct number of places. If they land on a 'question square' they have to answer *yes* or *no* using a short answer. If the other people in the group think a question isn't answered honestly or correctly using a short answer, that person has to go down.

3   There is room for disagreement – the questions give a very general profile of someone but you could obviously argue that having a bicycle doesn't mean you actually ride it!

Exam folder 9

SB pages 64–65

Reading Part 4

This prepares students for the kinds of question they will come across in this part of the exam. This part of the exam has five multiple-choice questions and this folder prepares them for the first four of these. In the exam, they have one long text rather than four short texts as here.

1   Read the first text together and discuss who has written it. Look at A, B, C and D and decide which matches text 1 (D). Students read the other three texts silently and choose A, B, C or D.

    Ask students to underline the words which helped them if possible. They should use a colour as they will do this three times.

A Text 2 is advising: *You should try it. You really shouldn't work hard all the time. Why don't you join the health club?*
B Text 4 is apologising: *It was very rude of me. I'm really sorry.*
C Text 3 is advertising: *special discount; Don't miss the chance to join.*
D Text 1 is complaining: *I am not happy about this because it is very dangerous.*

2   Students find the answers and discuss them. Ask them to underline the words that helped them in a different colour.

A The writer of text 4 has this opinion: *The equipment in the gym is old and is sometimes difficult to use.*
B The writer of text 3 has this opinion: *There is no other club in town which is as good as this one.*
C The writer of text 2 has this opinion: *I use the pool there because it's brilliant. The gym is OK.*
D The writer of text 1 has this opinion: *There were no instructors.*

3   Students find the answers, then underline the words that helped them in a different colour. Look at the Exam Advice box together.

A Text 3 states this: *phone me, Mick Smith, the manager*
B Text 1 states this: *I joined your health club last week. / I came in for the first time on Thursday.*
C Text 4 states this: *I go to the club every Sunday afternoon*
D Text 2 states this: *I go ... at least twice a week*

Speaking Part 2

1   Discuss the picture of Josh with the class. Elicit the fact that he has broken his leg. Discuss the Exam Advice box with the students. In the Speaking test, the students have no written instructions. The examiner explains the situation and gives the students a picture or pictures to discuss. They are not penalised if they ask the examiner to repeat something.

2   Ask students to look at the pictures and ask them to think about which things Josh can and can't use, which he needs and which he would like to have.

3   Ask students to work in pairs for about three or four minutes and discuss what to take him. Go through the phrases we can use for giving opinions, making suggestions and agreeing and disagreeing. It is not essential for them to reach agreement in the exam, but they should give each other reasons for their opinions.

4   See which thing(s) the class wanted to take him.

10 I look forward to hearing from you

In this unit:	
Grammar	Present perfect and past simple; *ago, for, since, in*; *ever*; *been* and *gone*
Functions and vocabulary	Beginning and ending letters; forms of correspondence (letter, card, email, etc.); UK addresses; making arrangements
Pronunciation	Plural nouns: /s/, /z/ and /ɪz/
PET skills	Letters (Writing Part 3); sentence transformations (Writing Part 1)
Revision	Present perfect forms (Unit 8); short answers (Units 6 and 9)
Exam folder	Listening Part 1
Writing folder	Writing Part 3

Preparation

Pronunciation Write out or make an OHT of sentences for Exercise 3 so that the class can do it together. Have three colour pens ready. Alternatively project them from the CD-ROM or webpage.

Activity *Did you …?* Write the names of famous people from the past (now dead) on cards. For small classes, have a different name for each student. For larger ones, divide them into groups of six or more and give each member of the group a different name.

SB pages 66–69

Introduction

1 Ask the class to look at the texts and suggest what they are. Write the answers on the board, including any reasonable alternatives.

> **Answers**
> 1 notice in window   2 birthday card
> 3 anniversary card   4 Post-it note   5 business letter
> 6 someone sending a text message   7 postcard
> 8 someone writing an email

2 Discuss/explain the answers as necessary with students.

> **Answers**
> a birthday card (2)   b Post-it note (4)
> c text message (6)   d anniversary card (3)
> e business letter (5)   f email (8)   g postcard (7)
> h notice in window (1)

(↘) Vocabulary spot

Beginning and ending letters and emails

> **Answers**
> We begin letters and emails: *Dear (Name)*. Emails are also often started with *Hi (Name)*.
> Remind students that it is not normal to write *Dear Friend* in English.
> We end a letter or email to a friend: *All the best, / (With) Best wishes, / (With) Love (from)*
> 'Love' is more commonly used by women and children, but men may use it to close female friends and relatives.
> We end a letter or email to a stranger: *Yours sincerely*. Students are not expected to write formal letters in PET, but they can learn that this is the most widely used form.

3 Encourage students to say whether they use any of these forms of written communication, and if so under what circumstances.

4 Your students may know many of these. Ask if they know any others. If they do not know most of them, put them in small teams to see which can work out the meanings of these shortcuts the fastest.

> **Answers**
> | :) | I'm happy. / This is a joke. |
> | :(| I'm sad. |
> | :{ | I have a moustache. |
> | :o | I'm surprised. |
> | CU | See you. |
> | 4U | For you. |
> | 2U | To you. |
> | CUL8R | See you later. |
> | RUOK? | Are you OK? |
> | YRUX? | Why are you cross? |
> | 2b/nt2b=? | To be or not to be, that is the question. (First line of soliloquy in *Hamlet*) |

Reading

1 This task practises scanning for specific information. Ask students to work in pairs. This can be done as a race to see which pair can sort the letters fastest. Make sure they understand that they have to separate the letters and emails into two groups. Encourage them to read silently, as quickly as they can.

> **Answers**
> Mike's letters/emails: **a, c, f, h**
> Maria's letters/emails: **b, d, e, g**

2 After checking Exercise 1, ask students to put the letters and emails in order. There are lots of clues to help them, such as the names, so students should be able to sort them out, even if they find some words or expressions they do not know.

Answers
Mike 2 – **f**	Mike 3 – **h**	Mike 4 – **c**
Maria 2 – **d**	Maria 3 – **g**	Maria 4 – **e**

3 Go through the questions with the class, writing the examples and other answers on the board, so that you end up with two lists of questions and answers: **a–e** and **f–j**. Do not clean the board if the lesson continues after this point.

Answers
b (Because) they've moved to another town.
c (Because) he hasn't studied English since secondary school.
d Yes, he has.
e She's reserved a room in the hostel for him.

f Five years ago.
g Last year.
h Three years ago.
i The Gibsons.
j When he was a child. / Ten years ago.

Language focus
Present perfect and past simple; *ago, for, since, in*

Language presentation

Ask students why the questions/answers **a–e** in Reading Exercise 3 are in the present perfect, but those in **f–j** are in the past simple. Elicit/Supply that the focus is on the present result in **a–e**, whereas in **f–j** the focus is on a point of time in the past.

The following presentation is more interesting if you use real biodata about yourself or the students. It builds the table in the Grammar spot.

Draw a time line on the board. Mark a point in the past and date it (see example).

↓2007   ↓ NOW

Ask a question using the present perfect, e.g. *How long have I worked here?* Elicit/supply the answer *for (three) years* and write *I've worked here for (three) years* on the board above the time line as shown, connecting it to the past time point and now.

←— I've worked here for (three) years. —→
↓2007   ↓ NOW

Ask students if they can make a sentence using *since*. Elicit/Supply *I've worked here since 2007* and add it to the time line.

←— I've worked here since 2007. —→
←— I've worked here for (three) years. —→
↓2007   ↓ NOW

Now ask a question using the past simple, e.g. *When did I start this job?* and elicit/supply the answer *in 2007*. Add it to the time line, connecting it to the past time point as shown.

←— I've worked here since 2007. —→
←— I've worked here for (three) years. —→
↓2007   ↓ NOW
↓
I started this job in 2007.

Ask students to make a sentence using *ago*. Elicit/Supply *I started this job (three) years ago* and add it to the time line as before.

←— I've worked here since 2007. —→
←— I've worked here for (three) years. —→
↓2007   ↓ NOW
↓
I started this job in 2007.
I started this job (three) years ago.

Practise further by asking a few questions round the class using the present perfect and the past simple.

Clean the board and ask students to complete the Grammar spot. Check their answers.

⬊ Grammar spot

Present perfect and past simple + *ago, for, since, in/on/at*

Answers
←— I've worked here *since* 2007. —→
←— I've worked here *for* (three) years. —→

I started this job *in* 2007.
I started this job (three) years *ago*.

a present perfect	**b** present perfect
c past simple	**d** past simple

1 Ask students to complete the dialogue alone, then work with a partner to check their answers.

Answers
b Did you have   **c** was   **d** met   **e** Have you been
f I've been   **g** I've learnt   **h** Have you been
i I have   **j** was   **k** I visited   **l** I didn't come
m I've found   **n** I arrived

2 Do the first two or three with the whole class, then let them work on through the exercise.

Answers
b 've/have already earned   **c** began   **d** gave
e told   **f** didn't want   **g** got   **h** 've/have sold
i bought   **j** 've/have spent

3 This exercise practises some of the grammar commonly tested in Writing Part 1. It also emphasises the parallel meanings of sentences in the present perfect and past simple.

Answers
b ago   **c** since   **d** for   **e** since   **f** ago

 Corpus spot   *For, since* or *ago*?

Answers
a since (It may be useful to point out that this means *since we were at college*.)
b ago   **c** since   **d** ago   **e** for

 Corpus spot   *Been* and *gone*

Discuss the examples with the class and the meaning of *been* as the present perfect of *go* when it means *go to and return from*.

Point out the example in Reading Exercise 1, text d: *I've never been to Birmingham before* and in Reading Exercise 2, question h: *Have you been to England before?*

Answers
a been   **b** gone   **c** gone   **d** been   **e** been
f gone   **g** been

Have you ever ...?

Explain that *ever* is used in this sort of question emphatically (meaning *at any time*).

Practise a few questions and answers round the class, then ask students to do the exercise in pairs.

If appropriate, ask them to write the exercise up as homework.

Answers (students' responses will vary)
b Have you ever bought something online?
c Have you ever been to Bangkok?
d Have you ever been to a pop concert?
e Have you ever ridden a bike?
f Have you ever been to a wedding?

«Pronunciation»

This practises the pronunciation of final *s* in plurals.

1 **1 39** Write up the word *glasses* and ask students to repeat it after you. Demonstrate the /ɪz/ sound. Then ask them to underline the word with that sound in each of the other sentences.

Play the recording for them to check their answers. Elicit the rule that we say /ɪz/ after /s/, /dʒ/, /ʃ/ and /tʃ/.

They copy the underlined words into the first column.

Answers
/ɪz/
glasses
bridges
hairbrushes
matches

Recording script

a He needs new <u>glasses</u>.
b There are ten <u>bridges</u> in the city.
c I bought two new <u>hairbrushes</u>.
d There are three football <u>matches</u> tomorrow.

2 **1 40** Write on the board: *lips books hats*. Say the words and then ask some students to say them. Elicit that they end in /s/.

Now write on the board: *games schools balls*. Do the same and elicit that this time the words end in /z/.

Ask students to look at the sentences in their books and listen to the recording. They should put the underlined words into the correct column.

Answers
/s/	/z/
books	schools
shops	legs
chips	shoes
cakes	lessons
boots	

Ask students if they can see a rule for the /s/ sound – it occurs after /k/, /p/ and /t/.

Recording script

a Those are my books.
b There are three schools in this street.
c Where are the shops?
d She's got really long legs.
e Her shoes are uncomfortable.
f We had chips for lunch.
g I like cakes.
h The lessons were boring.
i Her boots are black.

3 **1 41** If possible, put the sentences on the board (see Preparation), and ask students to come up and mark the different sounds in different colours (or underline, circle, box them). Play the recording and ask them to repeat each sentence.

Recording script and answers

a My father <u>plays</u> tennis very well. /z/
b My back <u>aches</u>. /s/
c He never <u>catches</u> the ball. /ɪz/
d She <u>swims</u> every day. /z/
e He <u>likes</u> travelling. /s/
f She <u>stays</u> at home on <u>Sundays</u>. /z/, /z/
g He never <u>finishes</u> work early. /ɪz/
h He <u>eats</u> salad every day. /s/
i She <u>always</u> <u>watches</u> him when he <u>plays</u> football. /z/, /ɪz/, /z/
j He <u>hopes</u> to be a scientist. /s/
k The hotel <u>arranges</u> everything. /ɪz/

≪Activity≫ Did you . . . ?

This activity practises past simple and present perfect questions and short answers.

Read through the example with one student to make sure they all understand what to do.

Hand out the cards (see Preparation).

Remind students that their questions and answers must be grammatical and ask them to refer doubts or disputed facts to you.

Exam folder 10

SB pages 70–71

Listening Part 1

Look together at the Summary box about this part of the exam. (This folder has only five questions, not seven as in the exam.)

1 Look at the question and pictures for question 1 in Exercise 3 with students and establish that it is about forms of transport – the words *car*, *bus* and *train* are almost certainly mentioned in the recording.

2 Ask students to work in pairs and do the same for the other questions.

Suggested answers
2 hotel, campsite, beach (tall, floor)
3 beard, short hair, glasses
4 journalist, photographer, actress
5 CD, calendar, picture

3 **1 42** Look at the Exam Advice box and remind students that they have two chances to get the answers.

Play the recordings (each one is heard twice), then check the answers.

Answers
1 A   2 C   3 A   4 B   5 B

Recording script

For each question, there are three pictures and a short recording.
Choose the correct picture and put a tick (✓) in the box below it.

1
How did the woman travel?
Woman: Hi, I got here safely. <u>I drove in the end</u> because I was late last time when I took the train. It was raining, so I didn't want to wait for the bus.

2
Where did the man stay?
Man: We were on the top floor of the hotel and we expected to have a lovely view. But <u>our hotel only had four floors</u> and there was a much taller hotel between us and the sea so we couldn't see much. There was a nice campsite next to the beach so next time we're going there.

3
Which is the girl's brother?
Boy: I was walking through town yesterday and your brother stopped to say hi. I didn't recognise him – he looks so different.
Girl: I suppose so. <u>He's grown a beard and he wears glasses</u> now.
Boy: And his hair's really short, too.

4

Which job is Alice doing now?

Man: Is Alice working as an actress now? She was still training last time I saw her.

Woman: Oh, she didn't finish that course. It's difficult to get a job, you know. She's working on the local newspaper now <u>as a photographer</u>.

Man: Really? I always expected her to be a journalist – she was so good at writing when she was at school.

5

What has the boy bought his mother?

Girl: Toby, have you bought a birthday present for Mum yet?

Boy: Of course I have. <u>I've got her a calendar</u>, a film one, with pictures of her favourite actors and singers.

Girl: Oh, that was a good idea. I've got her a CD.

Boy: I nearly got her a CD but I couldn't decide which one.

Writing folder

Writing Part 3

The aim of this folder is to help students to produce an appropriate and interesting answer of the right length.

1 Discuss the task with the class, using the questions to elicit suggestions about what the answer should contain.

2 Establish that Mirza's letter answers the questions, but that it is not a good answer because it is too short and simple.

3 Look at the Exam Advice box together. Ask students to choose from sentences a–i to add to Mirza's letter.

While they are looking at them, write Mirza's letter on the board with space between the sentences so that you can add sentences a–i as you go through the exercise with the class.

As you discuss the answers, point out that it is often a good idea to begin answering a letter by saying *thank you*; the extra sentences give more detailed facts about *when*, *how often* and *who with*; and these sentences also say how the writer feels about the facts.

Suggested answers (added sentences are underlined)

<u>Thanks for your letter.</u> I don't go to a fitness centre. <u>There's one near our house and my brother joined it last year. He says it's good.</u> I prefer to do sport outdoors. There's a sports ground near our house. <u>I go there on Saturdays and play football with my friends. On Sundays we have matches against other teams.</u> I go swimming quite often. <u>I usually go to the big pool in the city centre, but sometimes we go surfing in the sea. I really like that and I think it's a great way to keep fit.</u>

All the best,
Mirza

⬎ Grammar spot   Asking for a reply

Ask students to mark the correct words, then write the complete sentence on the board.

Answer
I *look forward to hearing from* you.
This idiom is widely used and, correctly expressed, will gain marks in PET Writing.
Discuss variants, e.g. *I look forward to seeing/meeting you.*

4 Ask students to write a few extra sentences to add to Liz's letter and put as many suggestions as possible on the board.

5 This exercise could be homework, if time is short.

Facts and figures

TOPIC: Geography, nationality and numbers

In this unit:

Grammar	Superlative adjectives; present simple passive
Functions and vocabulary	Countries, nationalities, languages; numbers and measurements; what to say when you're not sure
Pronunciation	/ʃ/ as in *shoe*; /tʃ/ as in *cheese*
PET skills	Answering multiple-choice questions (Listening Part 2); hesitation techniques (Speaking test); understanding and transcribing spoken numbers (Listening Part 3)
Revision	Comparative adjectives (Unit 7); descriptive adjectives (Units 2 and 6)
Exam folder	Reading Part 5

Preparation

It will be useful to have a world map, atlases, a globe or access to *Google Earth* available for this unit.

Activity *Numbers* Photocopy the cards (on page 181) and cut them up (one per student).

SB pages 72–75

Introduction

1   Students learn the names of countries and geographical features. Put them into groups and time them while they match the flags to the countries.

Answers
b 1 (Chile)   **c** 6 (Portugal)   **d** 5 (Italy)   **e** 2 (the USA)
f 7 (Australia)   **g** 4 (Kenya)   **h** 3 (Mexico)

2   This exercise introduces the words *continent, border, equator, island, desert, coast* and *ocean*.

Elicit the names of the continents and write them on the board: *Africa, North* and *South America, Australasia, Antarctica, Asia, Europe*. Do the same for the main oceans: *Atlantic, Pacific, Indian*. If you have an atlas or a globe, get students to point them out. You could also ask students to identify some deserts and islands.

Answers
b Italy   **c** The USA; Mexico   **d** Kenya
e Japan; Australia   **f** Chile   **g** Portugal

3   Look at the box of useful expressions together. Encourage students to note down words they don't know. Each group should now choose one country, anywhere in the world, and write three facts about it on a piece of paper. If they know the flag, they should draw that. Each group reads out their facts and shows their flag. The rest of the class write down which country they think it is. When everyone has finished, compare answers.

Listening

PET Listening Part 2

1   Ask students to work individually or in pairs. Pre-teach *planet* and *valley*. They read the quiz in their books and tick their guesses.

2   **2 02** Students listen to the radio quiz. They will hear a man called Rory answer the questions. They should use a different colour to mark the answers that Rory gives. Check students have marked Rory's answers as below.

Rory's answers
1 C   2 B   3 B   4 C   5 A   6 C   7 A   8 C   9 B   10 A

Recording script

(underlining refers to answers for Exercise 5 below)

Question master: And now, Rory – are you ready? You have ten questions. Number 1 – which is the smallest ocean in the world? Is it (A) the Atlantic Ocean, (B) the Indian Ocean, or (C) the Arctic Ocean?

Rory: The Arctic Ocean.

Question master: Number 2 – which is the longest border in the world? Is it (A) between the USA and Canada, (B) between the USA and Mexico, or (C) between Argentina and Chile?

Rory: Oh, just a moment. I think it's between the USA and Mexico.

Question master: Number 3 – where is the wettest place in the world? Is it (A) in India, (B) in Colombia, or (C) in Nigeria?

Rory: Er, I'm sorry, could you repeat that, please?

Question master: Of course. Where is the wettest place in the world? Is it (A) in India, (B) in Colombia, or (C) in Nigeria?

Rory: I think it's in Colombia.

Question master: Number 4 – which planet is the largest? Is it (A) Earth, (B) Venus, or (C) Jupiter?

Rory: Jupiter.

Question master: Number 5 – in which country is the busiest airport in the world? Is it (A) in the USA, (B) in Japan, or (C) in Greece?

Rory: Er, I'm not sure. The USA.

Question master: Number 6 – which island is the biggest? Is it (A) Great Britain, (B) Greenland, or (C) Cuba?

Rory: I think it's Great Britain. No, let me try again. Cuba – that's my answer.

Question master: Number 7 – which continent has the most people? Is it (A) Asia, (B) Australasia, or (C) Africa?

Rory: Let me think – it's not Australasia. I think it's Asia.

Question master: Number 8 – which city is the most expensive to live in? Is it (A) Geneva, in Switzerland, (B) Paris, in France, or (C) Tokyo, in Japan?

Rory: Tokyo.

Question master: Number 9 – where is the deepest valley in the world? Is it (A) in the USA, (B) in China, or (C) in Kenya?

Rory: I'm sorry, I don't know.

Question master: Have a guess.

Rory: China.

Question master: And the last question. Number 10 – which country is the farthest from the equator? Is it (A) Portugal, (B) Australia, or (C) Peru?

Rory: Just a moment. Portugal.

Question master: Thank you, Rory. You got seven correct answers and three wrong answers.

3   Students know that three of Rory's answers are wrong, so they work in groups to decide which ones.

4   **2 03** Now play the rest of the quiz. Students listen and check whether they had picked Rory's wrong answers.

Answer
Rory got 2, 6 and 9 wrong.

Recording script

Question master: And here are the answers.

Number 1: Rory, you were correct. The Arctic Ocean is the smallest ocean. It is 14,351,000 square kilometres.

Number 2: Rory, you were wrong. The longest border in the world is between the USA and Canada and it's 6,416 kilometres long.

Number 3: Rory, you were correct. The wettest place in the world is Tutunendo in Colombia and it has 11,770 millimetres of rain every year.

Number 4: Rory, you were correct. The largest planet is Jupiter and it is 142,800 kilometres wide.

Number 5: Rory, you were correct. The busiest airport is in Atlanta in the USA. About seventy-five million passengers use it every year.

Number 6: Rory, you were wrong. Greenland is the biggest island. It has an area of 2,175,000 square kilometres.

Number 7: Rory, you were correct. Asia is the continent with the most people. More than three billion people live there.

Number 8: Rory, you were correct. Tokyo is the most expensive city in the world to live in.

Number 9: Rory, you were wrong. The deepest valley in the world is in Kenya. The Great Rift Valley is 1,250 metres deep.

And number 10: Rory, you were correct. Portugal is 4,200 kilometres from the equator, so is the farthest.

Well, congratulations, Rory. You have won our fourth prize …

PET Speaking test

5   **2 03** Get students to try and fill in as much as they can. Either give them the answers (underlined in the recording script above) or let them listen again. Students can use these expressions in the Speaking test.

Answers
Oh, just a **moment**.
Er, I'm sorry, could you **repeat** that, please?
Er, I'm not **sure**.
Let me **try** again.
Let me **think**.
I'm sorry, I don't **know**.

Language focus
Superlative adjectives

Language presentation

Before going on to superlative adjectives, revise comparisons by asking students to compare the country they are in with another one which you give them, or two towns. Write some adjectives on the board, e.g. *cheap, wet, hot, fashionable, noisy, interesting,* and write the sentences they give you on the board, revising the rules for comparative adjectives (see Unit 7).

Now add a third country or town and make some sentences around the class using superlatives. Make sure students understand that when there are two things being compared we use the comparative and when there are more than two things being compared we use the superlative.

1   Ask students to complete the table in their books. Draw it on the board and go over it together.

Answers

Adjective	Comparative	Superlative
small	smaller	the smallest
long	longer	the longest
wet	wetter	the wettest
large	larger	the largest
busy	busier	the busiest
big	bigger	the biggest
expensive	more expensive	the most expensive
deep	deeper	the deepest
far	farther/further	the farthest/furthest
good	better	the best
bad	worse	the worst

 Grammar spot   Superlative adjectives

Students should use the previous exercise to help them complete the table. Remind students about the similar table they completed in Unit 7 (comparative adjectives).

Answers

Most one-syllable adjectives (e.g. *small*) add **est**.

One-syllable adjectives ending in *e* (e.g. *large*) add **st**.

Most adjectives ending in a **vowel** and a consonant (e.g. *wet*) double the consonant and add **est**.

Most adjectives with more than one **syllable** (e.g. *expensive*) use *the* **most**.

Adjectives ending in *y* (e.g. *busy*) usually change *y* to *i* and add **est**.

Far, **good** and **bad** are irregular and become *the farthest/furthest*, **the best** and **the worst**.

Language presentation

If necessary, ask some questions to practise *best* and *worst*, e.g.:

Who is the best footballer in the world?
Who is the worst singer in the world?

Point out that we can use *the most* with a noun. Talk about the city you live in or the capital city: *X has many people but Y has more people than X. Do you remember which city in the world has the most people?*
Write on the board *many/more/most*.

2   Look at the three photographs and the example.

Suggested answers
William is the happiest, the friendliest and the most confident.
Charlie is the most serious, the shyest and the kindest.
Michael is the angriest, the most hard-working and the most interesting.

Ask students to compare their answers and suggest corrections before you check them.

 Corpus spot   Superlative adjectives

Answers
a Vilnius is the <u>biggest</u> town in my country.
b That's the <u>worst</u> joke I've ever heard.
c The <u>cheapest</u> hotels are near the railway station.
d Those four days were the <u>happiest</u> in my life.

Numbers and measurements

PET Listening Part 3

1   Ask students to write the abbreviations in words.

Answers
mm millimetre(s)   **cm** centimetre(s)   **m** metre(s)
km kilometre(s)   **km²** square kilometre(s)

Language presentation

Check students know the word *area*. Teach *about* as in *about three metres*.
Ask some questions round the class to practise numbers:
How tall are you?
How tall am I?
How tall is (the tallest building in your town)?
How far are we from (another city)?
How wide is this classroom?
What is the area of this classroom?

2   Check how familiar students are with saying numbers in English. Read some numbers out, e.g. 39   102   456   912   3,790   54,687   145,201   3,965,342 and ask them to write them down. The numbers should get progressively longer, working up to millions.

In Listening Part 3, students nearly always have to write a number down, so it is important they can do this fairly quickly.

3   **2 03** Now play the answers to questions 1–6 from the quiz again (Listening Exercise 4). Ask students to write the answers to the questions in their books. Stop the recording after 'Greenland is the biggest island. It has an area of 2,175,000 square kilometres.'

Answers
b 6,416 km   c 11,770 mm   d 142,800 km
e 75,000,000   f 2,175,000 km²

Countries, nationalities, languages

1   **2 04** Students listen to six people saying the same thing in different languages. They guess the answers and then complete the table.

Answers

	Language	Nationality	Country
a	Greek	Greek	Greece
b	Polish	Polish	Poland
c	Japanese	Japanese	Japan
d	Russian	Russian	Russia
e	German	German	Germany
f	Italian	Italian	Italy

2   Now complete the table for other countries. Add any others that are relevant for your students. Students may like to add other languages which are spoken in these countries, e.g. in Spain – Catalan, Basque, Gallego, etc.

Answers

Language	Nationality	Country
Spanish	Spanish	Spain
Spanish	Mexican	Mexico
French	French	France
Portugese	Brazilian	Brazil
English	Australian	Australia

EXTRA

If you wish, talk about the different parts of the United Kingdom – England, Wales, Scotland and Northern Ireland (also called Ulster). The Republic of Ireland (also called Eire) is an independent country. It was part of the United Kingdom until 1921. Britain, or Great Britain, is England, Scotland and Wales. The British Isles is a geographical name for all the islands of Britain and Ireland. Scotland, Wales and England are all one island, and although Scottish and Welsh people are British, they are not English.

3   Discuss how many languages students speak and let them guess how many languages are spoken in the world (www.ethnologue.com says there are 6,912 languages – 1,002 in the Americas, 2,092 in Africa, 239 in Europe, 2,269 in Asia and 1,310 in the Pacific).

Present passive

Language presentation

Look at the example in Exercise 1 and discuss what the arrows mean (the object of the active sentence becomes the subject of the passive sentence). Talk about how the present passive is formed (present tense of the verb *to be* and past participle).

Look at the summary together and talk about how the negative and questions are formed in the passive.

If relevant, point out that the passive is used where the impersonal pronoun *one* is used in a lot of other languages. *One* is very formal in English.

1   Ask students to make other sentences about languages around the class using both the positive and negative forms.

2   Remind students that they need to use the same past participle as for the present perfect tense. They should revise the irregular ones (see Irregular verb list on Student's Book page 216). The past participles in this exercise are used in Exercise 3.

Answers
invented   led   made   carried   kept   lit   played

3   Students do the exercise in pairs or alone.

Answers
b is lit   **c** is carried   **d** is kept   **e** is invented
f are not / aren't made   **g** are always led
h are not / aren't played

4   Look at the example and remind students about how to make a question and a negative in the present simple passive. Students use the same pattern to write questions and then answer them.

Answers
Questions
Are cars driven on the left in Australia or Italy?
Is baseball played in the United States or Russia?
Are kilometres used in Canada or Mexico?
Is rice produced in China or Switzerland?

Answers
Cars are driven on the left in Australia. They aren't driven on the left in Italy.
Baseball is played in the United States. It isn't played in Russia.
Kilometres are used in Mexico. They aren't used in Canada.
Rice is produced in China. It isn't produced in Switzerland.

«Pronunciation»

This practises making and distinguishing between the sounds /tʃ/ and /ʃ/.

1   Put the phonetic symbols /tʃ/ and /ʃ/ on the board if you think this will help students.

Answers
cheese /tʃ/   shampoo /ʃ/

2   Ask students to say which words are in the wrong column. Do not give them the answers yet as they will hear them on the recording in the next exercise.

3   **2 05** Play the recording and get students to repeat each word. Get them to make any changes to their decisions.

Answers and recording script (the words in bold are in the wrong column)

cheese	shampoo
Chinese	shy
teacher	special
much	information
cheap	ocean
brush	**lunch**
question	**picture**
temperature	machine

◀Activity▶ Quiz

Students should work in small groups to produce six questions about their town, school, region or country. Each group has two pieces of paper – one for the questions and one for the answers. Tell each group which number questions they are writing (one group writes 1–6, another group writes 7–12 so you end up with a complete quiz). The questions must be similar to the questions in the radio quiz, i.e. they should use superlatives.

Write a couple of questions together on the board to start, e.g. *Which is the highest mountain in Italy?* When everyone is ready, they give you the answers and their set of questions is passed to the next group until everyone has seen all the questions. Each group ends up with a numbered list of answers. The teacher reads out the correct answers.

◀Activity▶ Numbers

Each student has a number on a card (see Preparation). They shouldn't show it to anyone and should memorise it if they can so they can say it without looking at the card. Either the whole class or smaller groups work together. Each person moves around saying their number. They should gather more and more people together so they end up forming a line with the largest number at one end and the smallest at the other. Everyone should then say their number to check they are in the right order.

In a class where students can't move around, students sit in groups and each person says their number. In turn, students have to put their card on the table, starting with the student with the lowest number. They can then be given the cards from another group and do the same again.

Exam folder 11

SB pages 76–77

Reading Part 5

Some questions in Reading Part 5 test lexis and others test structure. Some lexical items are also dependent on structure. Some items are about connectives, which tests students' understanding of a whole sentence or more. This exam folder teaches students to look around the space before choosing their answers.

1   Do this together. Discuss the fact that it is the meaning which makes each answer correct.

Answers
1 D   2 A   3 B   4 C

2   Students do this in pairs. They need to realise that only C fits in 1 because *look* is followed by *at*. The other words all fit 2–4 structurally, so it is the meaning which differentiates them. Explain the difference between *watched* and *saw*.

Answers
1 C   2 D   3 B   4 A

3, 4 Students do these exercises in pairs.

Answers
3   1 D   2 A   3 C   4 B
4   1 B   2 A   3 C   4 D

5   The photograph is of Alan Chambers and Charlie Paton on their expedition to the North Pole. Give students a minute to think about the answers to the questions and then discuss them together.

6   Give students time to read the text but without looking at the questions underneath it. Ask them to think about questions a–e which test their general understanding. Refer students to the Exam Advice box. If they read a text through first to get an idea of what it is about, this will help them answer the questions.

Answers
a to the North Pole   b they walked   c in a freezer; to prepare for the trip   d by plane   e a cake

7   Students now choose the correct word for each space.

Answers
1 B   2 C   3 A   4 C   5 D   6 D   7 B   8 C   9 A   10 B

12 A good read

In this unit:	
Grammar	Past continuous; past continuous versus past simple; past continuous and past simple + *while* or *when*; *still*
Functions and vocabulary	Telling a story; saying what happened and what was happening; kinds of books; book reviews
Pronunciation	/uː/ as in *two*; /ʊ/ as in *took*
PET skills	Describing a book and giving an opinion about it (Speaking Part 4, Writing Part 3); using past tenses for narrative (Writing Part 3)
Revision	Saying what you like and why; giving opinions (Units 2, 4 and 6)
Exam folder	Speaking Part 1
Writing folder	Writing Part 3

Preparation

Activity *What can you say about a book?* Students will work in groups of four. Prepare four sheets of paper for each group, with the following headings (one on each sheet):
Sentences which mean *I love this book*:
Sentences which mean *Other people like this book*:
Sentences which mean *I don't like this book*:
Sentences which tell you a fact about the book:

Activity *Write a review* Prepare blank cards (about 15 x 10cm so they are big enough for students to write on).
Writing folder Photocopy the sample answers (on page 172).

SB pages 78–81

Introduction

PET Speaking Part 4

1 **2 06** This exercise practises past simple narrative. Play the recording and ask students to say what they think happened. The sequence of events is described in Exercises 7 and 8 on page 81.

2 Ask students which book the story comes from.

> **Answer**
> The obvious answer is book **d**, but it is possible to make a case for several of the others.

3 Ask the class to match the covers a–f with the kinds of books 1–6. Check the meaning of *novel*, *story* and *short story*. These are false friends in some languages.

> **Answers**
> **2** c **3** a **4** e **5** d **6** b

4 Teach the terms *fiction* and *non-fiction*.

> **Answers**
> Biography is non-fiction. The others are fiction.

5 Encourage students to talk about the books they like.

Reading

1 Before students read the extract, check they understand the summary of the story so far. Pre-teach *double bass*, *violinist*, *conductor*, *scream*, *trumpet* and *harp*.

2 Go through the questions with the class.

> **Answers**
> **a** Somebody was screaming very loudly.
> **b** She got out of bed. She put on a T-shirt and some jeans and went out of her room.
> **c** (She talked to) Adriana and Martin Audley.
> **d** (They saw) a police car, some people and something else / Frank Shepherd's body.
> **e** Because she was frightened. / Because Frank was dead.

3 Ask students to discuss what they think happened next.

Language focus
Past continuous and past simple

1 Ask students to do the matching exercise.

> **Answers**
> **a** 3 **b** 2 **c** 1

> ### Language presentation
>
> Ask questions about each pair of sentences in the Grammar spot, e.g. *Was someone screaming before Penny woke up?* (*Yes.*) *Was someone screaming after she woke up?* (*Yes.*) to elicit the fact that the past continuous suggests something was going on for a period of time. Explain that it is often used to contrast with, or give background to, events which are expressed in the past simple. Complete the Grammar spot together.

Grammar spot

Past continuous and past simple meaning

> **Answers**
> Sentences **a–c** tell us about events that happened.
> Sentences **1–3** tell us what was happening around the time of those events.

Language presentation

Look at the table of Past continuous forms with the class, drawing attention to the parallels with present continuous forms (Unit 3). Remind students that the continuous tense does not tell us exactly when somebody started screaming, or when they stopped. In the story on page 79 we know only that they were doing it before and after Penny woke.

2   Ask students to write their answers.

> **Answers**
> **b** were waiting   **c** was walking   **d** was standing
> **e** was carrying   **f** was helping   **g** were getting
> **h** was reading   **i** wasn't lying   **j** was sitting
> **k** was laughing

3   Ask students to speculate about what was happening. (A spy was passing a secret message to another spy?) Then ask them to answer the questions.

> **Suggested answers**
> **a** the girl / the doctor / the writer / all three   **b** nothing
> **c** a secret message   **d** because her plan was successful

Language presentation

Look at the Grammar spot together. Explain/Elicit that we can use *while* + the past continuous for two activities that were both happening for a period of time.

Compare this to the second example, *when* + the past simple, contrasted with the past continuous.

Invite students to give real-life examples, for example *While you were having breakfast, I was marking your homework.* Draw attention to the commas mid-sentence.

Grammar spot

Past continuous and past simple + *while* or *when*

> **Answers**
> *While + past continuous + past continuous* describes two activities that were happening at the same time.
> *When + past simple + past continuous* describes an event that happened during a longer activity, or interrupted it.

4   This exercise practises *while* + past continuous for simultaneous activities.

Draw attention to sentence **a** (*While Georg was getting up, Kurt was driving home from work*).

Then do **b–h** round the class. Teach the meaning of *still* if necessary.

> **Answers**
> **b** While Georg was cooking breakfast, Kurt was having a shower.
> **c** While Georg was playing basketball, Kurt was sleeping.
> **d** While Georg was having lunch, Kurt was still sleeping.
> **e** While Georg was working in the library, Kurt was buying some new CDs.
> **f** While Georg was walking home, Kurt was listening to music.
> **g** While Georg was watching television, Kurt was still listening to music.
> **h** While Georg was going to bed, Kurt was driving to work.

5   This practises past continuous versus past simple.

Language presentation

Introduce the exercise by saying something like *I phoned my parents last night, but they didn't answer. Why didn't they answer, do you think?* (Use a plural to practise *were -ing*.) Elicit suggestions from students in the past continuous. Write some more examples on the board.

Ask students to complete the exercise.

> **Suggested answers**
> **b** were playing tennis.   **c** was cooking.   **d** were going home on their motorbike.   **e** was putting petrol in his car.

6   This exercise practises past continuous negative forms.

Look at the example with the class and do **b** with them. Let them continue in pairs. If appropriate, ask them to write up the answers for homework.

> **Suggested answers**
> **b** Were Georg and Kurt watching football on television when the phone rang?
> No, they weren't watching football on television, they were playing tennis.
> **c** Was Kurt having a shower when the phone rang?
> No, he wasn't having a shower, he was cooking.
> **d** Were Georg and Kurt sitting in a café when the phone rang?
> No, they weren't sitting in a café, they were going home on their motorbike.
> **e** Was Kurt writing an email when the phone rang?
> No, he wasn't writing an email, he was putting petrol in his car.

7   This is the story in the Introduction, Exercise 1. Ask students to work through the exercise. Remind them that *when* can go with both past simple and continuous tenses, but *while* is usually followed by the continuous.

Answers
b shut   **c** pulled   **d** switched   **e** took
f was reading   **g** heard   **h** switched   **i** listened
j was happening   **k** was looking   **l** was walking
m was standing   **n** came

8   This is a continuation of the same story. Tell students to read the whole text before they begin (this is useful practice for all types of cloze tests including Part 5 of PET Reading – see Exam folder 11).

Answers
b tried   **c** hit   **d** fell   **e** was trying   **f** heard
g ran   **h** jumped   **i** drove   **j** was still lying
k arrived

≪Pronunciation≫

This practises making and distinguishing between the sounds /uː/ and /ʊ/.

1   Model the sounds /uː/ as in *two* and /ʊ/ as in *took*. Practise them round the class.

Ask students to identify them in the two sentences in their books.

Answers
Don't sh<u>oo</u>t! /uː/   P<u>u</u>t the gun down! /ʊ/

2   **2 07** Play the recording for students to repeat. Ask them to mark the sounds in different colours.

Answers
/uː/   *pool*, *too*, you, too, school, rules, blue, cool, suit, true, you
/ʊ/   *full*, would, book, look, good, cook, put, pull, stood, foot

3   Go through the answers and ask the students to put the words into the table.

4   Check they are pronouncing /uː/ and /ʊ/ correctly.

≪Activity≫ What can you say about a book?

Put students in groups of four. Give each student in the group a piece of paper with a different heading (see Preparation). Together they must decide which sentences belong under each heading and the student with that piece of paper copies out those sentences, so that at the end they have four lists of sentences.

Suggested answers*
Sentences which mean *I love this book*: **a, c, i, j, p**
Sentences which mean *Other people like this book*:
   b, e, g, m, r
Sentences which mean *I don't like this book*: **f, h, l, n**
Sentences which tell you a fact about the book: **d, k, o, q, s**
*Some sentences may appear in more than one list (e.g. **b** and **m** might also be facts).

≪Activity≫ Writing a review   PET Writing Part 3

If appropriate, choose a book all the students know and write a 'review card' together (see Preparation) on the board to show them how to use the questions listed here, e.g. *The book is called* The Double Bass Mystery *and it's by Jeremy Harmer. It's fiction. It's a crime story about a murder and it takes place in Barcelona. The heroine is Penny, an English musician. It's an exciting story and I think it's a great book for a boring journey.*

Students then write their own review card about a book they have enjoyed in any language.

Exam folder 12

SB pages 82–83

Speaking Part 1

1   **2 08** Begin by discussing the photograph with the class. Explain that they take the Speaking test in pairs, and that there are two examiners, one who talks to them, and one who only listens.

Play the recording, then discuss with the class the information the examiner wants, i.e. names, where they come from, where they are studying and how long they have been there. **Note:** the speakers on the recording have very slight foreign accents. Students can pass the Speaking test with much stronger accents.

2 **2 08** ▷ Play the recording again, pausing as necessary for students to complete the questions. Draw attention to the Exam Advice box.

Answers
b what's your surname
c How do you spell it?
d where do you come from?
e do you work or are you a student
f What do you study?
g where do you live?
h And what do you do?
i Could you speak more slowly, please?
j do you enjoy studying English?
k Could you repeat that, please?

Discuss with students the topics the examiner might ask them about, e.g. what part of the city they live in, what school they go to, their job, how long they have lived/worked in the city, hobbies, etc. Tell students that it is all right to ask the examiner to repeat or speak more slowly, if they do so in correct English.

Ask which of Luca and Paulina's replies are good and which are not so good. (The long replies are better.)

3 If necessary, revise the alphabet briefly by asking students to spell names as appropriate.

4 Ask students to practise in pairs.

Writing folder

Writing Part 3

1   Look at the titles with the class and discuss what kinds of story each might belong to.

2   Ask them to read the beginnings and endings of the stories and decide which title they match.

Answers
a 3   **b** 4   **c** 6   **d** 2   **e** 5   **f** 1

3   Ask students to work in groups of three or four. Allocate a story to each group, but do not let the other groups know which one. Tell them to write the middle part of the story in not more than fifty words. Explain to students that they have to choose a letter or a story in the exam, so it's good to practise writing stories in case they don't want to do the letter. See page 172 for photocopiable sample answers.

4   When they have finished, ask each group to pass their writing to the next group. They decide which story it belongs to. Ask each group to read its complete story and ask other students which title goes with which story.

5   Draw students' attention to the Exam Advice box. Students could write their story for homework and then read it to the class. Ask students to decide which title other students' stories go with.

> ### ⬎ Corpus spot
>
> *search / search for / look for*
>
> Look at the two examples with the class. *Search for* is more emphatic than *look for*. For non-material things, such as *a job*, *look for* is more likely to be used.
>
> This exercise could be homework.
>
> **Answers**
> **a** looking for   **b** searched   **c** looking for
> **d** looked for   **e** searched

Units 7–12 Revision

Speaking

1 Follow the procedure outlined on page 42 of the Teacher's Book.

Exercises 2–6 could be set for homework and discussed afterwards in class.

Grammar

2

Answers
b ever **c** never **d** in **e** since **f** already
g yet **h** while **i** for **j** on

Reading

3

Answers
1 B **2** D **3** C **4** A **5** B **6** A **7** D **8** A **9** B **10** C

Grammar

4

Answers
b This is the <u>funniest</u> book I've ever read.
c Portuguese is <u>spoken</u> in Brazil.
d This cinema is less modern <u>than</u> the one in my town.
e The café is in <u>a/the</u> corner of the park.
f Why <u>don't you</u> phone the doctor?
g The weather here is <u>hottest</u> in July.
h This is the <u>worst</u> painting I've ever done.
i Could you <u>speak</u> more slowly, please?
j My racket wasn't as expensive <u>as</u> my teacher's.
k Natalya is from <u>Russia</u>. / Natalya is <u>Russian</u>.

Vocabulary

5

Answers
b straight **c** crossroads **d** down/along/up
e roundabout **f** over **g** on **h** pedestrian
i across **j** past **k** right **l** one-way **m** left
n on **o** opposite

6

Answers
roundabout corner entrance fountain stadium turning
wedding anniversary birthday carnival festival honeymoon
cough ankle neck thermometer throat tongue
border continent desert island ocean valley

Progress Test 2 Key

1 C 2 B 3 C 4 B 5 A 6 C 7 B 8 A 9 B

10 B 11 A 12 B 13 C 14 A 15 B 16 B 17 A

18 C 19 B 20 C 21 A 22 B 23 B

24 through 25 quietest 26 museum 27 anniversary

28 cough 29 unfortunately 30 recently

Progress Test 2

Choose the correct answer, A, B or C.

1 Andy _____ my wallet while he was walking home from college.
A was finding   B has found   C found

2 I'm sorry, Dad's not here this weekend, he's _____ to my uncle's house.
A been   B gone   C went

3 We can meet at the café _____ the cinema.
A across   B next   C opposite

4 I haven't read any English books _____ last year.
A yet   B since   C before

5 The sports stadium isn't as modern _____ the skateboard park.
A as   B than   C so

6 _____ this author written many books?
A Did   B Is   C Has

7 My family arrived in this country fifty years _____ .
A already   B ago   C time

8 Several languages _____ taught at this school.
A are   B have   C do

9 Thank you very much _____ the presents you have given us.
A to   B for   C of

10 It's best to go around the city centre on _____ .
A bus   B foot   C bicycle

11 Could you tell me _____ to the bus station, please?
A the way   B where   C reach

12 We can use the pedestrian _____ near the traffic lights.
A cross   B crossing   C across

13 I've thrown _____ all the old newspapers and tidied the sitting room.
A off   B down   C away

14 James is not well. I think _____ better go home early.
A he'd   B he   C he's

15 Has your brother got _____ or does he feel sick?
A temperature   B a temperature
C high temperature

16 Can we sit down? I've _____ my leg.
A sore   B hurt   C pain

17 I can't write any homework because I've broken my _____ .
A wrist   B throat   C ankle

18 I'm really looking forward _____ your brothers and sisters.
A meet   B to meet   C to meeting

19 The six o'clock train is the most _____ for me.
A available   B convenient   C popular

20 Go down this road and take the second turning _____ the left.
A by   B of   C on

21 You should ask your teacher for some _____ about this problem.
A advice   B idea   C opinion

22 I'm reading a magazine article _____ my favourite singer's last concert.
A of   B about   C by

23 I'm sorry I can't come out with you but I don't feel well _____ the moment.
A in   B at   C on

Find one spelling mistake in each sentence. Write the correction in the space.

24 The train went throught a tunnel underneath the mountain. _____

25 The accommodation office is quiettest between one and two o'clock. _____

26 Is the entrance to the musuem near the library?
_____

27 My parents are celebrating their aniversary with a barbecue. _____

28 I've got a couph and a pain in my stomach.
_____

29 I wanted to reserve a room in the hostel but unfortunatly it's full. _____

30 I ricently read an amazing biography. _____

TOPIC: Furniture and homes

In this unit:

Grammar	Modal verbs (probability and possibility): it *could/might/must/can't be*; prepositions of place
Functions and vocabulary	Describing styles and what you prefer; price; rooms and furniture
Pronunciation	/ʒ/ as in *television*; /dʒ/ as in *joke*
PET skills	Solving a problem (Speaking Part 3); saying where things are and making guesses (Speaking Part 3)
Revision	Present and past tenses; prepositions (Unit 7); giving advice (Unit 9)
Exam folder	Reading Part 2

Preparation

Language focus, Exercise 1 If possible, bring a mysterious or ambiguous object or picture to class, e.g. a strangely shaped stone or an unusual ornament.

Activity *Comparing pictures* Make enough photocopies of the pictures on page 181 to give a pair of pictures to each pair of students in the class.

SB pages 86–89

Introduction

1   Elicit/Supply the names of the objects. Discuss the meaning of the adjectives and which can be used for each of these objects.

> **Answers**
> a mirror   b chest of drawers   c telephone
> d cupboard   e dishwasher   f (desk) lamp
> g sofa   h chair

2   Direct students to the speech bubbles. Ask them to match the words to the objects in the photographs, encouraging them to guess/ignore any words they do not know until you go through the exercise with the whole class.

Go through the exercise, drawing attention to the way people express their attitudes to the objects. Remind students that *furniture* is an uncountable noun and briefly revisit the grammatical implications of this. Teach *I can/can't afford; it was(n't) worth the price* and *X matches Y*.

Encourage students to say what they feel about the objects shown.

> **Answers**
> 1 h   2 b   3 a   4 e   5 d   6 g   7 f   8 c

3   Let students briefly tell each other about the kind of furniture they like, using words from Exercises 1 and 2.

⬇ Vocabulary spot

Talking about the price of things

Ask students to complete the sentences. This can be homework.

Refer students to examples in the texts above when checking answers.

> **Answers**
> a cost   b afford   c is   d worth

Listening

1   **2 09** Ask students to spend a few moments looking at the photographs and thinking about what it is like to live in these places.

Tell them to listen to the four speakers and match them to the places. Say that there are probably some words they do not understand, but they should listen for the general meaning. Play the recording for them to match the photographs to the speakers and check their answers.

> **Answers**
> a 4 (Neil)   b 2 (Patricia)   c 1 (Ian)   d 3 (Adam)

Recording script

1   I'm Ian. I'm a student, so I'm not rich but I've found a good way to save money. I don't pay rent. My home has a very small kitchen and a living room downstairs. There are curtains and carpets – it's very comfortable. I've got central heating, and on the first floor there's a little bathroom and my bedroom. I can't give you my address because I often move. You see, when I get bored of the view, I can drive my home away and park somewhere new!

2   I'm Patricia. My husband and I were looking for a traditional house when we found our unusual home. It's in two old railway carriages. They've been here since 1902. The carriages stand side by side, the sitting room and dining room are between them and there's a normal roof over the whole building. We enjoy living here and our guests enjoy visiting us.

3 My name's Adam. I'm fifteen. My home is twelve metres above the ground. I made it myself. I didn't use any nails, only ropes, so I haven't damaged any branches. I use <u>solar power</u> to heat it and I have a proper kitchen, and a <u>shower</u> and so on. I've got my <u>hi-fi</u> up here and there's plenty of space for guests. Sometimes the tree moves when the wind blows, but my house hasn't fallen down yet, so I'm not really worried.

4 I'm Neil and I rent this amazing place between London and Brighton. It's two <u>towers</u>. The <u>windows</u> have a view of the railway line and it could be noisy for some people, because you hear the trains passing through the tunnel under it every hour, but I don't mind the noise because I'm a party animal. I enjoy giving enormous parties with really loud music because there aren't any neighbours to complain. It's perfect for me.

2 Go through the words listed and elicit/supply meanings.

2 09 Play the recording again and ask students to mark the grid when they hear the words.

Answers

	Ian	Patricia	Adam	Neil
dining room		✓		
bathroom	✓			
shower			✓	
roof	✓			
towers				✓
windows				✓
curtains	✓			
carpets	✓			
hi-fi			✓	
central heating	✓			
solar power			✓	

3 **2 09** Offer to play the recording once more before students answer the questions. Go through the answers with the class, playing the recording of each speaker after the two questions referring to them. Discuss any new language, encouraging guessing as much as possible.

Answers
b He drives his home away and parks somewhere new.
c They were looking for a traditional house.
d (It's) between the two railway carriages.

e He used ropes.
f Because it hasn't fallen down yet.
g Because he's a party animal.
h Because (he enjoys giving enormous parties with loud music but) there aren't any neighbours to complain.

Language focus
could/might/must/can't + be

Language presentation

Write on the board: *It could be noisy for some people.* Elicit/Supply what Neil means when he says this (e.g. perhaps the house is noisy for some people). We use *it could be* to talk about something we are not sure about. Elicit/Supply the alternative *it might be*. Write the phrases on the board.

If you have brought an object/picture to class (see Preparation), use it to practise the structure. (If you cannot find a suitable object, use one of the photographs in Exercise 1 with the whole class.) Suggest to students that it is somehow special or unusual, and encourage them to make wild guesses about what it is, using *It could be / It might be ... a piece of the moon / a toy / a very old apple.*

When someone offers a really unlikely suggestion (e.g. *It might be a piece of cheese*), take the opportunity to introduce *it can't be*, and explain that this means *I'm sure it is not.* Give a reason (e.g. *because it doesn't smell bad!*). Write the phrase on the board. Let students practise by offering further unlikely suggestions for others to disagree with. Encourage them to give a reason for disagreeing.

When they come up with something close to the answer, ask them for a reason and teach *it must be*.

Grammar spot   Modals

Ask students to read the dialogue and complete the table. Check the answers together.

Answers
1 must be   2 can't be   3/4 might be / could be

PET Speaking Part 3

1 Ask students to do the exercise orally in pairs. Give individual help with vocabulary as needed, but don't give away the names of the items. At the end, give the answers to the class, writing the names of the objects on the board.

Answers
a double bass and a football boot

2 This exercise could be homework, if time is short.

Answers
2 must   3 can't   4 might   5 could

Prepositions of place

Do the exercise with the class, discussing the meanings of the prepositions as you go through it. They met all of them in Unit 7, except *below*, *facing*, *on top of* and *beyond*.

Answers (corrections are suggested for false sentences)
b The toilet is near/beside a cupboard.
c There's a mirror above the basin.
d true
e There's a window behind the toilet.
f true
g There's a tall cupboard in the corner.
h true
i We can see towels inside some of the drawers.
j true

Rooms and furniture

1   Ask students to work in pairs naming the rooms and furniture. Go through the answers with the class.

Rooms	Furniture
kitchen	cupboards, fridge, table, chairs
bedroom	bed, wardrobe
bathroom	shower, toilet
living room	chairs, coffee table
study	table, chair, bookshelves
hall	

2   Ask students to look at the list of words and check meanings in their dictionaries. This is a chance to talk about using an English–English dictionary carefully, and possibly to remind students of the shortcomings of small bilingual dictionaries. (E.g. is the difference between *basin* and *sink* clear?) Students then decide which rooms to put the things in.

Suggested answers

bathroom	basin, bath, mirror
living room	sofa, clock, television
bedroom	clock, chest of drawers, wastepaper basket, bedside table, poster, mirror, desk, pillows
kitchen	cooker, sink, dishwasher, washing machine
study	desk, wastepaper basket, poster, clock
all/most rooms	central heating, curtains, carpet, air conditioning

3   This exercise revises giving advice (see Unit 9). Invite students to suggest other things they could put in the flat, using the structure *Why don't you / You should have a television in the living room*, etc.

Ask students to write some of their suggestions.

(↘) Vocabulary spot

This encourages students to use visualisation as an aid to memorising vocabulary.

«Pronunciation»

This practises making and distinguishing between the sounds /ʒ/ and /dʒ/.

1   Model the sounds /ʒ/ and /dʒ/. Ask students to identify them in the sentence in their books.

Practise the sounds round the class.

Answers
/ʒ/ television   /dʒ/ joke

2   **2 10** Ask students to read the sentences quickly to themselves. Teach any unfamiliar vocabulary.

Play the recording for students to repeat. Then ask them to mark the words containing the sounds /ʒ/ and /dʒ/ in different colours. ◄ You may need to play the recording again.

Answers
/ʒ/   *measure*, revision, pleasure, usually, leisure, decision, unusual
/dʒ/ *jeans*, fridge, lounge, college, jogging, generous, wages, Bridge, just, giraffe

3   Go through the answers (see Exercise 2) and ask students to put the words into the table.

Draw attention to the fact that /ʒ/ is almost always found in words ending in *-ision* and in many words ending in *-sure* (and in *usual*). It is not such a common sound in English as /dʒ/, which is normally spelt *j* at the beginning of words and *-ege/-dge* at the end, but there are exceptions (usually words beginning *ge-* or *gi-*).

4   When students have finished, ask them to work in pairs and take turns to say the sentences and listen to each other's pronunciation.

«Activity» Comparing pictures   PET Speaking Part 3

This activity practises prepositions of place. It is useful practice for Speaking Part 3 when students talk about a photograph. Although in the exam candidates do not have to find differences, the ability to express accurately where things are is important.

Give one picture to each student in a pair (see Preparation).

Tell them not to look at each other's pictures. They must find out the differences by saying where things are. The writing is done as they work.

When they have finished, ask the pair with the fewest sentences to write them on the board. The other students check that they are factually and grammatically correct. If there is an error, another pair takes over. When they have finished, a pair with more sentences takes over, and so on, until all the class's sentences are written up correctly.

Point out anything they have missed.

Exam folder 13

SB pages 90–91

Reading Part 2

1 Look at the Summary box. Read the descriptions of people together and ask students to underline the important information. They will then look for this information in the advertisements. Check vocabulary as necessary.

Answers

1 Alma <u>doesn't like cities</u> and wants to live <u>somewhere quiet with an English family</u>. She wants to do a <u>full-time course</u>.

2 Kostas enjoys <u>city life</u>. He wants to do a <u>part-time course</u> and have a part-time job as well. <u>He is not interested in going on trips or doing activities with the college after his classes</u>. He wants to <u>rent his own flat</u>.

3 Margarita would like to live in a <u>hostel with other students</u>. She wants to do a <u>full-time course</u>. She likes to play <u>sport</u> in her free time.

4 Tomek is looking for a <u>full-time four-week course</u> at a college which organises <u>social activities for students</u>. He <u>doesn't mind living in the city or the country</u> but he wants to <u>stay with a family</u>.

5 Hiroki wants to do a <u>part-time course</u> at a <u>college which can arrange his accommodation</u>. He loves <u>walking</u>, so he wants to be <u>near the countryside</u>. He <u>doesn't enjoy organised trips and activities</u>.

2 Look at what students have underlined for Alma and go through the questions together to find the right text.

Answers

a A C H b A H c H d H

3 Get students to do the same for the other people on their own. They need to remember the word *hostel* from Unit 10. Look at the Exam Advice box and remind them that three texts do not match any of the people.

When they have finished, check the answers and any vocabulary as necessary.

Answers

2 B 3 E 4 G 5 C
A, D and F are not used.

 Corpus spot   *Do* and *take*

You may like to mention that *do* + a course of study is more common.

Answers

1
a I want to *do/take* a course here in England.
b We're going to *do/take* the same course.
c Last year I *did/took* an English course in Bristol.

2
a did/took   b is doing/taking
c Have (you) done/taken

What's in fashion?

In this unit:

Grammar	*used to*; *too* and *enough* with adjectives; adjective order; *it looks …*
Functions and vocabulary	Guessing unknown words; clothes; colours; centuries and decades
Pronunciation	Pronunciation of *gh* and *ph*
PET skills	Describing a photo (Speaking Part 3); sentence transformation (Writing Part 1)
Revision	Describing things; years and decades (Unit 6); superlative adjectives (Unit 11); adjectives
Exam folder	Listening Part 4
Writing folder	Writing Parts 2 and 3

Preparation

Language focus *Too* and *enough*, **Exercise 2** Make copies of the recording script (from CD-ROM or webpage) for students.

Writing folder Photocopy the sample answer (on page 172).

SB pages 92–95

Introduction

1 Look at the pictures together and introduce the words *fashion show* and *model*. Look at the unit title – we say something is *in fashion* or *it's the latest fashion*. If you think your students have enough basic vocabulary, talk briefly about what's in fashion at the moment. Ask if anyone has been to a fashion show.

2 **2 11** Tell students they are going to hear some remarks from people in the fashion show audience (numbered 1–12). For each one they should write down which model the person is talking about – A, B, C or D.

Play the recording.

Answers
1 A 2 C 3 B 4 B 5 D 6 D
7 C 8 B 9 D 10 A 11 C 12 A

Recording script

1 Those heels are too high for her.
2 That jacket is very fashionable.
3 Those leather trousers are extremely tight.
4 That's a lovely striped scarf.
5 The shorts are enormous – they're very big and loose.
6 Those trainers look comfortable.
7 I love the material that the grey suit is made of but the colour's very dull.
8 The dark blue hat is very nice.
9 He should take that awful baseball cap off.
10 The sleeveless dress looks fairly cool because of the thin material.
11 What a horrible pattern on that silk tie. I prefer plain ties.
12 The colours are too bright and the orange belt doesn't match.

3 **2 11** Students listen again and write down the nouns from the recording. Teach or revise: names of clothes, *fashionable, tight, striped, comfortable, material, sleeveless* (compare *long sleeves* in C), *pattern, bright* and *doesn't match.*

Answers
high heels	fashionable jacket
leather trousers	striped scarf
enormous shorts	comfortable trainers
grey suit	dark blue hat
awful baseball cap	sleeveless dress
silk tie	orange belt

4 Get students to talk about what clothes they like to wear.

Reading

1 Students read the four paragraphs quickly and match them to the photographs. Tell them not to worry about any words they don't know at this stage. The paragraphs are not in chronological order.

Answers
top left paragraph – photo c
top right paragraph – photos a
bottom left paragraph – photos b
bottom right paragraph – photo d

Explain that each paragraph talks about a decade. Elicit/Tell students how we say decades (*in the nineteen nineties*, etc.) and ask the name of the last century (*twentieth*) and what the present century is called (*twenty-first*). (There is more work on past dates in Unit 24.) Put students into groups to guess a decade for each paragraph and its photograph.

EXTRA

These dates are for fashions in Britain and may vary around the world. If some of the fashions were not popular in the countries your students come from, this could be a point for discussion.

> **Answers**
> top left paragraph – 1960s
> top right paragraph – 1920s
> bottom left paragraph – 1950s
> bottom right paragraph – 1990s

2 Tell students they are going to read the text more slowly on their own, underlining any new words.

Look at the Vocabulary spot. Ask students what else they can use apart from the photographs to guess the meaning of words. (They can use the context and they can also see if the words look like any words in their own language.)

Students work in groups, helping each other with words they don't know.

Go through the texts together, getting students to write down any new vocabulary and asking them how they guessed what the words meant.

3 In the recording you heard in Introduction, Exercise 2, Speaker 6 says *Those trainers look comfortable*. Write this on the board and ask students what *look* means here (*seem / I think they are*). Discuss which of the clothes in the photographs look *comfortable/uncomfortable, cool/warm* or *boring/exciting*. They should decide which are the most uncomfortable (revising the superlative).

Ask students to guess what material some of the clothes are made from – silk, wool, cotton, leather or man-made material. Ask round the class what students' clothes are made from.

Compare round the class when they have finished. Have a vote on which period or fashion students prefer, including present-day.

Language focus
Used to

> ### Language presentation
> Look at the examples in Exercise 1. Point out that *used to* only refers to the past. It refers to something that was a habit or continued over a prolonged period of time but no longer happens. Look at the time line in the Grammar spot.
>
> Tell students that *used to* behaves like a regular verb ending in *-e* (compare *danced / didn't dance*). A common error is to add *-d* in the question and negative: *did men ~~used~~ to* and *men didn't ~~used~~ to*. *Used to* cannot be used in the present tense *~~I use to~~*.

1 Write more sentences together or get students to do them and compare.

> **Suggested answers**
> In the 1920s men used to wear flat caps.
> In the 1920s women used to wear beads.
> In the 1950s women didn't use to wear very short skirts.
> In the 1950s men used to wear narrow trousers.
> In the 1950s men didn't use to wear big ties.
> In the 1950s women used to wear gloves.
> In the 1960s men used to wear big ties.
> In the 1960s men didn't use to wear baseball caps.
> In the 1990s women didn't use to wear shiny black boots.
> In the 1990s teenagers didn't use to wear white socks.

 Grammar spot   *Used to*

Students fill in the summary.

> **Answers**
> + In the 1920s, women *used to* wear hats.
> − In the 1950s, women *didn't use to* have short skirts.
> ? In the 1970s, did men *use to* wear ties?

2 Students work in pairs to practise making and answering questions. They ask each other about the past – referring back to a time when they were very young, so they no longer do these things. Practise a couple of questions and answers together to make sure they form the question correctly.

> **Answers**
> b What time did you use to get up?
> c What time did you use to go to bed?
> d What did you use to do at weekends?
> e What did you use to enjoy doing?

3 When they have finished, they should write three sentences about what their partner used to do.

1   Divide students into pairs. Student A looks at the photograph on page 200 and Student B looks at the photograph on page 202 (in the Student's Book). They ask each other questions about the photographs using *used to*.

2   Students write down at least five things which have and haven't changed in the photograph.

Suggested answers
The statue used to be near the building on the left.
The building at the back used to be narrower.
The building on the right used to be a shop.
People used to meet there.
There used to be a kind of seat.
There didn't use to be a tree / any cars / traffic lights / street lights / street signs / railings / marks on the road.

«Activity» Colours

Revise colours including *dark/light blue* etc. by looking at the colour wheel. Talk about students' favourite colours and how they make them feel. Get them to work alone matching the adjectives to a colour and then compare with another student.

«Pronunciation»

This practises the pronunciation of *gh* and *ph*.

1   Do the first one together. The odd word out is *cough* because here *gh* is pronounced /f/ but is silent in the other words. Ask students to look at the spelling and pronunciation of the words in lists **b** and **c** and choose the odd one out. Do not give them the answers at this point.

2   **2** **12** Play the recording and have students repeat the words, then ask them for their answers.

Answers
b The odd word out is *enough* – all the words have a /f/ sound but it is spelt *gh* in *enough* and *ph* in the other words.
c The odd word out is *fashion* – all the words have a /f/ sound but it is spelt *f* in *fashion* and *ph* in the other words.

Recording script

a   bright   light   cough   through
b   enough   photograph   telephone   alphabet
c   paragraph   fashion   geography   physics

3   Give students a few minutes to think and then discuss the answers.

Answers
f – this is the most common spelling of the sound /f/
ph – a few words spell the sound /f/ as **ph**
gh – there are some common words in which **gh** is pronounced /f/, e.g. *laugh, cough, enough* and *rough*. But also, **gh** is often silent, e.g. *right, might, sight, thought, bought*.

Too and *enough*

Language presentation

Try to reach something high up in the room. Write on the board: *I'm too* .... and students provide *short*.

Underneath write: *I'm not* .... *enough* and students provide *tall*. Get students to confirm that these two sentences mean the same.

1   Start doing the exercise together until students seem confident enough to do it alone. Then complete the Grammar spot together.

Answers
b are too big   **c** aren't long enough
d is too bright   **e** are too dark

↘ Grammar spot   *Too* and *enough*

Answers
We use *not* with *enough*.
Too goes before an adjective.
Enough goes after an adjective.

2   Give students the photocopied recording scripts from Introduction, Exercise 2 (see Preparation) so they can check any adjectives they don't know against the pictures.

They work in pairs to match the opposites. They have come across all of these adjectives in this unit except *thick*, *large* and *small*.

Answers
short–long   thin–thick   loose–tight   large–small
low–high   narrow–wide   plain–patterned

PET Writing Part 1

3   These pairs of sentences give students practice in transformations like those in Writing Part 1.

Look at the example together and ask students to work on the other sentences. They use adjectives with opposite meanings as practised in the previous exercise.

Point out that *to* is often used after *too* and *enough* (e.g. *It's too hot to eat*).

Answers
b wide enough   **c** high enough   **d** is too   **e** is too

4   In pairs or individually, students write about four sentences using the adjectives provided and others if they wish.

Adjective order

1   Complete the table together. The rules for adjective order are fairly complicated and this exercise covers the most important ones.

Answers

Opinion	Size	Description	Colour	Material	Noun
–	long	shiny	black	plastic	boots
wonderful	–	patterned	–	–	shirts
–	short	–	white	cotton	socks

2   The columns are in the correct order, so this provides a summary. Students could learn some of the descriptions as a memory aid to adjective order.

3   Students should now use the table to do the next part of the exercise.

Answers
b a warm brown coat
c a beautiful old wooden desk
d an amazing short silk dress
e a brilliant new film
f some fashionable black cotton shorts
g a shiny glass table

EXTRA

If students are interested, you could talk about whether they think colours and clothes reflect people's personalities.

«Activity» Clothes

Students write a description of what they were wearing yesterday. Check which tense they will use – the past simple or continuous, not *used to*. Check they understand why *used to* is incorrect (because it is used for a habit in the past, not to talk about something you were doing at a particular time, e.g. yesterday). Students should write their descriptions on a piece of paper without their name on it and give it to you. You read them out or give them to individual students to read out. They guess who the description is of.

Exam folder 14

SB pages 96–97

Listening Part 4

The instructions for Listening Part 4 are more complicated than for the other parts, so it is worth spending time practising what students will have to do.

1   Discuss with students the usefulness of reading the instructions carefully before they listen. This part of the exam is always a conversation between two people, usually one male and one female. Before they listen, it is important that students find out from the instructions which name is female and which is male (if they aren't names they know) so they can identify the speakers. The instruction also tells them what the conversation is about. Look at the Exam Advice box together.

Answers
Sandy is a boy; Megan is a girl; their conversation is about jobs.

2   In the exam, students should read the sentences before they listen, to get an idea of what they will hear.

Answers
1 Megan's new job   **2** photography/models   **3** bookshops
4 Sandy's job   **5** photography   **6** a magazine
Their jobs could be photographer, working in a bookshop or working for a magazine.

3   In the exam, students put a tick on their answer sheet under A for YES and B for NO. At the end of the exam, they transfer these to the answer sheet, writing A or B for each answer. They need to get used to the idea that A means correct and B means incorrect as in Reading Part 3 (see Exam folder 7). This exercise practises that. The questions in the exam, of course, will never be about general knowledge – they will always test what is heard.

Answers
1 B   **2** B   **3** A   **4** A   **5** B

4 Students can do Exercises 4 and 5 in pairs. These words are used in the listening text and are all words students have come across (except *depressing*).

Answers
like: interesting, great, brilliant, exciting
dislike: awful, not interesting enough, miserable, depressing, boring

5 In this part of the exam, the speakers always agree or disagree and students need to recognise different ways of doing this.

Answers
agree: Of course, Exactly
disagree: You're wrong there, I don't think so, That's not a good idea.

6 **2 13** Play the recording and get students to mark their answers.

◄ Play it a second time.

Answers
1 A 2 B 3 B 4 B 5 A 6 B

Recording script

You will hear a conversation between a boy, Sandy, and a girl, Megan, about their jobs. Decide if each sentence is correct or incorrect. If it is correct, put a tick (✔) in the box under A for YES. If it is not correct, put a tick (✔) in the box under B for NO.

Megan: Hi, Sandy. How are you? I haven't seen you for ages.
Sandy: OK, I suppose. Are you OK?
Megan: Oh, yes. I've got this <u>great job</u>, you see. I work on a fashion magazine. <u>It's what I've always wanted to do. It's brilliant</u>. And it's in the centre of town, near where I live.
Sandy: So what do you do exactly?

Megan: Well, at the moment I go along with the photographer when he takes the photos of the models for the magazine. They have lots of pages of the latest fashions.
Sandy: So you're a photographer now?
Megan: Well, not yet … I'm doing a course. <u>I help him to carry the equipment</u>. What about you? I haven't seen you since we left art college. Are you working?
Sandy: Well, I am, but I want to be a photographer too, you know. And I've got a really awful job at the moment in a bookshop.
Megan: What's wrong with that? Why are you miserable about it? Bookshops are very interesting places.
Sandy: Not this one. It's an extremely depressing bookshop – like all bookshops, in fact.
Megan: Well, <u>you're wrong there</u>. Why don't you try to get a job in that new bookshop, you know, in Spring Street? It opened last week. It looks interesting.
Sandy: Not interesting enough for me. <u>I want to do something more exciting</u> – that's why I want to become a photographer.
Megan: But photography is a very tiring job – busy all day. And no time to relax.
Sandy: Exactly, so it's not boring. And <u>I've already done a photography course</u>. I'm always out taking photographs.
Megan: Are you?
Sandy: Yes, so could you ask if I can have a job on your magazine?
Megan: <u>I don't think so. That's not a good idea.</u> You see, the photographer only needs one assistant and that's my job.
Sandy: Oh. But could I come and watch one day?
Megan: Of course. People often come and watch. But don't talk to anyone – they're all too busy.

7 **2 13 ◄** Play the recording again. The words underlined in the recording script give the answers to the questions.

Writing folder

Writing Parts 2 and 3

1 Read the question together. Students will probably write about the names and styles of furniture.

2 Ask students to read the answer and tell you how many different things the writer bought. Check vocabulary as necessary.

Answer
The writer bought five things: lamp, cushions, mirror, (bed) cover, (three) posters

3 Check students understand all the adjectives, then ask them to do this in pairs.

Possible answers
There are lots of possible answers.
I went shopping this morning and I bought some things for my *new* flat. I got a *lovely/amazing, large/big/tiny/small, new/modern/shiny, any colour, plastic* lamp in that new shop near the station. Then I found some *lovely/amazing, large/big/tiny/small, new/modern/soft, any colour/colourful, cotton* cushions to match my *comfortable, new, leather* sofa. They look nice. Then I bought a *lovely/amazing, large/big/tiny/small, new/modern/shiny, any colour, plastic* mirror which I've put on my *large/big/tiny/small, new/modern/wooden* chest of drawers. It was cheap. I'd like to buy a *large, new/modern, wooden* bed but I can't afford it, so I bought a *lovely/amazing, new, any colour/colourful, cotton* cover instead. The bed I've got is old. When I was coming home I walked through the market and I saw some *amazing/crazy/lovely, colourful* posters, so I bought three.

4 Read the question together.

5 Students can work in pairs to think of suitable adjectives. Look at the Exam Advice box together.

Possible answers
Dear Sarah,
We had a very *long/difficult/bad* journey here because the weather was *wet/windy/bad*, so the ferry was late. We are staying in a(n) *interesting/pretty/small* town. We have a *nice/big/pretty* room with a *beautiful/wonderful/lovely* view. I like the sea best. The water is *clean/warm*.
Love,
Rosie

6 Remind students to make a plan and to look back at the Writing folder in Unit 6 to see what 100 words look like. If necessary, make a plan together. See page 172 for a photocopiable sample answer.

Sample plan
What kind of?
modern fashionable comfortable unusual
names of clothes/shops

Bought recently
one or two things
where
expensive/cheap
colour
how I feel

15 Risk!

In this unit:

Grammar	Modal verbs (permission and obligation): *can* and *can't* (permission); *have to* and *don't have to*; *had to* and *didn't have to* (obligation); adverbs
Functions and vocabulary	Rules (permission, obligation and prohibition); phrasal verbs with *get*; activities and experiences
Pronunciation	Different pronunciations of *ou*
PET skills	Listening for detailed meaning; answering true/false questions (Reading Part 3 and Listening Part 4)
Revision	Adjectives; past tense
Exam folder	Reading Part 1

Preparation

Introduction It would be useful to make an OHT of the table so you can fill in the answers together. Alternatively, project the table from the CD-ROM or webpage onto the whiteboard. If you have time, find out what you can and can't do at 16 for the country in which you are teaching. If not, you and the class can just come to a consensus.

Activity *Jobs* Photocopy the list of jobs (on page 182) and cut them up (at least one job per student).

Language focus, Phrasal verbs with *get* Make copies of the recording script (from CD-ROM or webpage) for students.

Activity *Adverbs* Photocopy the sheet of adverbs (on page 182).

SB pages 98–101

Introduction

This introduction practises the use of *can* and *can't* to say what is allowed or not allowed. Later in the unit students learn *have to / don't have to* and *must/mustn't*. Students also practise agreeing and disagreeing.

1   Do the UK column with the whole class (see Preparation).

Answers for the UK
The second column here shows the age at which people are allowed to do these things in the UK.

When you are 16 …	UK	
you can buy a pet.	✓	12
you can vote in elections.	✗	18
you can get a tattoo.	✗	18
you can work full-time.	✓	16
you can buy fireworks.	✓	16
you can buy lottery tickets.	✓	16
you can get a pilot's licence.	✗	17
you can ride a scooter.	✓	16
you can learn to drive a car.	✗	17
you can give blood.	✗	17
you can get married (if your parents agree).	✓	16

2   Get students to complete the second column, about their own country. Very young students may prefer to do this in pairs. If students are not sure, encourage them to use the language they learnt in Unit 11 for hesitating and saying you don't know.

3   Students compare their answers in pairs or threes. In a mononational class they can try to come to a consensus. In a multinational class they can compare what they have put. Introduce the question *At what age can you …* and make sure students remember how to make a question with modal verbs. Then put the answers on the board. In a multinational class you can have a column for each country represented.

Check that students know that *can't* is the contracted form of *cannot* (spelt as one word).

4   Ask students to add more laws they can think of. In a multinational class they can go into the same nationality groups. Ideas (figure in brackets is for Britain): get married without parental consent (18, except in Scotland, where it is 16), join the army (16), leave home (16 with parental consent), adopt children (18), drive a bus or a lorry (21).

5   Have a brief class discussion about the various ages that people are allowed to do things in different countries.

Listening

PET Reading Part 3 and PET Listening Part 4

Language presentation

Look at the photograph with the students and discuss what is happening. This is a real event which takes place every year in north Africa. Talk about the unit title – *Risk!* – and what it means (students get a chance to talk about their own opinions and experiences of risk-taking later in the unit).

Introduce/Revise the following words – *race, marathon, competition, desert, sand, tent, camp* and *temperature* by asking: *What are the people doing? Why? Where are they? Where will they sleep? How hot is it, do you think?* Write on the board *organisers* and *competitors* and make sure students know which is which.

Ask students to guess what the competitors will need to take, e.g. a tent, food, running shoes, water, a backpack and so on.

2 **14** Students listen for general understanding and answer the questions.

Answers
b false **c** false **d** true **e** true

Recording script

Ryan: You know, Martha, I want to do something really exciting this summer. I went sky-diving last year and it was great. I'd really like to know more about the marathon you did in Morocco. How did you get on?

Martha: Well, I enjoyed it. It's not really dangerous if you behave sensibly, but it certainly tests your strength and personality. When I set off, I didn't know if I was strong enough to do it. You have to pass a medical examination before you go but apart from that anybody can do it. In fact the oldest competitor to finish was 76.

Ryan: I'm a bit younger than that so maybe I have a chance. So, what do you have to do? Why is it so hard?

Martha: Well, it's a 230-kilometre marathon across the desert and you have to finish the run in seven days.

Ryan: And I suppose it's hard running on sand.

Martha: Yes, it is, but the worst thing is that you have to carry your own food for the seven days.

Ryan: And I'm sure you need a lot of water as well.

Martha: You don't have to carry water for seven days because you're given water each day. You have to take a good water bottle with you. It's very important to drink enough. You can take other drinks to mix with the water if you like.

Ryan: And where do you sleep?

Martha: In tents. You don't have to carry those. The organisers do that, but you have to bring your own sleeping bag. You fall asleep very quickly in the evening because you're so tired but you can't stay in your tent after sunrise in the morning. You have to get up quickly when the organisers call everyone. They do it very noisily because some people are amazingly heavy sleepers.

Ryan: So, do you have your own tent?

Martha: No, and you need to get on with the other people in your tent because you spend a lot of time with them.

Ryan: And what about the organisers?

Martha: They don't run with you, of course. And they live separately. The competitors can't go into their camps. They have much nicer food and are more comfortable.

Ryan: So, does it get boring running for hours at a time?

Martha: Not really, but you can take an MP3 player if you want. Just remember everything goes in your backpack and you carry it in the heat. It's normally about 40 degrees in the daytime and it sometimes gets hotter than that, but it's cold at night. When you first arrive, when you get off the plane, you can't believe how hot it is! Anyway, I have some work that I need to get on with. Why don't you look at the website – then you can decide. And I'll find my photographs to show you.

Ryan: Oh, thanks.

Language focus

Can, can't; *have to, don't have to*

1 **2** **14** Play the recording again and ask students to listen for the expressions and put them into the correct columns.

Answers
You have to: **a, b, f**   You can't: **g, h**
You can: **d, i**   You don't have to: **c, e**

Language presentation

Discuss the difference between the four columns: the things in the *You have to* and the *You can't* columns are the rules of the competition – there is no choice. The things in the *You can* and *You don't have to* columns are not rules: *you can = it is allowed or possible; you don't have to = it is not necessary.*

Ask students about some of the things they *have to do / don't have to do* in the college where they are studying. Get students to ask each other some questions round the class about their home lives. One student answers, then that student asks another student, etc. Ideas: wash up, clean your bedroom, babysit, wash the car, cook, etc. Make sure they answer with short forms – *Yes, I do* or *No, I don't.*

It is not necessary for students to know the difference between *must* and *have to* for PET, but you could discuss it with them so they have an awareness. *Must* is used when the obligation comes from the speaker, e.g. *You must try to be more patient, I must see you, I must go shopping – we haven't got any food. Have to* is also possible in these cases but less strong. *Have to* is used where the obligation comes from someone else, not the speaker, e.g. *I have to wash up every night.*

Grammar spot

Modal verbs: permission and obligation

Students use the previous exercise to help them complete the summary.

> **Answers**
> It is a rule: *have to*   *can't*
> If you want: *can*   *don't have to*

2 Look at the table with the students to check they can form questions and negatives.

> **Answers**
> **b** do we have to
> **c** don't have to
> **d** can
> **e** can't
> **f** have to
> **g** do students have to
> **h** don't have to

❰❰Activity❱❱ Jobs

This practises questions with *have to*.

Photocopy the list of jobs (see Preparation) and cut them up (at least one job per student).

Choose a job (e.g. your own) and ask students to tell you what you have to and don't have to do. Then think of another job and ask students to guess what it is using the questions in their books.

Put students into small groups and give them a pile of cards face down. Tell students they can come and ask you if they don't know what the job on their card is. Each student takes a turn to take a card without showing it to the others and they guess what the job is by asking questions with *have to*. They have 20 questions. The student can only answer *Yes, I do* or *No, I don't* but they can give one clue.

Phrasal verbs with *get*

This is the first formal introduction to phrasal verbs.

> ### Language presentation
>
> All these verbs are in the listening text. Look at the example. Explain what a phrasal verb is – a verb of two or three parts which can have a literal meaning, e.g. *go down*, or a less transparent meaning, e.g. *get on*. Ask if there is another meaning of *get on* – e.g. *get on a bus* – and point out that some phrasal verbs have more than one meaning.
>
> Ask students to do the exercise and check they understand what the phrasal verbs mean. If they can't remember them or don't know them, give them the photocopied recording script (see Preparation) and ask them to highlight or underline the phrasal verbs with *get*.
>
> Ask them if they can see another phrasal verb near the beginning which isn't in the exercise – *set off* – and if they know any other phrasal verbs. Encourage students to keep a list of phrasal verbs as they come across them, with a translation and an example in English (see Vocabulary spot).

> **Answers**
> **b** up   **c** on with   **d** off   **e** on with

Had to, didn't have to

1 This introduces students to the past tense of *have to* – both form and context. Point out that this is the past form of both *have to* and *must*.

> **Answers**
> I had to arrive several hours before the jump.
> I didn't have to take any special clothes with me.

2 Discuss what the people are doing in the photographs – sky-diving, scuba diving in underwater caves, bungee jumping, and going on a fairground ride. This gives students a chance to talk about their own experiences of the unit topic.

3 Give students a few minutes to think of the riskiest thing they've ever done and ask them to write three sentences about it using *have to*. If necessary, write some prompts on the board. Ask a few students to describe their experiences. Check that students can form the negative and question form of *had to*.

4 Students complete the exercise.

> **Answers**
> **b** didn't have to   **c** Did you have to   **d** didn't have to
> **e** had to   **f** didn't have to   **g** Did they have to
> **h** had to

This practises the different pronunciations of *ou*.

1 Ask students to say the four words. If they are pronouncing them wrongly, say them yourself or play them on the recording.

The written letters *ou* are pronounced as /ə/ in *nervous*, /ʌ/ in *young*, /ɔː/ in *bought* and /aʊ/ in *house*. You could write these on the board with the phonetic symbols.

2 **2 15** Play the recording and ask students to repeat if you haven't already done so.

> **Recording script**
>
> nervous young bought house

3 **2 16** Ask students to put the words into the correct column, then play the recording to check their answers.

> **Answers**
>
> | /ə/ **nervous** | /ʌ/ **young** | /ɔː/ **bought** | /aʊ/ **house** |
> |---|---|---|---|
> | dangerous | enough | thought | shout |
> | flavour | touch | ought | out |

> **Recording script**
>
> dangerous thought shout enough
> ought out touch flavour

4

> **Answers**
>
> Other words that could be added to the columns include:
> /ə/ nervous: colour, famous
> /ʌ/ young: couple, double
> /ɔː/ bought: your, pour
> /aʊ/ house: about, loud

Adverbs

1 Ask students to write down the adjectives from the underlined adverbs.

> **Answers**
>
> **b** comfortable **c** noisy

Go through the rules together (see Grammar spot). Remind students they have already come across similar rules for forming comparative and superlative adjectives. Look at the exceptions together and make some sentences, e.g.
He is a fast runner. He runs fast.
We caught an early/late train. We arrived early/late.
She is a hard worker. She works hard.

 Grammar spot Making adverbs from adjectives

> **Answers**
> Add *ly* (*perfect* → *perfectly*)
> Change *y* to *i* and add *ly* (*noisy* → *noisily*)
> For adjectives ending in *le*, take off *e* and add *y*
> (*comfortable* → *comfortably*)

2 Students use the information in the Grammar spot to help them form more adverbs.

> **Answers**
> cheerfully heavily perfectly confidently loudly
> quickly gently

3 Read through the rest of Ryan's letter together. Then ask students to put the adverbs in the spaces.

> **Answers**
> **b** cheerfully **c** loudly **d** confidently **e** quickly
> **f** gently **g** heavily **h** perfectly

Corpus spot Spelling of adverbs

> **Answers**
> **a** easily **b** luckily **c** completely

«Activity» Adverbs

1 Check that students can form adverbs correctly from these adjectives. Write the ones with a spelling change on the board. **Note:** the ones with a spelling change are underlined in the answer box.

> **Answers**
> <u>angrily</u> quickly quietly nervously <u>miserably</u> <u>lazily</u>
> <u>happily</u> secretly seriously slowly loudly <u>sleepily</u>
> excitedly

2 Explain you are going to say the sentence in the book in a way which fits one of the adverbs. They have to guess which adverb. Read the example sentence aloud, demonstrating *anxiously*. Divide the class into two or four teams and give each team some of the adverbs which you have photocopied (see Preparation).

They place the adverbs in a pile and take one each. The other team must guess which adverb they have from the way they say the sentence. They can only have two guesses. See which team gets the most marks.

The activity could continue with students providing their own adverbs.

◀◀Activity▶▶ Taking risks

1 Ask students to look at the questions in the mini-survey and say you are going to find out how many students in the class like taking risks. Students may like to add other questions to the list before you begin. Ask students to interview each other in pairs.

Answers
Give one point for the following answers:
a yes **b** yes **c** no **d** yes **e** yes **f** yes **g** no **h** no

2 Sum up whether the class likes taking risks or not by asking how many people got eight points, seven points, and so on.

Exam folder 15

SB pages 102–103

Reading Part 1

This part of the exam consists of five questions, some of which are signs and notices and some of which are slightly longer texts like messages, notes, etc. (see Exam folder 1). This exam folder practises signs and notices.

1 Read the sign together and talk about questions **a**–**c**.

Answers
a in a fair or theme park
b children less than five years old
c children five years old or older

2 Ask students to look at the explanations. Decide together which is the correct explanation and why the others are wrong.

Answers
A is correct (*less than five years old* = under five; *cannot go alone* = must have an adult with them)
B is wrong because the sign says nothing about groups
C is wrong because adults can go on the ride with children

3 For question **a**, read the sign together. Add the missing words to the sign, with the class prompting you. Tell students they do not need to do this but it helps them to realise that words are often left out in signs. They are usually articles and verbs.

Answers
a This entrance *is* closed until 11 am today. Use *the* other entrance beside *the* café.

Discuss together questions **b**–**d**.

Answers
b by an entrance **c** one **d** two

4 Give students a few minutes to look at the explanations and answer questions **a**–**d**.

Answers
a yes **b** no (*after today* means *forever*)
c B
d A is wrong because *after* today doesn't mean the same as *until 11 am* today.
C is wrong because the park is open before 11 am.

5 Let students try this before you discuss it with the class.

Answers
Please remain in *your* seats until *the* ride stops completely.

6 Ask students to answer the question.

Answers
B is correct.
A is wrong because the notice is about when the ride stops, not when it starts.
C is wrong because the notice does not tell people to wait after the ride stops.

7, 8 This could be homework, if time is short. When checking the answers, ask students if there are any missing words in the signs.

Answers
7 A (*the* is missing before *park*)
8 B (Hot food is available at lunchtime at *the* restaurant (*which is*) by *the* lake.)

16 Free time

In this unit:

Grammar	*going to* future; present tense after *when, after, until* in future time
Functions and vocabulary	Giving, accepting and refusing invitations; study and leisure; the time; making arrangements
Pronunciation	The time
PET skills	Present tense after time adverbs (Writing Part 1); Making arrangements (Speaking Part 2)
Revision	Giving, accepting and refusing invitations (Unit 2); present continuous for future plans (Unit 4)
Exam folder	Listening Part 2
Writing folder	Writing Part 1

Preparation

Introduction You may wish to ask students to read the quiz for homework before coming to class.
Activity *I'm going to …* Photocopy the cards (on page 182) and cut them up.

SB pages 104–107

Introduction

1, 2 If they haven't read it for homework (see Preparation) give students a time limit (between five and ten minutes as appropriate) to do the quiz before going on to teach any new vocabulary. Ask them their opinions of the results.

   Note: the use of the informal word *mates* for *friends* is very common in magazines aimed at teenagers, but is otherwise usually only encountered in spoken English.

3 Elicit brief descriptions of the pictures, supplying vocabulary as necessary. Discuss whether they are good things to do the day before an English test. If appropriate, spend a few minutes talking about time management and the importance of planned revision. (The implication of the pictures could be: it's better to do something enjoyable which is good for your English, e.g. listening to pop songs in English, watching an English-language film or having some fun and exercise; last-minute cramming is not recommended, and should not be necessary if you have planned your revision time.) This discussion is followed up in **Activity** *Making plans.*

 Corpus spot   *Homework*

Remind students of Corpus spot Unit 8, verb + noun pairs.

Answers
a did   **b** do

Reading

This reading task introduces *going to* and *when, until* and *after* + present tense in context.

1 Elicit the theme of the message board by asking the class to look at the first message.

2 Ask students to match the questions and answers by reading the messages again.

Answers
2 a   **3** g   **4** c   **5** b   **6** e   **7** h   **8** f

3 Ask which people have the best and worst ideas.

   Discuss the class's reactions and teach any new vocabulary as you do so, e.g. can students distinguish between *all night* and *every night*? (There is practice of this in Unit 27.)

Language focus

Going to

Language presentation

Direct students' attention to the use of *going to* in the message board texts. Elicit/Explain that *going to* is used to describe future intentions and situations where we can already see what is about to happen. Look at the table together as necessary. (Most students will have met *going to* before.) Demonstrate the interrogative form by asking a few questions about the website messages on p.105, including *yes/no* ones, e.g. *Is Anthony going to go to bed early?*

1 Discuss the pictures and supply any vocabulary as necessary. This exercise can be done orally in class then written up for homework, if time is short.

Suggested answers
b She's going to take a photo.
c He's going to dive into the water.
d They're going to borrow some books.
e He's going to ride his motorbike.

2 This exercise can be done around the class, or in groups of about six students in large classes. Each student who answers a question can ask the next one, directing it at someone else, so that the questions and answers go round the class/group. Tell students that they do not have to be truthful and encourage outrageous (but grammatically accurate) answers.

3 When all students have answered at least one question, invite individuals to come and write the best answers on the board, e.g. *Miranda's going to catch a plane to New York after this lesson.*

Let students copy some of the sentences to help them remember the exercise.

4 Encourage students to read to the end of the dialogue, then read all the sentences **a–h** before trying to fit them into place. This approach is good practice for exam tasks such as cloze tests.

5 **2 17** Play the recording for students to check their answers. Discuss any problems and play it again if necessary. At the end, if appropriate, invite students to read it aloud together in pairs.

Answers
2 h   3 a   4 c   5 b   6 f   7 e   8 g

Recording script

Liz: Hi, Sam. What are you doing?

Sam: I'm making a poster. Do you want to help me?

Liz: I'm afraid I can't. I'm going to watch the football on television. Aren't you going to watch it?

Sam: No, not this time. I'm going to join a demonstration in the city centre.

Liz: Why?

Sam: Because the council is going to build a new car park.

Liz: So what's wrong with that?

Sam: Because they're going to put it by the market, you know, where Space Party is? The club we went to last week. That's where they're going to build it. Would you like to come on the demonstration?

Liz: Another time perhaps. Anyway, I think the car park's a good idea. There isn't enough parking in the town.

Sam: But it's a really bad idea. It isn't going to make things better for teenagers.

Liz: Why not?

Sam: Because they're going to knock down Space Party. So what are we going to do at weekends? Space Party's the only place to go to in this town.

Liz: OK, but what are you and your friends going to do to stop it?

Sam: We're going to stand in the shopping centre and we're going to tell people what's happening.

Liz: Well, good luck. Now I'm going to watch the match.

Sam: OK. You can tell me about it when I get home.

《Activity》 I'm going to . . .

Distribute the cards (see Preparation) to individuals or pairs (especially for less confident students).

Make sure students understand that they must mime preparations for the activity, not the activity itself. If necessary, give them some suggestions privately as to what they should do in their mime. For example, if the card says *drive a car*, they can mime studying a road map, getting their coat and bag, looking for the car keys, going out of the house, locking the front door, unlocking the car and getting into it.

Ask more confident students to mime first. If appropriate, maximise opportunities for humour by allocating activities that students are unlikely to do in real life.

Present tense following *when, until, after*

PET Writing Part 1

Language presentation

Direct students' attention to the first message on the message board on page 105 and elicit that the present simple is used after *when, until* and *after* in the messages although it refers to the future. Explain that English uses a present tense after time adverbs like *when, after* and *until*, **not** a future.

Note: The present perfect may also follow *after, when* and *until* but PET candidates are not tested on this. They are expected to know that the future is incorrect.

(↓) Grammar spot

When, until, after + present tense

Ask students to complete the Grammar spot and check it before they do the exercise below it:

When we talk about *future* time, a *present* tense follows the adverbs *when, until* and *after*.

The exercise could be homework, if time is short.

Suggested answers
b comes   c gets   d pay   e finish   f gets   g get

The time

1 **2 18** Look at column **A** with the class. Play the recording while students write the times in column **A** using figures.

2 **2 18** Play the recording again so students can check their answers.

> **Answers**
> **b** 3.25 **c** 4.45 **d** 7.30 **e** 8.35 **f** 11.57

Recording script

a **Man:** Excuse me, what's the time, please?
Woman: It's <u>ten to one</u>.

b **Woman:** Can you tell me the time, please?
Man: It's <u>twenty-five past three</u>.

c **Man:** What time does the bus leave?
Woman: At <u>quarter to five</u>.

d **Woman:** What time is it now?
Man: It's <u>half past seven</u>.

e **Man:** What's the time of the next performance?
Woman: It starts at <u>twenty-five to nine</u>.

f **Woman:** Excuse me, can you tell me the time, please?
Man: Of course. It's exactly <u>three minutes to twelve</u>.

3 Ask students to write the times in words.

> **Answers**
> **b** twenty-five past three *or* three twenty-five
> **c** (a) quarter to five *or* four forty-five
> **d** half past seven *or* seven thirty
> **e** twenty-five to nine *or* eight thirty-five
> **f** three minutes to twelve *or* eleven fifty-seven
>
> Note: In Britain, the first alternatives are more common in speech and the second alternatives are more formal, used on the radio, etc. The twenty-four-hour clock is commonly used in timetables etc., but rarely in speech.

(↘) Vocabulary spot   Asking the time

Complete the table with the students so that they can refer to it later.

> **Answers**
> **a** what's **b** tell **c** know **d** it

«Pronunciation»

This practises asking about and saying the time.

1 Refer back to the Vocabulary spot. Point out that the word *time* is stressed in each question. Drill briefly round the class for stress.

Write *at quarter to five* on the board. Point out and mark the strong and weak stresses (if appropriate, remind students of the Pronunciation in Unit 5).

    ■   ■
at quarter to five

Ask individual students to say the other times they wrote down in *The time*, Exercise 1. Draw attention to the weak pronunciation of *at* /ət/ where relevant, and to any other pronunciation problems, such as the silent *l* in *half*. ◼ Briefly drill the questions and answers in the conversations they heard, using the recording if preferred.

2 Demonstrate the pair work by asking and answering question 1 with students before the class begins practising in pairs, e.g.

What time did you get up last Friday? At ten to seven.
Excuse me, what time is it now, please? It's four fifteen.

«Activity» Making plans

This activity revises present continuous for future plans in addition to practising *going to*.

1 **2 19** Direct students to the personal organiser and ask them to fill in Marco's plans while they listen. Play the recording.

> **Answers**
> *Sunday morning:* skateboarding at 10.45
> *Sunday afternoon:* cinema at 2.30

Recording script

1
George: Marco, <u>would you like to see</u> an English film on Sunday afternoon?
Marco: Oh, yes. <u>I'd really like that</u>. What time?
George: It starts at twenty-five to three.
Marco: Fine. I can be at the cinema at half past two.
George: Good. See you on Sunday.
Marco: Yeah. Bye.

2
Oscar: Hi, Marco. Oscar here. You know we have an exam on Monday?
Marco: How can I forget?
Oscar: Well, Philippe and I are spending Sunday afternoon together. We're going to study some English grammar. <u>Would you like to join us</u>?
Marco: <u>I'm afraid I can't</u>. <u>Another time perhaps</u>.
Oscar: Oh, OK.
Marco: <u>Thanks for asking me</u>, anyway.

3
Peter: Marco? <u>Do you want to</u> come skateboarding this weekend? Sunday afternoon?
Marco: <u>I'm sorry, I'm going to be busy then</u>. <u>What about</u> Sunday morning?
Peter: Yes, but not too early!
Marco: OK. <u>Let's meet at</u> quarter to eleven.
Peter: <u>All right. See you then</u>.

2 Check students' answers. Draw attention to *Philippe and I are spending Sunday afternoon together. We're going to study some English grammar.* Both sentences are about future plans.

You may like to refer to Unit 4. The first sentence is about a definite arrangement they've made. The second shows their intention. This may be too fine a distinction for some students and is not essential as long as they understand that both refer to the future.

2 19 ◁ Play the recording again and elicit the forms used to give, accept and refuse invitations (underlined in the recording script above). Practise round the class. Write them on the board if necessary.

3 Ask students to write down three things that they are going to do this weekend without talking to each other or looking at each other's notes.

4 Ask students to go round the class, making arrangements to meet as many other people as possible. For large classes, divide them into groups of about eight. It may be useful to set a time limit for this, e.g. ten minutes. Insist they talk about their plans using appropriate language for inviting, accepting and refusing, rather than simply comparing pages and copying each other's notes. (If appropriate, they could use their mobiles and phone each other, instead of talking face to face.)

5 Ask the class to count how many things they have planned, to find out who has the busiest weekend. Discuss their plans with the class to see if they can really fit everything into the two days.

Exam folder 16

SB pages 108–109

Listening Part 2

Look at the Summary box about this part of the exam.

1 Remind students that it is always important to read the instructions, which not only tell them what to do, but also contain information.

Discuss the instructions and elicit the answers to the questions.

> **Answers**
> **a** a radio interview
> **b** two (one woman and an interviewer)
> **c** It's about a trip she's going to make.

2 Tell students that in the exam, they will have 45 seconds to read the questions for Part 2 before they hear the recording. As they do this, they should take the opportunity to think what the questions tell them about the content of the recording.

Invite the class to make guesses about what they are going to hear, based on questions 1–6 (not options A, B and C, which may be misleading), and write their guesses down.

When they have done so, let them compare their guesses with those in the box at the bottom of the page and discuss any differences with the class. Look at the Exam Advice box together.

3 Ask students to read the options (A, B and C) for each question. Point out to them that the options must be treated with caution, because only one of the three can be correct. Nevertheless, the students need to get used to reading them before they listen, as the options are not recorded and there are no pauses.

Remind students about previous exercises they have done comparing different words with similar meanings (e.g. Exam folder 6, Exercise 5). Ask them to do the matching exercise quickly.

> **Answers**
> **2** e **3** f **4** d **5** b **6** a

4, 5 **2 20** Remind students that the questions follow the order of what they hear and that the interviewer's questions can help them to keep track of which item to think about. If they cannot answer a question, they should leave it and go on to the next one. They can answer the ones they missed during the second listening.

Play the recording twice. At the end, go through the answers, playing the recording and stopping it as necessary to clarify any parts the students did not catch.

Answers
1 A   2 A   3 B   4 B   5 C   6 A

Recording script

You will hear a radio interview with a woman called Philippa about a trip she is going to make.

For each question, put a tick (✔) in the correct box.

Jim: Welcome to Travellers' Talk, our weekly programme about travel and holidays. I'm Jim Baker and my first guest this morning is Philippa Berry, who won first prize in last month's competition. Philippa, remind listeners how you won the competition.

Philippa: I wrote a poem called *The Traveller*. It tells the life story of a very old man.

Jim: And Philippa has won a thousand pounds to spend on a holiday. Philippa, congratulations.

Philippa: Thank you.

Jim: Now tell us about the journey you've planned.

Philippa: Well, first of all, I decided that I didn't want to go alone because I haven't been abroad alone before. I asked my family and one or two friends to come with me. But I'm going to be away for six weeks and that's too long for most of them. My brother loves travelling, but he's got exams and my best friend says it's too expensive. So I'm joining a tour organised by a travel agent. We travel together but we don't have to stay together all the time, so that'll be just right for me.

Jim: And when are you leaving?

Philippa: Well, I have to use my ticket before the end of this year and these tours only go once a year so I had to decide immediately. In fact we set off two weeks from today.

Jim: And where are you going first?

Philippa: Well, we start by flying from London to Amsterdam, where we catch a plane for the United States. We spend three days in New York and then we travel by bus across the States to California.

Jim: I expect you're really excited about it.

Philippa: Yes, I am. But the part of the holiday I'm looking forward to most is the bus journey from one side of the States to the other. We're going to see all kinds of wonderful scenery and I'm hoping to take some good photographs of mountains and that kind of thing. It's my hobby. Of course, I'll be pleased to visit the big cities too.

Jim: And when your trip is over, what then?

Philippa: After I get home, I'm planning to have a show of the photographs I take. It's going to be in the city library, where I had a holiday job. They have space in the library for things like that and the librarian has very kindly said that I can use it for one week.

Jim: Well, that's great. Thank you, Philippa, for telling us about your plans. Now, we need to talk about this week's competition …

Writing folder

Writing Part 1

1   Ask students to look at the question and the three answers. Talk about which one is correct and why.

Answers
A and B are grammatically incorrect. C is correct.

2   Ask students to do the same with question 2.

Answers
A is correct.
B is grammatically incorrect. You cannot say *The new pool has been open since two days.*
C doesn't make sense.

3   In this part of the exam, it is important that students understand that what they write must make the second sentence mean exactly the same as the first. This part of the exam tests a range of grammatical structures.

Answers
3   bigger/larger than (tests comparatives)
4   open (tests *closed = not open*)
5   not go (tests the fact that *must* is not followed by *to*)
6   've/have never been (tests present perfect + *never*)
7   to go (tests *used to* followed by infinitive)
8   small (tests *too* + adjective and *not* + adjective + *enough*)
9   lent me (tests *borrow*, *lend* + pronoun without *to*)
10   spent (tests *spend* + time without *for*)

17 Next week's episode

TOPIC: Predictions

In this unit:

Grammar	*will* future; *will* versus *going to*; *everyone, no one, someone, anyone*
Functions and vocabulary	Predicting; TV and radio programmes
Pronunciation	/ɑː/ as in *car*; /ɔː/ as in *sore*; /ɜː/ as in *third*
PET skills	Listening for detail and attitude (Listening Part 4); guessing unknown words from context
Revision	*need* (Unit 5); telling a story (Unit 12); present continuous for present actions (Unit 3)
Exam folder	Reading Part 4

Preparation

Introduction, Exercise 2 If appropriate, you may wish to bring some real examples of TV guides in English into the classroom for students to look at when you discuss the TV programmes they like, or to browse through later.

Introduction, Exercise 3 Make an OHT of the blank crossword or project it from the CD-ROM or webpage.

Activity *A script for a soap* If students are going to write and act out soap episodes, you may need to plan where and when.

Activity *Predictions* Have ready suitable pieces of paper.

SB pages 110–113

Introduction

1 **2 21** Look at the words in the box with the class and elicit/supply definitions and examples of the types of programme.

Play the recording and discuss the answers.

Answers
1 News   2 Police drama   3 Children's programme
4 Costume drama

2 Ask students to label the columns and check the answers together. Avoid discussing the vocabulary in the texts until they have finished, as there are lots of clues.

Either have a brief discussion now about the types of programme they enjoy, using the English TV guides if you have brought any, or leave this until after they have done the crossword and use it as a lead-in to the Listening.

Answers
2 Children's programmes   3 Documentary
4 Game shows   5 Costume drama   6 Police drama
7 Soaps   8 Sport

3 Let students do the crossword in pairs or set for homework. To check the answers, if possible project the crossword onto the board or OHP (see Preparation). Ask students to come up and write in the words, or fill them in yourself as students call them out.

Answers

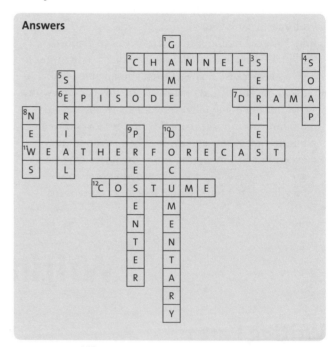

Listening

In this part of the lesson students practise listening for detailed understanding.

If this follows immediately after working through the Introduction, lead from the discussion about TV programmes to ask which, if any, soaps students follow on the radio or television.

If you wish, tell students that the term *soap* (originally *soap opera*) originates from the practice of soap powder manufacturers in the USA sponsoring serials on the radio in the days before television. If you are in the UK, some students may be able to recommend ones that they watch. Point out that this is a good way of learning English. Outside the UK, invite students to have a brief discussion of the merits or demerits of any soaps popular locally, saying why they do or do not watch / listen to them.

1 Direct the students to the photograph of the characters in *Café Europe*. Ask them to give their opinions on the characters based on the photograph.

2 Read the summary of last week's episode with the class and check that they understand it fully (e.g. *Why did the chef leave? Who is Adam? What did Claudia agree to do?*).

Check students understand 'prediction'. Ask if they think the predictions will come true. Ask them to write down at least one prediction each.

3 **2 22** Ask students to read the questions before they listen. Play the first part of the episode.

Answers
b a job, some money **c** to ask about the chef's job

Recording script

Nathalie: Hello, Mario, how are you?
Mario: Fine, Nathalie, but busy. <u>My chef left last week.</u> I have to do all the cooking myself and I'm so tired.
Nathalie: Perhaps I can help. <u>I'm looking for a job. I need to earn some money</u>.
Mario: But can you cook?
Nathalie: Cook? Oh, well, you know, yeah. I'm sure I'm exactly the person you're looking for.
Mario: Well, actually, I saw a woman yesterday, but she wasn't sure. Can you start tomorrow?
Nathalie: Sure. The sooner the better.
Mario: Because this woman lives a long way away. She's phoning me this morning. <u>Come and see me later. If she doesn't want the job, you can have it.</u>
Nathalie: Oh, thank you, Mario. Bye.

4 **2 23** Repeat the procedure, playing the second part.

Answers
b a picture of a car
c a red car like the one in the picture

Recording script

Adam: <u>Morning, Karim. Are you going to work already?</u>
Karim: Hi, Adam. Yes, Mario hasn't got a chef and I'm going to help him. Anyway, I want to talk to Claudia. You know I'm going to buy her car?
Adam: Yeah? That'll be really useful.
Karim: And it's good value. It's almost new. <u>Like this one in this magazine, see?</u>
Adam: Oh, right. <u>I saw one like that near Claudia's place yesterday</u>, it was a different colour. There was a fair-haired girl in it, but it had –
Karim: Claudia's car is red.
Adam: Really?
Karim: Anyway, I must go. See you.
Adam: But Karim, <u>that car I saw, that was red –</u>
Karim: Bye, Adam.
Adam: – but its headlights were smashed. Oh, well. Perhaps it wasn't Claudia's car.

PET Listening Part 4

5 **2 24** Play the third part of the episode (⏪ twice if necessary). Ask students to do the exercise and compare their answers with another student.

Answers
b true **c** false **d** false **e** false **f** true

Recording script

Karim: Hi, Claudia.
Claudia: Hi, Karim. Do you still want to buy my car?
Karim: Sure. <u>I can give you the money tomorrow.</u>
Claudia: Oh, Karim, that's great. I need the money this week. I have to pay my college fees for next year.
Karim: No problem. I know it's a good car. It's never been in an accident, has it?
Claudia: <u>Oh, no. I've looked after it very carefully.</u>
Nathalie: Hi, Claudia.
Claudia: Hey, Nathalie, what are you doing here? Oh, I forgot to ask you. Did you put some petrol in my car on Sunday? When you borrowed it?
Nathalie: Oh, er, yeah. Actually, I want to see Mario. I need to ask him something.
Claudia: Are you going to come and work as a waitress here with me, Nathalie? That'll be a good laugh. But <u>I don't think we need another waitress. He wants a new chef.</u> Go through to the kitchen.
Nathalie: Thanks, Claudia.
Karim: Perhaps Nathalie'll be the new chef.
Claudia: <u>I don't think so. She can't boil an egg!</u> Look, Karim, before we get busy in here, I'm going to go and buy a magazine, OK?

Karim: Sure.

Claudia: I'll be back in a minute.

Nathalie: Hey, Karim. Oh, where's Claudia? I want to tell her some news.

Karim: Yeah?

Nathalie: Yes. I'm going to be the new chef. She'll be really surprised when I tell her.

Karim: But Nathalie, you can't cook.

Nathalie: Why do you think that?

Karim: Claudia told me.

Nathalie: Well, Mario doesn't know. And Claudia won't tell him. She's my friend. I'm sure I can keep the job until Mario pays me at the end of the week. I need some money very quickly.

Karim: But the café will lose all its customers!

Nathalie: Oh, come on, Karim. Anyway, I must go now. Please don't tell Mario.

Adam: After you.

Nathalie: Thank you. Bye.

Adam: Hi, Karim. <u>Who was that?</u>

Karim: Oh, hello, Adam. <u>That was Nathalie.</u> She shares a flat with Claudia.

Adam: <u>But that's the girl –</u>

Mario: Hey, Karim, where's Claudia? I've got some good news. I've found a chef!

Claudia: Hey, I'm back.

Adam: Claudia …

Karim: Mario …

Mario: Good. We've got customers. We'll talk later.

Announcer: What will happen next? Will Mario find out about Nathalie's cooking? Will Claudia find out about her car?

Language focus

Will future

1 Ask students to look back at the predictions they wrote for Listening Exercise 2. Find out which members of the class made the best predictions. Are these the people who watch soap operas most often?

2 ◄◄ Replay the whole episode if necessary (some classes will have heard it enough times by now). Direct students' attention to the use of *will* in the questions. Elicit/Explain that *will* is used when we make predictions about future events. Refer to the table as necessary. Go through the questions, elicit the negative form and briefly drill positive and negative statements, using the ideas generated by question **d**.

Suggested answers
a To mend Claudia's car.
b Yes, he will probably find out.
c Yes, Adam will probably tell Karim, and he will tell Claudia.
d There will be problems in the kitchen! / Mario won't be happy. He won't pay Nathalie.

3 Ask the class to suggest answers and write them on the board.

Possible answers
b will go to university. **c** will be hotter.
d will give us less homework. **e** will have a good job.

4 Direct students to the sentences in Exercise 3 and ask them to write individual answers for Exercise 3, using their own ideas. Make sure they know they must be negative.

Possible answers
b I won't see them very often.
c we won't use any central heating.
d we won't be tired. **e** I won't go to school.

Talking about the future

These exercises focus on the use of *will*, *going to* and the present tense after time adverbials.

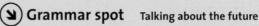

⤵ Grammar spot **Talking about the future**

Look at the example with the class. Ask why *tell* is in the present. Remind students about the use of the present after *when*, etc. (see Unit 16). Let students complete the gapped sentence and check it with them.

Answer
Nathalie uses *going to* for a definite plan, *will* for a prediction and *the present tense* after *when*.

1 Let students work through the exercise in pairs and check it round the class.

Answers
b is/'s going to leave   will/'ll get   hears
c am/'m not going to join   will/'ll be   tell
d is/'s going to give   will not/won't enjoy   gives   will/'ll help

2 Ask students to write two or three sentences modelled on the previous exercise. This could be homework.

Everyone/everybody, no one/nobody, someone/somebody or anyone/anybody

1 Refer students to the group photograph of the characters from *Café Europe*. Ask the questions in the Student's Book: *Who is looking at the camera? Who is wearing a hat?* etc. and elicit/supply the answers.

> **Answers**
> a Everyone/Everybody
> b No one/Nobody
> c Yes, Mario is.

Write on the board: *Everyone/Everybody is looking at the camera. No one / Nobody is wearing a hat.*

 Grammar spot *Anyone/anybody*, etc.

Fill the gaps together.

> **Answers**
> a No one b anyone c someone
> d anyone e anyone
> We use a *singular* verb with these words.

Remind students that the rules are the same as for *some* and *any* (see Unit 5).

Briefly drill some questions and answers about students in the room.

 Corpus spot

Ask students to correct the sentences and check answers together.

> **Answers**
> a There isn't <u>anybody</u> on the beach.
> b We looked for my ring but <u>no one</u> found it.
> c I saw that everybody <u>was</u> dancing.

2 Ask students to write as many true sentences as they can in five minutes. Ask them each to read one of their sentences, which must not be a repeat of someone else's. See who has the most correct, true sentences.

《**Activity**》 **Everyone has something**

1 This activity revises and extends vocabulary of household items and personal possessions and practises the use of *everyone* and *no one*. Check students know the names of the objects in the pictures. They are: laptop computer, mirror, sculpture, plant, blind, lipstick, desk, hairdryer, exercise bike, football boots.

2 Divide students into groups of about six. They must find which thing everyone has and which thing no one has in their bedroom. If necessary, they can add to the list.

Ask them what question they will ask: *Does anyone have a laptop/computer in their bedroom?*

When they have finished, they report back to the class.

《**Pronunciation**》

This practises making and distinguishing between the sounds /ɑː/, /ɔː/ and /ɜː/.

/ɑː/ is not a difficult sound for most students (see also Unit 3), but /ɔː/ (see also Unit 7) and /ɜː/ often cause problems.

1 **2 25** Play the recording of the three sentences and ask the students to say which vowel sound they hear twice in each sentence. Let them practise producing the individual sounds, then ask them to say first the pairs of words, and then the sentences together.

> **Answers**
> a /ɑː/ large car b /ɔː/ all sore c /ɜː/ third turning

> ### Recording script
> a She's got a large car.
> b My toes were all sore.
> c Take the third turning.

2 Ask students to work in pairs. They find words containing the sounds and complete the table.

> **Answers**
>
> | /ɑː/ | /ɔː/ | /ɜː/ |
> |------|------|------|
> | can't | talk | hurts |
> | dark | saw | shirt |
> | aren't | morning | earn |
> | harder | more | dirty |
> | half | doors | learn |
> | | story | work |
> | | | heard |

3 **2 26** Play the recording for students to check answers.

> ### Recording script
> a My head <u>hurts</u> when I <u>talk</u> too much.
> b I <u>saw</u> the <u>shirt</u> this <u>morning</u>.
> c I need to <u>earn</u> <u>more</u> money.
> d I <u>can't</u> see in the <u>dark</u>.
> e These <u>doors</u> <u>aren't</u> <u>dirty</u>.
> f You must <u>learn</u> to <u>work</u> <u>harder</u>.
> g I only <u>heard</u> <u>half</u> the <u>story</u>.

«Activity» A script for a soap

In these activities students can practise writing dialogue, speaking and/or writing narrative in the past. You may direct the class to do one or more of the activities or allow them to choose in groups, as appropriate.

For tasks **a**, **b** and **c**, divide the class into groups of four or five. Try to ensure that the best speakers are not all in one group. Ask them to decide which characters they will play and think about the story. Discourage them from writing. If possible, give them time and space to improvise and rehearse, then have the groups perform for the rest of the class. Ask the class to decide which group's prediction is most likely to be the next episode.

For task **d** students write a summary of the story they prefer. This can be done in groups or could be homework, if time is short.

EXTRA

Most UK soaps have websites with summaries of recent episodes. Some classes might enjoy looking at these.

Alternative where improvisation is inappropriate
Ask students to work in pairs to invent and write a summary of next week's episode. Let them compare their ideas with other pairs and see if they had similar ideas.

«Activity» Predictions

For large classes, put students into groups of about eight. Ask each student to write their name on a piece of paper (add yours if you wish to participate). Then ask each student to take one and not to reveal the name. Ask them to write four predictions about that person. Encourage amusing or fantastic ideas but not unkind ones.

Let students take turns to read out their predictions. Ask them to write down who they think is the subject, then see how many people guessed correctly.

Exam folder 17

SB pages 114–115

Reading Part 4

Look at the Summary box about this part of the exam and read through the Exam Advice box with the class.

1   Look at the stem of question 1 together. Elicit what can be learnt from it.

> **Answer**
> The text is a letter, and it is from a class of students.

Explain that reading the options is not necessary yet, and may be confusing. (This is different from the Listening test, where they need to use the time before hearing the text to read all the questions. In the Reading test, they can refer back and forth between the text and the questions as they work.)

2   Go through questions 2–5 in the same way.

> **Answers**
> 2   The reason(s) why the students think Parson's Place is important.
> 3   Something will cause traffic jams.
> 4   What the ordinary people will do, or what will happen to them.
> 5   The students have made a poster.

Point out that question 4 is an incomplete sentence. The options A, B, C or D will complete the sentence. This question form occurs quite often in PET multiple choice.

3   Ask students to read the text quickly. Reassure them that you will explain any new words at the end of the lesson, but remind them that they need to practise reading texts without checking unknown words because they will not be able to do so in the exam.

4   Discuss question **a** together.

Read the options for question 1 and discuss which is correct (D). Ask students to work in pairs and do questions **b–e** in the same way.

> **Answers**
> a   Few people know ... our town (lines 2–3)
> b   It is a beautiful natural area ... roads nearby (lines 4–6)
> c   the second paragraph
> d   the average family
> 1 D   2 C   3 A   4 D   5 B

18 Shooting a film

TOPIC: Films

In this unit:

Grammar	Past perfect; past perfect versus past simple
Functions and vocabulary	Talking about the order of past events; films; telling a story
Pronunciation	/ə/ at the end of words
PET skills	Reading for specific information (Reading Part 2); reading for detail, answering true/false questions (Reading Part 3, Listening Part 4)
Revision	Past simple (Unit 6); giving opinions (Units 2 and 6)
Exam folder	Listening Part 3
Writing folder	Writing Part 2

Preparation

Activity *Telling a story* Photocopy the pictures (on page 183). Each student (or pair) should have one picture.
Activity *Films* Photocopy the quiz (on page 183), enough for students to share in pairs.
Exam folder 18 Make copies of the recording script (from CD-ROM or webpage) for students.

SB pages 116–119

Introduction

1 Students work in small groups to look at the photographs and try to identify the kind of film they represent. See if anyone knows the titles of the films.

Answers
a comedy *Mr Bean*   b musical *Mamma Mia!*
c science fiction film *Star Wars*
d horror film *The Mummy*
e cartoon/animation *Ice Age*
f action film *The Dark Knight*   g love story *Titanic*
h historical film *The Other Boleyn Girl*

2 Ask students to work in groups. Each student should think of a film they have seen recently (it could be on TV). They are going to tell the story of the film (briefly!) to other students who will guess what the title is.

3 Students decide what kinds of film they have described (*horror*, *cartoon*, etc.).

4 When they have finished, ask a few students to tell you which films they talked about, what kinds of film they were and what kinds of film their group likes best. Ask students who their favourite film star is.

Reading

PET Reading Part 2

1 Look at the picture and talk about what is happening. Check the vocabulary.

Discuss which things the actors have to do and which things the film crew have to do.

EXTRA
If there is time, talk about a scene from a film which most of the students have seen and enjoyed and discuss what preparations were made before they filmed it.

2 Tell students that they are going to read an article about a film company who are shooting a film at the seaside. Ask them to read the article in their books quickly and answer the question. (Answer: ten minutes)

3 Students read the text more slowly, checking what the film crew and the actors did.

Answers

The actors ...	The film crew ...
went to the make-up room ✓	set up the lights ✓
went to the dressing room ✓	moved the cameras ✓
read the scripts ✗	checked the microphones ✓

PET Reading Part 3 and Listening Part 4

4 Get students to do these questions in pairs to check they have understood what they read.

Answers
b false   c true   d false   e false

5 Have a class discussion about the unit topic and read the Vocabulary spot together. Get students to underline words and expressions in the text that they could use in the Speaking test.

Language focus
Past perfect

Language presentation

Write on the board: *By the time you got here today, I'd ...* Either tell students, or get them to suggest, some of the things you had and hadn't done. Make sure they understand that all these things happened before they got here. Point out that *had* is shortened to *'d*.

1 Look at the table together and check the formation of the past perfect.

Look at **a** and **b** together, then students can do the rest of the exercise alone.

Answers
b had visited the make-up artist.
c had set up the lights.
d had cleared the rubbish.
e had told everyone what to do.
f hadn't checked the microphones.
g had shot ten minutes of the film.
h had been there for ten hours.

2 First, ask students to write down an age next to each event. Ask a few students *How old were you when you first ...?*

Next, ask students to write two sentences.

Finally, students work in pairs, practising the question form of the past perfect. Ask individual students to report back to the whole class saying what they have found out about each other.

Past perfect and past simple

1 Use the sentences and the Grammar spot to compare the use of the past perfect and the past simple.

Answers
Two things happened almost at the same time in Sentence B.
One thing happened before another in Sentence A.

 Grammar spot   Past perfect and past simple

Answers
When two things happen almost at the same time, we use the *past simple* tense in both sentences.
When one event happens before another, we use the *past perfect* tense for the event that happened first and the *past simple* tense for the second event.

---

2 Do a few of the questions together.

Answers
b had   **c** hadn't finished   **d** welcomed   **e** had been
f was   **g** had changed   **h** didn't recognise

3 Look at the picture and discuss what is happening. Do the first few questions together, then students can finish the exercise in class. If they are having trouble, divide the events into two groups – things that happened when they walked along the beach and things that happened before that.

Answers
b had lived   **c** met   **d** hadn't seen   **e** reminded
f had dug   **g** had put   **h** had written   **i** had covered
j decided   **k** found   **l** started   **m** was   **n** took
o read   **p** had written   **q** were   **r** didn't know

《Pronunciation》

This practises words ending in a weak syllable with the vowel sound /ə/.

1 All the words except *holiday* and *telephone* have the weak sound /ə/ in the last syllable. Most words ending in *ant*, *ent*, *tion*, *or* and *er* end with a weak syllable.

2 **2 27** Play the recording for students to listen and repeat.

Recording script

woman important holiday camera letter appointment newspaper horror preparation telephone actor answer

3 Students work in pairs to guess the words, then they write them in the correct column.

Answers

ending in er(s)	ending in or(s)	ending in tion	ending in ant or ent
teenager	*actors*	fiction	different
letters	visitor	action	assistant
teacher	director	question	instrument

4 **2 28** Students listen and repeat.

Recording script

actors fiction different visitor teenager letters action assistant question director instrument teacher

《Activity》 Telling a story

1 This activity practises telling a story in the past simple and using sequencing adverbs. There are twenty cards, each with a scene from a film on them (see Preparation). There are four film sequences altogether, each one made up of five cards. If you have 20 students, give them one card each. If you have 15 students, leave out one of the films. If you have more than 20 students or a number which is not a multiple of five, get some students to work in pairs. Students go round the room trying to find someone whose card is part of the same sequence. Slowly they arrange themselves into four groups.

2 Their task is then to put the cards in order. The last scene from each film is missing, so they have to invent the ending. Each group tells the story of their film sequence to the rest of the class, providing the ending. Encourage them to use the sequencing adverbs they have learnt.

⟪Activity⟫ Films

Either use the photocopiable quiz (see Preparation) or ask students to write questions themselves. Divide the class into several teams. Give each team the quiz questions. Set a time limit. Students work together to answer the questions. They could do the quiz as homework and then compare their answers in their teams. Discuss the answers with the whole class and decide which team has won.

Answers
1 *Harry Potter and the Philosopher's Stone*
2 James Bond
3 Silent comedies
4 *Titanic*
5 Frankenstein
6 *Snow White and the Seven Dwarfs*
7 New Zealand
8 A lion
9 1927 (*The Jazz Singer*)
10 India (over 800 per year)

Exam folder 18

SB pages 120–121

Listening Part 3

Look at the Summary box together.

1 The advertisement practises some cinema vocabulary.

Answers
a a programme   **b** Box office   **c** performances
d screens   **e** Discounts

2 This exercise trains students to guess what kind of word they need to put in the space by looking at the words around it. Look at the Exam Advice box together.

Answers
a a time
b a day of the week or a date
c a place, e.g. a bank or a supermarket
d director, photography, actor, etc.
e a foreign language
f a type of person, e.g. children, adults
g a price
h a phone number

3 Students look at the notes about the cinema and tell you what kinds of word they are going to listen for. In the exam they have time to read through the questions.

Answers
1 a day of the week or a date   2 a person
3 something that is connected with the film (see **2d**)
4 a language   5 a person   6 a time

4 **2 29** Read the instructions together. These give students an idea of what the recording is about.

Play the recording twice and then check the answers.

5 **2 29 ◁** Give out the photocopied recording script (see Preparation) and play the recording again.

Answers
1 Monday   2 director   3 photography   4 Spanish
5 Princess   6 9.30

Recording script

You will hear a recorded message giving you information about films.
For each question, fill in the missing information in the numbered space.
Message: Welcome to the Victoria Cinema Information Line.
Here is a list of films for the week starting July 7th. There are three performances each day of *One Summer Night* at 5 pm, 7.30 pm and 10 pm, except <u>Monday</u>, when there is only one chance to see it at 7.30 and Sunday, when there is no performance.
Every afternoon there is a showing of *The Violinist* at 2.30 pm and after the performance on Wednesday, the <u>director</u>, Mark Hawkins, will give a lecture about the film. This is included in the ticket price.
Our late-night film is *Dead Men's Shoes*, which is coming to the cinema for the second time. It is set in the Canadian mountains and stars the well-known actor Jim Harrison. It recently won a prize for its <u>photography</u>.

Our foreign-language film this week is called *A Dangerous Game* and is showing on Saturday afternoon at 5 pm. Although the director is actually Swedish, the film is in <u>Spanish</u> with subtitles in English.

There are two films showing in our Saturday morning Film Club for children. The film at 10 am is suitable for children aged between 5 and 10 and is called *The Young <u>Princess</u>*. It is about the adventures of a young girl whose father becomes king of his country by mistake. At 11.30 we are showing *The Mad Professor*, which is a comedy.

All tickets are £4.50 except for children and senior citizens who pay £3.50.

The box office is open from 2 pm until 8.30 pm but our telephone booking line is open in the morning from 10.30 am and you can book tickets with a credit card until <u>9.30 pm</u> if you ring 0987 34872. There is a charge of 50p for tickets bought by telephone.

Thank you for calling the Victoria Cinema Information Line.

Writing folder

Writing Part 2

1 Ask students to complete the sentences quickly and check the answers round the class. Ask them how they decided and remind them as necessary that the present continuous can be used for future plans and that the present perfect cannot be used for a definite time in the past which is finished, e.g. last night.

Answers
a tomorrow afternoon   b this weekend   c last night

2 This exercise can be done by students in groups, or by students working individually. Draw attention to the Exam Advice box.

Suggested answers (useful language is in brackets)
1
- say what the house is like: **present simple** (*It's a traditional farmhouse.*)
- say what you have done this morning: **present perfect** (*I've helped with the animals.*)
- tell him/her your plans for the rest of the weekend: **present continuous / going to** (*We're going (to go) for a walk in the woods tomorrow.*)

2
- say how you plan to get there: **present continuous / going to** (*I'm coming / I'm going to come by train.*)
- ask about what you will all do: **future / going to** (*What will we do? / What are we going to do?*)
- tell them what time you will arrive: **present continuous / future / going to** (*I'm arriving at 10.30. / I'll be at the station at 10.30. / I'm going to arrive at 10.30.*)

3
- say what you enjoyed most: **past simple** (*I really enjoyed helping with the animals.*)
- tell him/her about your journey home: **past simple** (*I had an easy journey home.*)
- tell him/her your plans for next weekend: **present continuous / going to** (*Next weekend I'm having a party / I'm going to have a party.*)

3 Ask students to work in small groups. Tell each group which question to answer, but do not let the rest of the class hear. Give them a time limit of seven minutes.

4 Ask them to pass their answer to the next group to be checked. That group says which question is answered, and if the right tenses have been used.

Units 13–18 Revision

Speaking

1 Follow the procedure outlined on page 42 of the Teacher's Book.

Exercises 2–7 could be set for homework and discussed afterwards in class.

Vocabulary

2

Answers
b tower   **c** coast   **d** rope   **e** tunnel   **f** on
g square   **h** in   **i** from   **j** entrance   **k** instructions

3

Answers
Dear Hanna
How are you? I *hope* you're well.
I'm fine. I went *shopping* yesterday with my *friend* Emilia *because* it was my birthday and I *received / had received* some money.
I saw a *beautiful* jacket in my *favourite clothes* shop.
I tried it on *and* it was *comfortable*. But I *thought* it was *too* expensive. Then Emilia showed me the ticket – it was half *price*! I bought it, *then* we decided to go to a *restaurant* which is near *there*. We had a very good day.

4

Answers
b sofa   **c** curtain   **d** amazing   **e** gloves
f sensible   **g** cooker   **h** save

Grammar

5

Answers
2 A   **3** C   **4** B   **5** B   **6** C

6

Answers
2 B   **3** C   **4** A   **5** A   **6** B

7

Answers
b could/might   **c** mustn't/can't   **d** can't
e don't have to   **f** used to   **g** has to
h don't have to   **i** have to   **j** could/might   **k** need

Progress Test 3 Key

1 C   **2** B   **3** C   **4** A   **5** B   **6** A   **7** A   **8** C   **9** C

10 A   **11** C   **12** A   **13** C   **14** B   **15** C   **16** C   **17** B

18 B   **19** A   **20** C   **21** A   **22** C   **23** A

24 scarf   **25** handsome   **26** embarrassed

27 comfortable   **28** gloves   **29** floating   **30** competitors

Progress Test 3

Choose the correct answer, A, B or C.

1 Clare usually wears plain skirts and .... shirts.
  A pattern **B** patterns **C** patterned

2 We have three rooms .... the ground floor and five upstairs.
  A at **B** on **C** in

3 That plastic watch isn't .... €50.
  A cost **B** afford **C** worth

4 It's nearly eleven o'clock and Zoe is still asleep. She .... be tired.
  A must **B** might **C** could

5 My father .... to cycle to work, but now he drives.
  A use **B** used **C** uses

6 I gave my silk jacket to my sister because it was too small .... me.
  A for **B** by **C** to

7 We .... catch a bus because I've got my car.
  A don't have to **B** mustn't **C** can't

8 Is your granny .... to carry all those boxes?
  A enough strong **B** enough stronger
  C strong enough

9 .... your brother come to the film with us or is he too young?
  A Must **B** Does **C** Can

10 Does Bobby speak any other languages, ... from Spanish?
  A apart **B** along **C** away

11 I didn't get .... with my brother when we were little, but we're good friends now.
  A up **B** off **C** on

12 Where did you get those .... boots?
  A lovely black leather **B** lovely leather black
  C black lovely leather

13 Excuse me, please. .... the train?
  A What's time **B** What time comes
  C What time is

14 Those shoes .... pretty, but I'm sure they're very uncomfortable.
  A look like **B** look **C** are look

15 What .... to do after dinner?
  A does everyone going **B** everyone is going
  C is everyone going

16 The plane took off at .... past nine.
  A fifteen **B** twenty-three **C** twenty-five

17 Alec really wanted to watch television, but .... the end he agreed to come out with us.
  A at **B** in **C** on

18 The guests .... already started dancing when my parents came in.
  A were **B** had **C** have

19 I was looking for a shop assistant but there was no one .... sight.
  A in **B** on **C** at

20 This picture .... me of my parents' house.
  A remembers **B** recognises **C** reminds

21 The students will wait here until someone .... them.
  A calls **B** will call **C** call

22 Thank you for .... me to watch your match, but I'm afraid I'm busy.
  A ask **B** asked **C** asking

23 I've got an exam tomorrow, so I'm going to .... at home this evening.
  A stay **B** spend **C** stand

Find one spelling mistake in each sentence. Write the correction in the space.

24 That scharf matches your lipstick perfectly.
  ....

25 Everyone agrees that your brother-in-law's very handsom. ....

26 The journalists were embarassed when they met the professor after the conference. ....

27 That armchair is very confortable but it isn't fashionable. ....

28 Don't forget your glouves, because it's extremely cold outside. ....

29 After the heavy rain, there was a lot of wood floting down the river. ....

30 It's important that the competetors all listen to the organisers' instructions carefully.

19 Happy families

TOPIC: Family life

In this unit:	
Grammar	Verbs and expressions followed by *to* and *-ing*; *make* and *let*
Functions and vocabulary	Families; agreeing and disagreeing
Pronunciation	/ð/ as in *this*; /θ/ as in *thin*
PET skills	Talking about yourself and your family (Speaking); giving opinions, agreeing and disagreeing (Speaking Part 2)
Revision	Giving opinions; giving advice (Unit 9)
Exam folder	Reading Part 5

Preparation

Note: If there are any sensitive family situations among your students, you may want to change some of the exercises or activities to make them less personal (e.g. Introduction, Exercise 2 and Listening, Exercise 4). They could talk about famous families, for example.

Language focus, Exercise 2 Make copies of the recording script (from CD-ROM or webpage) for students.

Activity *Families* Photocopy the cards (on page 184) – one per student. There are 12 cards, so some students may need to work in pairs or take two cards, depending on the number of students in the class.

SB pages 124–127

Introduction

1 Look at the family tree together. Check students understand the layout. Before students start reading the text, make sure they realise that it is described by Daniel. Find Daniel in the family tree. Students fill in the spaces alone or with a partner.

> **Answers**
> **b** daughter **c** uncle **d** husband **e** sister
> **f** stepmother **g** half-sister **h** nephew **i** niece
> **j** brother-in-law **k** cousin **l** ex-wife

Language presentation

Check that students know what an 'in-law' is (relative by marriage) and the difference between a *stepsister* (the daughter of a stepmother or stepfather, i.e. not a blood relation) and a *half-sister* (the daughter of your father or mother but not both). Check other family vocabulary, e.g. *Who is Daniel to Tony?* (*son*); *Who is Clare to Michael?* (*aunt*); *Who is Lily to Clare?* (*mother-in-law*), etc.

Point out that *cousin* is used for males and females, *aunt* and *uncle* are also used for the husbands and wives of aunts and uncles (related by marriage); *brother-in-law* is your husband's brother but also your sister's husband.

Check the meaning of *parents* and *relations*, as *parents* is a false friend in some languages. Talk about what English children call their parents and grandparents – *Mum/ Mummy/Mom* (American), *Dad/Daddy*, *Granny/Grandma/ Nanna*, *Grandad/Grandpa*.

PET Speaking

2 Students work in pairs with a blank piece of paper each. One student tells another student about his or her family and the other student makes a family tree, keeping it fairly simple. Then they exchange roles. If they prefer, students can do the family tree of a family they know or a famous family.

You could ask individual students to tell the class about their partner's family tree.

Tell students that they might want to speak about their own family in the Speaking test.

Listening

1 **2 30** Look at the photographs and discuss when they were taken and what the relationships are between the people.

Students listen to the recording and note down which position each person is in their family and the disadvantage they mention. Check the meaning of *fed up* and *spoilt*.

> **Answers**
> **Rebecca (oldest):** Your parents worry about you.
> **George (youngest):** You're always the baby. / They never let you grow up.
> **Charlotte (middle):** You don't have a special place in the family.
> **Peter (only):** It's difficult to make friends.

Recording script

a My name's Rebecca. My brother's five years younger than me. My parents didn't make me look after him but I enjoyed it. I used to <u>look forward to playing</u> with him when I came home from school but I sometimes got <u>fed up with reading</u> the same stories hundreds of times. But all those afternoons with my brother were good practice because now I have my own son and <u>I'd like to have</u> more children. My son is like me in lots of ways except he's really untidy and I'm the opposite. The worst thing about being the oldest is that your parents <u>begin to worry</u> about you from the moment you're born and they continue to worry because you're always the first to do everything.

b I'm George and I have three older sisters so I was really spoilt when I was a child but I didn't mind that. I never worried about anything – I was always laughing and I think I <u>started to tell</u> jokes when I was about two years old. But when I was about 14 I <u>stopped doing</u> what everyone told me and then I had two parents and three sisters getting angry with me. That's the problem really with being the youngest – everyone <u>continues seeing</u> you as the baby even when you're an adult. They never let you grow up.

c I'm Charlotte and I have an older sister who is clever, pretty and has a lovely singing voice, in fact she's good at everything, and a younger brother who is good-looking, clever, oh what else, he's really good at playing football. Then there's me. I <u>try to be</u> nice to them both but I'm really jealous because they always <u>seem to do</u> everything right and I do everything wrong. So I always <u>arrange to spend</u> a lot of time with my mates. I think it's hard for middle children because they don't have a special place in the family.

d My name is Peter. I was never jealous of my friends who had brothers and sisters because my parents loved taking me with them when they went out so I spent a lot of time with adults. I enjoyed that. I have quite a few cousins and I used to see them sometimes but I didn't <u>want to share</u> my parents with anyone. I don't think I ever <u>learnt to play</u> with other children – I <u>preferred reading</u> and I spent a lot of time doing homework. I think only children sometimes find it difficult to make friends so that's a disadvantage. I only really <u>began making</u> friends when I went to university and <u>started spending</u> a lot of time with people of my own age.

---

2 Read the descriptions together, checking understanding and the meaning of any new words such as *keeping rules*, *solving arguments*, *don't mind*, *sense of humour* and *artistic subjects*. Get students to write the names of the people from Exercise 1 in the correct space and to add their own name to one of the descriptions.

3 **2 30 ◁** Ask students to look at the list of points in the section under *oldest children*. Tell them you are going to play Rebecca's part again and ask them to tick the points she mentions. Then continue through the recording in the same way. They should put a tick or a cross according to whether each point is mentioned or not.

> **Answers**
> **Oldest children**   *Rebecca*
> - <u>expect</u> to do well ✗
> - are <u>good at</u> looking after other people ✓
> - <u>need</u> to keep everything tidy ✓
> - <u>like</u> keeping rules ✗
>
> **Youngest children**   *George*
> - <u>love</u> taking risks ✗
> - have a good sense of humour ✓
> - often <u>refuse</u> to do what other people tell them ✓
> - are <u>interested in</u> studying artistic subjects ✗
>
> **Middle children**   *Charlotte*
> - are <u>good at</u> solving arguments ✗
> - enjoy being with other people ✓
> - are good managers and leaders ✗
> - <u>don't mind</u> changing their plans ✗
>
> **Only children**   *Peter*
> - <u>prefer</u> being with adults ✓
> - are quite serious ✓
> - are <u>afraid of</u> failing ✗
> - are hard-working ✓

PET Speaking Part 2

4 Students move around the room, getting themselves into groups with other people who have the same position in their family – oldest, middle, youngest and only child.

In a very large class where students cannot walk about, allocate different parts of the room for different groups and students can change seats. If your class is small, or most students belong to the same group, have a whole-class discussion instead here and in Exercise 5 below. You can then extend the discussion to friends and people students know, as well as talking about their own situation.

In their groups, students discuss whether they agree with the points in the descriptions which refer to their position in the family. Encourage them to use the expressions in their books.

5   Get them to think of other things which they agree should be added to the list, e.g. *only children are friendly/shy.*

Have a feedback session from each group.

 Corpus spot   *Agree*

Answers
a <u>I agree</u> with you about the new restaurant.
b <u>Do</u> you agree about that?
c I hope she <u>will agree</u> to come with us tomorrow.
d My friend <u>agreed</u> to meet me at 7.30.

Language focus
Words followed by *to* or *-ing*

1   Write on the board: *Oldest children expect to do well. They are good at looking after other people.* Discuss the two different structures and then do the exercise.

Answers

Verbs and expressions followed by *to*	Verbs and expressions followed by *-ing*
expect need refuse	*be good at* like enjoy don't mind love be interested in be afraid of

2   Give students the recording scripts (see Preparation), either for checking or to copy from, depending on how much they already know.

Answers

Verbs and expressions followed by *to*	Verbs and expressions followed by *-ing*
would like begin continue start try seem arrange want learn	look forward to be fed up with stop continue prefer begin start

Remind students of the difference between *like doing* and *would like to do* (Unit 2).

Answers
begin, continue and *start* are in both columns
Note: *Try* and *stop* can also be followed by either *to* or *-ing*, but with a change in meaning. Students are only taught one meaning here, which is how they are used in the texts. *Like, love, hate* and *prefer* can be followed by either *to* or *-ing*, sometimes with a change of meaning and sometimes not. They are taught here followed by *-ing*. Students may encounter these verbs followed by *to*, but at a more advanced stage.

3   Students complete their table with these words. They then have a list for reference.

Answers
hope, agree, promise, plan, decide and *offer* are all followed by *to*

Look at the Vocabulary spot together. For homework, students could copy out the sentences containing the verbs – it is easier to remember them if they are in an example sentence.

4   Get students to tell you that *make* and *let* are followed by the infinitive without *to*. Ask what the verbs mean here – *make* means to force or to insist; *let* means to allow.

Possible answers
When I was five years old …
… my parents let me buy sweets on Saturdays.
… my parents made me go to bed at 7.30.

When I was ten years old …
… my parents let me go to the shops with a friend.
… my parents made me do my homework before dinner.

 Corpus spot   *to and -ing*

Answers
a Don't forget <u>to write</u> to me.
b I am enjoying <u>being</u> here on holiday.
c I am looking forward to <u>hearing</u> from you soon.
d We decided <u>to catch</u> the train back.
e My parents didn't <u>let me stay</u> in the hotel alone.
f When we finished <u>eating</u>, I went to my house.
g I would like to <u>meet</u> you and your family.
h I am <u>interested in joining</u> this club.

5   Talk briefly about problem pages in magazines and on the Internet. Do students think such pages can help? Would they write to a magazine or website if they had a problem? Pre-teach as necessary *hall of residence.*

Get students to do this exercise without looking back at their lists in Exercises 1–3. They can then go back to their lists to check.

Go through the answers.

Giving advice

1   Read the reply together. Does everyone agree with the advice?

2   Students write the advice expressions down. They learnt all these in Unit 9 except for *ought to*. Point out that *ought* is always followed by *to*.

3   If there is time, students can work in a group to write a reply to the other letter, using the different ways of giving advice. Or they could do this as homework and read some of them out next lesson.

⟪Pronunciation⟫

This practises the sounds /ð/ and /θ/.

1   **2 31** Play the recording and ask students to repeat.

Recording script

this   the   think   there   then   mother   thing   father   other

Then ask if they can work out which two words are the odd ones out (*th* in *think* and *thing* is pronounced /θ/ and *th* in the other words is pronounced /ð/).

Language presentation

Explain that *th* can be pronounced in two different ways in English. Write *this* and *thin* on the board. Tell students to put the tips of their tongues on the cutting edge of their front teeth. Demonstrate the two sounds – /ð/ in *this* is voiced and /θ/ in *thin* is unvoiced. Tell them to blow more air through their teeth when saying /θ/ than when saying /ð/. Get students to try making the sounds.

2   **2 32** Say the words *their* and *thirsty*. Play the recording and ask students to decide which column to put the words in.

◀◀ Play the recording again and ask students to repeat and check.

Recording script

their   thirsty   thank   that   both   birthday   thirty
they   bath   although   teeth   Thursday   weather
mouth   thousand

3   **2 33** Play the sentences and get students to repeat them.

Recording script

a   They're both thirsty on Thursdays.
b   I think his birthday is on the fourth Thursday of the month.
c   The weather is better in the north these days.
d   This thing is worth one thousand and thirteen pounds.
e   Their mother had healthy teeth then.

4   Students work in pairs saying the sentences to each other as fast as they can.

⟪Activity⟫ Families

Give one of the photocopied cards to each student (see Preparation).

The names they have to write in the family tree are written in their books. Students move around the room asking each other who they are in order to fill in the family tree. They may have to put a name in several places to start with until they have more information. If students find this very difficult, you could give them a clue, e.g. *Jane has three children.*

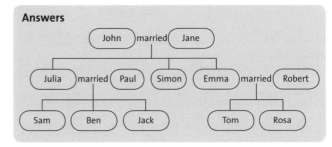

Exam folder 19

Reading Part 5

Look at the Summary box and discuss what students have to do in this part of the exam.

Look at the Check! box.

> **Answers**
> a Read through the whole text.
> b (o)
> c Read the words around the space and check the grammar and meaning.
> d Guess.
> e On the separate answer sheet.

1 Students do questions 1–10 on their own and then check the answers with you. Remind them to check for both grammar and meaning.

> **Answers**
> 1 A 2 C 3 B 4 B 5 D 6 C 7 D 8 B
> 9 B 10 D

2 Look at the photograph and the title of the text. There is not always a picture in the exam but the text always has a title.

Point out to students before they start reading that one of the sons has the same name as his father, so they are referred to as Frank senior and Frank junior. Give students eight minutes to do the task. This is the maximum amount of time they should spend in the exam.

> **Answers**
> 1 A 2 A 3 B 4 A 5 B 6 D 7 B
> 8 A 9 C 10 D

So you think you've got talent?

In this unit:

Grammar	Comparison of adverbs; *so* and *such*; connectives
Functions and vocabulary	Music; congratulating; saying what you like and prefer; jobs
Pronunciation	Words that sound the same but are spelt differently
PET skills	Scanning for specific information (Reading Part 2); sentence transformations (Writing Part 1); choosing the right connectives in a cloze test (Reading Part 5)
Revision	Comparative adjectives (Unit 7); superlative adjectives (Unit 11)
Exam folder	Listening Part 1
Writing folder	Writing Part 3

Preparation

Language focus, Congratulating and choosing Make copies of the recording script (from CD-ROM or webpage) for students.

Exam folder 20 Make copies of the recording script (from CD-ROM or webpage) for students.

Writing folder Photocopy the sample answers (on page 173).

SB pages 130–133

Introduction

This introduces musical instruments and types of music and revises comparative and superlative adjectives.

1   **2 34** Play the recording of different instruments and ask students to say what they are.

Answers
a drum   b flute   c electric guitar
d keyboard / electronic piano   e trumpet   f violin

2   Ask students if they play an instrument and write any other instruments on the board.

3   **2 34** ◁ Play the pieces of music again and ask students to think about the words in their books while they listen. Check they remember how to use comparative and superlative adjectives.

4   Discuss together the kinds of instrument you would hear in the different concerts. Write on the board any new names for students to copy.

Suggested answers
in a classical concert: violin, flute, piano, trumpet (also cello, double bass, oboe, drums, clarinet, horn, etc.)
in a jazz concert: drums, trumpet, piano (also saxophone, clarinet, double bass, etc.)
in a rock concert: drums, electronic piano/keyboard, electric guitar, etc.

5   Spend a few minutes discussing the kinds of music students enjoy listening to.

Possible answers
hip-hop, pop, heavy metal, dance music, blues, country, traditional music

6   Elicit *trumpeter, pianist, violinist* and *drummer* and write them on the board. Ask students for a word which describes them all – musicians. Point out that there is a double *m* in *drummer* and talk about spelling rules (they have come across them before in Units 3, 7 and 11). Ask them what they think will happen to verbs ending in *-e*, e.g. *dance* (they add *-r* not *-er*).

Get students to complete the table in pairs, adding the relevant suffixes.

Refer students to the Vocabulary spot and encourage them to keep vocabulary in categories in their vocabulary books.

Answers

-er	-or	-r	-ist
trumpeter	actor	dancer	*guitarist*
drummer	director	manager	pianist
employer		diver	violinist
farmer			artist
photographer			journalist
reporter			novelist
teacher			

Reading

1   Read the question together and talk about what is happening. Ask students if they have ever entered a competition. How did they feel? Do they watch talent shows on TV? What do they think of them?

Students read the text quickly to themselves and match the pictures to the bands.

Answers
a Eastside   b Texas Team   c The Storm   d Third Avenue

2 Put students in pairs and ask them to put the bands in order and make a note of their decision (they are given the answer later on).

Language focus
PET Reading Part 2
Comparison of adverbs

1 Students work in pairs. Give them a couple of minutes to find the answers to the questions.

> **Answers**
> **b** Third Avenue **c** Texas Team **d** The Storm
> **e** Eastside **f** Third Avenue **g** The Storm

This exercise introduces comparison of adverbs, the structure of which is very similar to comparison of adjectives. Remind students of the irregular adverbs (*best* and *worst*) and point out that you can often omit *the* in the superlative.

PET Writing Part 1

2 Ask students to underline the relevant parts of the notes and point out that these are the three ways of comparing adverbs. Then look at the Grammar spot together.

> **Answers**
> **a** Mara, the singer, sang more confidently than the other singers.
> **b** They danced less professionally than the other bands.
> **c** The violinist didn't play as loudly as the other musicians.

 Grammar spot Comparison of adverbs

> **Answer**
> They have the same meaning.

---

3 Do these together.

> **Answers**
> **a** Texas Team danced less professionally than the other bands.
> Texas Team didn't dance as professionally as the other bands.
> The other bands danced more professionally than Texas Team.
> **b** The violinist in Texas Team didn't play as loudly as the other musicians.
> The violinist in Texas Team played less loudly / more quietly than the other musicians.
> The other musicians played more loudly / less quietly than the violinist in Texas Team.

4 Students then go on and do these sentences, either alone or in pairs, or give each pair just one to do and then compare answers around the class. This kind of transformation often appears in PET Writing Part 1.

> **Answers**
> **a** The Storm's drummer didn't play as loudly as the other drummers.
> The Storm's drummer played more quietly / less loudly than the other drummers.
> The other drummers played less quietly / more loudly than The Storm's drummer.
> **b** Jason played much better than the other guitarists.
> The other guitarists didn't play as well as Jason.
> The other guitarists played less well than Jason.
> **c** The Eastside singers didn't sing as well as the other singers.
> The Eastside singers sang less well than the other singers.
> The other singers sang better than the Eastside singers.

So and *such*

1 **2 35** Play the judge's conclusion and ask students to write the results in order.

> **Answers**
> **First:** The Storm   **Second:** Third Avenue
> **Third:** Eastside   **Fourth:** Texas Team

Recording script
and answers to Congratulating and choosing

Judge: Thank you to all the competitors. I won't say much because I know you're all anxious to hear the results – it was a very difficult decision and I'll start with the band which came fourth. That's Texas Team, who are the youngest group here today. Unfortunately, the violinist played so quietly that we couldn't hear him. So <u>bad luck</u> to Texas Team. Third was Eastside. They are such good dancers they should enter for a dance competition. And with a bit more practice on the music they'll do very well. In second place is Third Avenue. They did well, especially their young guitarist, but the singer looked so unhappy we thought maybe he didn't want to win! <u>Never mind</u> – you nearly won, so <u>better luck next time</u>. <u>Congratulations</u> to The Storm who are our winners today. The singer had such a great voice that we had to give them first place. <u>Well done</u>.

---

2 **2 35** Play the recording again and ask students to complete the sentences.

Answers
b such good dancers   **c** so unhappy   **d** such a great voice

---

Grammar spot   *So, such* and *such a*

Answers
So is used before *an adjective* or *an adverb*.
Such is used before *an adjective + noun* or *a noun*.

Such + (adjective) + plural noun or uncountable noun	*Such a* + (adjective) + singular noun
good dancers loud drums nice food	great voice difficult decision

---

Corpus spot   *So* and *such*

Answers
a She is <u>such a</u> kind woman.
b My grandparents are always <u>so</u> happy together.
c She has <u>such a</u> pretty face.

---

3 Ask students to work in pairs to make six sentences from the table – *that* can be included or omitted.

Answers
b They danced so well (that) I wanted to watch them for ever.
c The concert was in such a small room (that) there wasn't space for everyone.
d The seats were so expensive (that) we couldn't afford to go.
e The fans made such a terrible noise (that) we couldn't hear the band.
f We had such good seats (that) we could see very well.

Congratulating and choosing

1 Photocopy the recording script (see Preparation). Students underline the expressions (see recording script on page 113).

Answers
Expressions to use when someone has won:
Congratulations, Well done

Expressions to use when someone has lost:
Bad luck, Never mind, Better luck next time.

Check they know what to say before a competition or exam, etc. – *Good luck*.

2 **2 36** Play the three different kinds of music. Students work in groups. Tell them they are the judges this time. In their groups they come to a consensus about who won, who came second, etc. Ask students how they will tell other people in the group about what they think and like. Put these expressions on the board:
I prefer A to B. My favourite is A. I like B best. I don't like C. The worst band is C.

When they have made their decisions, they should make some notes in the same way as the judges in the previous round. Their notes will be much briefer, as their judgement is based on the sound alone, but they should use comparisons and congratulating expressions.

Each group reads their decisions out to the class. Keep a chart on the board to decide who is the winner.

«Pronunciation»

This practises words that sound the same but are spelt differently.

1 **2 37** Play the recording. The words can all be spelt in two different ways. Ask students to write down one spelling and add a second spelling if they can think of it.

Check answers, writing both spellings on the board.

Answers and recording script
see/sea   sun/son   there/their   where/wear
wood/would   hour/our   hear/here   won/one

2 Ask students to decide which pair of words goes in which pair of sentences.

Answers
b Where wear   **c** here hear   **d** their there
e sea see   **f** would wood   **g** son sun   **h** Our hour

Connectives   PET Reading Part 5

Language presentation

Because* and *so
Look at the example in Exercise 1 and discuss the difference between *because* and *so*. (*Because* gives a reason and *so* gives the result of something.)
*We'd heard all the groups **so** we knew they were brilliant.*
*We knew all the groups were brilliant **because** we'd heard them.*

Because* and *as
Elicit the fact that *because* and *as* mean the same and can be in the middle or at the beginning of the sentence.

But and *although*

Write on the board *I'd really hoped to win **but** I still couldn't believe it.*

Ask if you can put any of the other words instead of *but* – you can't, but you can turn the sentence around to use *although*:

***Although** I'd really hoped to win, I still couldn't believe it.*

1 Students read the text first, then fill in the gaps.

Answers
b but **c** Although **d** so **e** because/as **f** as/because
g as soon as **h** either **i** or

2 Students do the exercise alone or, if they are having problems, do it with them.

Answers
Michelle: I try to go to the gym three times a week **because** I like to keep fit.
Anika: I go shopping **or** (I go) swimming.
Mark: I go racing on my motorbike, **although** I'm not very good at it.
Tanya: I'm busy writing songs for the band, **so** I don't have much spare time at the moment.

⊌ Grammar spot   Connectives

Students use their answers above to complete the rules.

Answers
a We use *because* or *as* when we give a reason for something.
   *I didn't go swimming **because/as** I had a cold.*
b We use *so* to give the result of something.
   *The bus didn't come **so** I walked to the city centre.*
c We use *either* and *or* in the same sentence to give two different choices.
   *We can **either** stay at home **or** go for a walk.*
d We use *although* or *but* to contrast or compare two ideas.
   *The film was funny **but** it was too long.*
   ***Although** the film was funny, it was too long.*

《Activity》 Music quiz

1 Students should write five questions and answers about music and give the questions to you.

2 Then put them all in a big bag, divide the class into teams, pull questions out at random and ask each team a question in turn. If a team answers correctly, they get two marks. If they can't answer, the next team is given a chance and they get one mark if they get it right.

Exam folder 20

Listening Part 1

Look at the information in the Summary box and answer the questions in the Check! box together.

Answers
a the pictures and the questions
b what the people will talk about / vocabulary
c listen carefully the second time
d guess
e twice

2 **38** Play the five recordings, which will be heard twice each, then go back and check the answers. In the exam there are seven questions.

1 C   **2** C   **3** B   **4** C   **5** A

Recording script

For each question, there are three pictures and a short recording.

Choose the correct picture and put a tick (✓) in the box below it.

1
Where will they meet?
Woman: Are you going to the city centre?
Man: Yes, do you want a lift?
Woman: Yes, please. Can you take me to the library? Then I need to go to the supermarket.
Man: OK. I'm going to the bank so I'll see you in the supermarket car park at four. Oh, and can you take back these library books for me?

2
What time will the boy catch the bus?
Girl: Hi, Alex, this is Mandy. You know we agreed to meet at a quarter past six? Well, we'll have to meet an

SO YOU THINK YOU'VE GOT TALENT?   115

hour later at a quarter past seven because I have to look after my sister while my mum is out.

Boy: Mm ... my bus only leaves once an hour so I can get the one <u>at a quarter to six or at a quarter to seven.</u>

Girl: Well, <u>get the later one.</u> That'll give me more time too.

Boy: OK. See you tonight then.

3

Which band does Robert play in?

Girl: Robert's just joined a band, you know.

Boy: Is he playing guitar in it?

Girl: <u>They've already got a guitarist, so he's the singer. There's a keyboard player too.</u> They used to have a drummer but he left.

Boy: We must go and see them play.

4

Which is Lisa's new T-shirt?

Girl 1: Have you seen Lisa's new T-shirt? It's amazing.

Girl 2: What's it like?

Girl 1: <u>It's sleeveless with a high neck and it's got red and green stripes.</u>

Girl 2: Ugh.

5

What will the weather be like tomorrow?

Man: And here is the weather forecast for today and tomorrow. The fine weather will continue today, so enjoy it while it lasts because <u>tomorrow we'll have cloudy skies</u> again. There won't be any rain but it won't be very warm, I'm afraid.

Look at the Exam Advice box.

2 38 ◀ Give out the photocopied recording scripts (see Preparation) and play the recordings again to check the answers. Discuss where the answers come and how much of the recording is relevant. (1 The answer is near the end and they shouldn't be distracted by *library* being mentioned again after the answer. 2 The confirmation of the answer comes after it is given, so the second listening is crucial. 3 Several pieces of information are needed to answer – *already got a guitarist, singer, keyboard player, no drummer.* 4 Three pieces of information are needed – *sleeveless, high neck and striped.* 5 The word *cloudy* gives the answer.)

Writing folder

Writing Part 3

1 Discuss the exam task with the class. Ask them to suggest how this beginning could fit the suggested kinds of story.

2 Allocate the different kinds of story around the class and give students two minutes to think of a story.

3 Ask them to write down the most important words they need for that story. Students should listen to the words other groups have listed and say what kind of story they think they are going to write.

   Warn students that they need to think carefully about what they will write and the language they will need. Discuss any problems that might arise from choosing some of these subjects, and strategies for avoiding them. For example, if they choose to write about a ghost, do they have all the vocabulary they need, or can they devise a storyline which uses only everyday words?

   Suggest that in the exam it is better to write a simple story in good English rather than an ambitious one for which they do not have enough language.

   Examiners will penalise answers which use a prepared story which does not fit the task.

4 Elicit ideas for making the story more interesting.

5 Use this exercise to show that students can make their story interesting by using a variety of vocabulary and structures, rather than by a complicated plot.

> **Answers**
> a adjectives added: *tall, long, white, large, brown*
> b adverbs added: *yesterday, rather, nervously, suddenly*
> c direct speech: *What's your name? You've won a prize!*
> d other changes: see italics below for all other changes
> *Yesterday,* I went into town to buy a CD. A *tall* man *with a long white beard was standing* outside the shop. He *seemed rather* worried *and he was looking nervously at* a piece of paper. *When he saw me,* he asked, '*What's your name?' Although I didn't know him,* I told him. *Suddenly* he smiled. '*You've won a prize!*' he announced, *and* gave me *a large brown envelope with my name on it.*

6 Read the Exam Advice box with the class. Give them two minutes to think about a story, make some notes and write down some useful vocabulary.

7 Tell students they have three minutes to tell their story. This will help them to find out if they can express their ideas, or whether they need to simplify them.

8 Give students fifteen minutes for this. See page 173 for photocopiable sample answers.

Keep in touch!

In this unit:

Grammar	Having something done; reported commands and requests; possessive pronouns and adjectives
Functions and vocabulary	Making phone calls
Pronunciation	Telephone numbers
PET skills	Listening for gist (Listening Part 1); listening for and writing phone numbers (Listening Part 3); sentence transformation (Writing Part 1)
Revision	Present simple (Unit 1); commands (Unit 7); making plans (Unit 16); past perfect (Unit 18)
Exam folder	Reading Part 3

SB pages 136–139

Introduction

1   Ask students to do the quiz, supplying explanations only when absolutely necessary.

2   Ask them about their results. If appropriate, discuss with them whether the conclusions of the quiz are accurate, and why or why not.

3   Ask the class to supply the answers and check that they understand all the language in the quiz.

   Note: The words *phone* and *mobile* are largely interchangable unless the context makes it necessary to specify mobile rather than landline phone.

Answers
a top up your mobile   b switch on   c a missed call
d hang up   e call someone back

4   Briefly discuss the question. In the UK, as in many other countries, it is illegal to use a hand-held phone while driving. Other places where people might think a mobile should not be used are: theatres, concert halls, etc., places of worship, classrooms, etc., libraries, restaurants, some offices and family mealtimes.

Listening

1   **3 02** As two of the conversations are between friends and two are between strangers, the concept of spoken register (informal and formal language) can be introduced here if appropriate.

   Play the recording, stopping it after each conversation to discuss whether the people are friends or strangers.

Answers
Strangers: **a, d**   Friends: **b, c**

PET Listening Part 1

2   This exercise practises listening for gist.

   3 02 Play the recording again without stopping and ask students to note down the order in which the conversations take place.

Answers
The order of the conversations is **b, a, d, c**.

Recording script

a
Secretary: Lee and Company.
Ivan: Oh, er, hello. May I speak to Mrs Lee?
Secretary: I'm afraid Mrs Lee isn't available this afternoon. Can you call back tomorrow?
Ivan: Er, yes. Thank you.
Secretary: Goodbye.
Ivan: Goodbye.

b
Helen: Hello?
Ivan: Hi. This is Ivan.
Helen: Hi, Ivan.
Ivan: Helen. I'm ringing to ask for your help.
Helen: Oh, yeah?
Ivan: You told me to ring you. The teacher's asked me to write about a journalist.
Helen: Oh, yes.
Ivan: Well, you said a friend of yours is a freelance journalist. She can give me some advice.
Helen: She's a friend of my dad's, really. But she's very nice.

Ivan: <u>Can you give me her phone number?</u>

Helen: Oh, right, er, I've got it here somewhere. <u>Hang on a minute.</u> Mm. Yes. It's <u>307669</u>. Ask for Mrs Lee. And say you're a friend of Helen Solomon's.

Ivan: OK. Thanks very much.

Helen: That's OK. Let me know how you get on.

c

Helen: Hi. Sorry I can't speak to you just now. Leave your name and number and I'll call you back when I'm free. Wait for the beep!

Ivan: Oh. Helen. This is Ivan. I'm seeing Mrs Lee on Monday afternoon. Thanks for giving me her number. Would you like to meet me afterwards? About four o'clock? I'd like to buy you a coffee or something to say thank you. Ring me if that's OK and say where.

d

Secretary: Amy Lee's office.

Ivan: May I speak to Mrs Lee, please?

Secretary: <u>Could I have your name?</u>

Ivan: Oh, yes. It's Ivan Finn. I'm a friend of Helen Solomon's.

Secretary: <u>One moment, please.</u>

Mrs Lee: Hello, Mr Finn? <u>How can I help you?</u>

Ivan: Er, I'm doing a project about journalism for my media studies course. Helen told me to contact you. Would it be possible for me to interview you one day this week?

Mrs Lee: I see. Well, this week's not good; I'm working to a deadline and I'm having my office painted. But what about Monday at, um, quarter past two?

Ivan: Oh, thanks very much. It's very kind of you to help me.

Mrs Lee: Not at all. I look forward to meeting you.

3 **3 03** Play the next track. Students will now hear the first three conversations in the correct order. Stop the recording if necessary to give them time to write. Recording scripts as for previous exercise, in the order **b**, **a**, **d**.

Go through the exercise, writing the answers up for students to check their work. The answers are underlined in the recording script.

Answers
Conversation 1
b I'm ringing to ask for your help.
c Can you give me her phone number?
d Hang on a minute.

Conversation 2
a May I speak to Mrs Lee?
b I'm afraid Mrs Lee isn't available this afternoon.
c Can you call back tomorrow?

Conversation 3
a Could I have your name?
b One moment, please.
c How can I help you?

«Pronunciation» PET Listening Part 3

This practises saying telephone numbers.

1 **3 04** Ask students to listen to the last part of Conversation 1 once more and to write down the number, first in figures and then in the words Helen uses. Telephone numbers are often tested in PET.

Answer
307669   three oh seven double six nine

2 Ask some students to say the numbers and have the rest of the class listen and correct them if necessary. Ask the students to write the numbers in words.

3 **3 05** Play the recording for them to check their answers.

Answers and recording script
a *three five double seven nine eight*
b oh one double two three, two double seven, two oh three
c oh two oh, seven five eight four, double three oh four
d double four, one two seven three, five oh nine, six seven two

Language focus
Making phone calls

1 Do the first conversation with the class and then ask them to write the answers to the second conversation individually.

Answers
Conversation 1
b I'm ringing   **c** to ring you   **d** give me the number
e Hang on   **f** Ask for   **g** a friend   **h** Let me know

Conversation 2
i May I speak   **j** a friend of   **k** One moment
l How can I   **m** told me   **n** Would you like to
o How about   **p** very kind of   **q** meeting you

2 Direct students to the business card. Read the instructions for the exercise with them. If they have not just completed Exercise 1, suggest they can look back at it for helpful language. Ask students to get into groups of four and work through the conversations. The four roles are:

Student A: wants to buy a motorbike

Student B: knows someone who sells motorbikes

Student C: Steve's assistant

Student D: Steve, someone who sells motorbikes

Reported speech is common in real life, but PET candidates are rarely asked to transform from direct to reported speech. However, reported to direct speech transformations, which are more straightforward, are quite common in PET Writing Part 1 (see also Unit 22).

Have something done

Remind students of Mrs Lee's sentence from the Listening. Ask *Is Mrs Lee painting the office?* to elicit that this structure is about someone else doing something.

Look at the table with the students. Drill briefly if necessary.

1   Read the instructions with the class and do the exercise orally, then ask them to write the answers.

> **Answers**
> **b** has his car washed   **c** has his hair styled   **d** has his contract checked   **e** is having his autobiography written

The class may like to discuss briefly who does each thing for him.

2   Read the instructions with the class and point out that it is about last year, then ask students to write answers and check them together.

> **Answers**
> **b** had an indoor swimming pool built.
> **c** had the garden redesigned.
> **d** had all the carpets changed.
>
> **Possible answers**
> **e** She had new furniture made for the living room.
> **f** She had gold taps put on all the basins.

If appropriate, you could discuss with students what they (or their families) have done for them.

Reported commands and requests

PET Writing Part 1

> **Language presentation**   **Commands**
>
> Direct students to the first example sentence from the Listening: *Helen told me to contact you.*
>
> Ask what Helen actually said. (*Contact Mrs Lee.*) Look at the top half of the table (**Commands**) together.

1   Read the instructions to the exercise with the class. Look at the example and do one or two more together as appropriate.

Check answers together for grammatical accuracy. The suggested answers are probably the most appropriate, but they are largely interchangeable!

> **Suggested answers**
> **b** Tell the coach to leave the club and not to come back.
> **c** Tell the rest of the team not to go clubbing every night.
> **d** Tell the goalkeeper to have his eyes tested.
> **e** Tell the ref to learn the rules of the game.

> **Language presentation**   **Requests**
>
> Direct students to the second example sentence from the Listening: *The teacher's asked me to write about a journalist.* Ask what the teacher actually said. (*Please write about a journalist.*)
>
> Look at the bottom half of the table together. Discuss the difference between a command and a request. Understanding the importance of *please* in everyday English is really important.

> ## ⬎ Corpus spot   **Reported speech**
>
> Ask students which sentences in the exercise are commands and which are requests before they write their answers. Check them together.
>
> > **Answers**
> > **a** Please read some of your poems.
> > **b** Go to the hospital immediately.
> > **c** Please help me.
> > **d** Don't lose the stone.
> > **e** Call me at nine o'clock.

2   Do questions **a** and **b** with the class, then let them try questions **c–e** individually before checking them together.

> **Answers**
> **b** Michael not to forget his wallet.
> **c** asked her/Angela to phone her dad from the airport.
> **d** asked Mandy not to use her shampoo.
> **e** told Ronnie to phone the doctor immediately.

Possessive pronouns and adjectives

Discuss the examples with the class. Point out that we use the apostrophe with *of* + a noun. If necessary, refer students to the table in the Grammar folder, Student's Book page 212.

Do questions **c** and **d** with the whole class, then let them complete the exercise individually before going through it.

> **Answers**
> **c** A classmate of yours said you were ill.
> **d** She saw a friend of hers on television last week.
> **e** Kamran's lucky because a cousin of his owns a hotel in London.
> **f** A colleague of Pedro's lives in our road.
> **g** I didn't realise that a friend of theirs played football for England.
> **h** I heard that a student of mine met the Prime Minister last week.
> **i** I believe a neighbour of ours has won the lottery.

≪Activity≫ Tell me about your life

1 Divide the class into two groups. Let them prepare separately.

Group A are the journalists who will interview Alexi. Direct them to discuss the questions they can ask him.

Group B are Alexi. Tell them to think about the questions in their book.

2 After a few minutes put A and B students in pairs for the first interview. Tell the journalists they can take notes if they want to, but don't let them spend too much time writing at this point.

3, 4 When they have finished their interviews, repeat the exercise, swapping the roles, with Group A as Lucilla and Group B as the journalists, so that all students both ask and answer questions.

5 Ask students to write up their interviews (this could be homework, if time is short). If you have the facilities, you could ask them to provide photographs and make a display of 'articles' for the classroom.

≪Activity≫ Mobile messages

3 **06** Play the recording and stop it as necessary for students to write down the wording of the message. Let them write messages for their own phones individually, then read out their wording to the class (or to each other in small groups) and suggest any improvements or corrections.

> ### Recording script
>
> **Helen:** Hi. Sorry I can't speak to you just now. Leave your name and number and I'll call you back when I'm free. Wait for the beep!

Exam folder 21

Reading Part 3

1 Look at the Summary box about this part of the exam. Give students a minute to think about the expressions in the two columns and then go through the answers. These words all come up in the task.

Answers
a most **b** less **c** maximum **d** allowed **e** outside

2 Look at the sentences together to get a general idea of what the text is about.

3 Look at the Exam Advice box together. Ask students to read the text silently, underlining where they find the answers. Give them a time limit of two minutes.

Answers
THE SOUTH LAKES MALL
The South Lakes Mall offers 200 shops, a swimming pool, restaurants, a bowling alley and two nightclubs as well as 30 acres of parkland with three lakes.

Opening hours
(1) <u>Shops</u>   <u>Mon–Fri</u> 10 am–<u>9 pm</u>
           <u>Sat</u>   9 am–<u>8 pm</u>
           <u>Sun</u>   10 am–<u>5 pm</u>
    Park   9 am–5 pm in winter
           <u>9 am–8 pm in summer</u>

We have thousands of visitors every day, (2) <u>our busiest day of the week being Friday</u>. To avoid the crowds, come on a Monday or Tuesday.

Inside the mall
When you arrive, go to (3) <u>one of our information offices to get a map. There is one by the main bus stop and another at the bottom of the escalator which goes up to the cinema.</u>
The shops are all on the ground floor and you will find everything from specialised furniture stores to clothes shops and department stores as well as restaurants, a bowling alley and a swimming pool. (4) <u>On the first floor above the pool you will find a 12-screen cinema and two nightclubs.</u> If you wish, you can buy entrance tickets for any of these facilities except the nightclubs from the information centres. (5) <u>Before 5 pm, entrance tickets to all facilities are reduced for students</u> and the over-sixties. If you wish to stay overnight, (6) <u>the information centres can give you a list of accommodation in the area, ranging from grand hotels</u> to Bed and Breakfast accommodation.

Outside the mall
Make time to visit the 30 acres of parkland which surround the mall. (7) <u>Boats for up to six people</u> can be hired and taken out onto one of the lakes for £12 an hour. Bicycles can be hired every day for £6 an hour. There are 4 km of paths but (8) <u>you are not allowed to take hired bicycles beyond the park.</u>

Travel
The mall is located one mile from the M49. Just follow the signs from Junction 13. There is free parking for 10,000 cars and there are six car parks. Car parking spaces are never more than five minutes' walk away from an entrance. (9) <u>Remember where your car is parked by looking at the coloured signs – no car park uses the same colour and each level in the car parks is numbered.</u> It is just as easy to visit the mall by train. There is a rail service every 15 minutes from Central London. (10) <u>When you reach Barnwell station, jump on a number 19 bus to the mall. It's a five-minute journey</u> and there's a bus every 15 minutes.

4 Give the students five minutes to read carefully the parts of the text they have underlined and answer the questions. Make sure they understand the use of A for correct and B for incorrect.

Answers
1 B 2 A 3 B 4 B 5 A 6 B 7 A 8 A 9 B 10 B

 Corpus spot

A different kind of false friend!

Let students do the exercise, then check the answers.

Answers
a campsites
b shops / shopping centres / (shopping) malls
c police station
d car park

EXTRA

If time allows, discuss the words with your students. If appropriate, you may like to point out that **a**, **b** and **c** are examples of words which exist in English but with different meanings, i.e. they are uncountable abstract nouns rather than places.

You and the class could make up sentences using them correctly, e.g. *I sometimes go camping in the summer holidays. Shopping is boring. Parking is free in this car park.*

You and your students may come up with examples of other English words that are 'misused' in their language(s).

22 Strange but true?

In this unit:

Grammar	Reported speech
Functions and vocabulary	Reporting what people said; saying what you (don't) believe; reporting verbs; science fiction
Pronunciation	Silent consonants
PET skills	Describing objects and events and expressing your opinion about them (Speaking Part 3); guessing unknown words from context; reading for gist (Reading Part 4); sentence transformation (Writing Part 1)
Revision	*it could/might/must/can't be* (Unit 13); present and past tenses; giving opinions; agreeing and disagreeing
Exam folder	Listening Part 4
Writing folder	Writing Part 1

Preparation

Language focus You may find it useful to make OHTs of the tables for Exercise 1 and the Grammar spot, so that you fill them in with the class. Alternatively, project them from the CD-ROM or webpage onto the whiteboard.

Activity *Who am I?* Think of some appropriate famous living people your students will have heard of and prepare 'clues' like the examples in the instructions for this exercise on page 125. Use present simple, present perfect and past simple tenses. Order the sentences so that they provide increasingly obvious clues to the identity of the subject.

Note: Students may meet reported speech where the verb is past but the reported verb is not changed, e.g. *He said he lives in Spain.* This is not introduced in this course as it is not required for PET. Changing the reported verb will not be wrong, but not changing it may be. Students at this level may become confused if they realise there is sometimes a choice.

SB pages 142–145

Introduction

PET Speaking Part 3

1 Check the meaning of the unit title (*strange* is a false friend for speakers of some languages).

Direct students to the photographs and invite them to describe them and speculate about them, using the language suggested and any other expressions the students come up with. The photographs show the following: **a** a glowing UFO in the sky in South Carolina, USA; **b** a flying button over Venezuela (a trick photograph); **c** lenticular clouds over Santos, Brazil; **d** the Northern Lights. Supply any essential vocabulary, but encourage the use of discourse strategies for talking about things we do not know the word for (see also Unit 1).

Make sure that students are given the opportunity to express scepticism and offer commonsense explanations. Teach the word *trick* (and perhaps also *fake*) and revise with them the modal verbs from Unit 13 as necessary.

2 This exercise could be done in groups (especially in large classes) to allow time for more students to talk. Groups can choose one story/description each to tell the whole class. If students are very sceptical and unable to think of any examples, ask them to think of unexplained events in films or TV series they have seen.

Go on to ask them to suggest reasons why science fiction stories are so popular, citing television series or films. If they need prompting, ask questions such as *Are they exciting? Do people like to imagine strange worlds? Are they frightening?*

Reading

1 Briefly discuss with the class what the photographs show.

PET Reading Part 4

2 In this exercise students practise reading for gist and guessing unknown words from context.

Ask students to read the magazine reports and say which match the photographs.

Answers
The top photograph matches the report on the left; the bottom photograph matches the report on the bottom right.

Language focus
Reported speech

1 See Preparation. Go through the exercise with the class, identifying who said each sentence, and write the answer in the column under *Who?*

2   Ask students to find the original sentences in the text and copy the missing words into the reported speech column.

Go through the exercise, writing up the correct answers.

3   Elicit from the students the changes made in each pair of sentences. Ask students to underline anything in the reported speech column which is different from the direct speech column.

Ask students to look over the sentences again and ask them the following questions:
a What kinds of words have changed? (Verbs, pronouns and adverbs.)
b What words have been added? (The speaker(s) and a verb, e.g. *said*.)
c Why? (This is reported speech.)
d Why have some verbs been changed? (Because they are introduced by a past tense, e.g. *he said*.)
e How have they changed? (Present simple becomes past simple; past simple becomes past perfect.)

f Why have some other words changed? (Pronouns and adverbs change because we are in a different place and the reporter is not the same person as the speaker, e.g. *here* becomes *there* and *we* becomes *they*.)

If appropriate, remind students that they studied the formation of the past perfect in Unit 18.

⮯ Grammar spot   Reported speech

What people say →	Reporting what people said
(a) Present simple → I see aliens quite often.	**Past simple** She said she saw aliens quite often.
Present continuous → I'm feeling ill.	**(b) Past continuous** She said she was feeling ill.
(c) *will* + verb → We'll meet you later.	*would* + verb They said they'd (would) meet us later.
(d) Present perfect → I've seen lots of aliens here.	**Past perfect** She said she'd (had) seen lots of aliens there.
Past simple → I saw some aliens last week.	**(e) Past perfect** She said she'd (had) seen some aliens last week.

4   Put two columns up on the board, as in the example, or project them. Ask students to read the magazine report and tell you the sentences which report what the people said, and write them in the right-hand column.

Then let students complete the left-hand column alone.

Students then underline the words that change when the speech is reported.

'Aliens took me to their spacecraft and I woke up a week later in the middle of a field.'	Franck said aliens had taken him to their spacecraft and he had woken up a week later in the middle of a field.
'The aliens will return in August 1980 and I am meeting them in the field.'	He said the aliens would return in August 1980 and he was meeting them in the field.
'We/I believe him/you.'	Two hundred people said they believed him.

5   Ask students to discuss the reports in groups and try to come up with explanations for them.

When they have done this, direct them to the box at the bottom of page 147 for possible explanations. Ask whether they accept these explanations.

PET Writing Part 1

6, 7   These exercises give practice in PET transformations, which often include reported speech. Ask students to work in pairs, taking turns to say the answers.

6

Answers
b   I work in London.
c   We live in New York.
d   We don't have any money. / We haven't got any money.
e   I visited Paris last year.

7   Direct students to the example and remind them that verbs in the present perfect become past perfect in reported speech, like verbs in the past simple.

Answers
b   We've lost the keys and don't know what to do.
c   I haven't seen a UFO yet but I hope to see one soon.
d   I've already met some aliens and they speak good English.
e   I've never eaten Martian food before.

8   This exercise practises transforming direct to reported speech.

Answers
b   She said she didn't enjoy cartoons.
c   They said they were both fans of Manchester United.
d   She said she hadn't seen her brother for three weeks.
e   He said his mum was making him a great birthday cake.
f   She said her friend hadn't invited her to her party.

«Pronunciation»

This exercise practises silent consonants.

1   Write the words *comb*, *when* and *honest* on the board and elicit/supply the meanings. Check that students remember what consonants are. Ask which are silent in these words and put a line through them (*comb when honest*). Ask students to say the words.

2   Students work in pairs to see which pair can find and mark the words containing silent consonants the fastest.

Answers
b   The knives might be in the high cupboard. 4
c   I've broken my wrist, my thumb, my knee and my foot. 3
d   That foreigner could be a scientist. 3
e   You need a bright light to write the receipt. 4
f   Let's meet in half an hour. 2

3   Let the students make a table like the example in their books while you draw the outline on the board.

When they have finished, go through the answers, letting students come up to write the words on the board, and cross out the silent letters.

Elicit/Supply the rules that, at the beginning of a word, *w* is always silent before *r*, *k* is always silent before *n*; in the middle of a word *gh* is always silent after *i*; and at the end of a word, *b* is always silent after *m*. *Honest* and *hour* are the only PET-level words beginning with a silent *h*.

Answers

Beginning	Middle	End
know knives	what answer	high thumb
wrist knee	might cupboard	
write hour	foreigner could	
	scientist bright	
	light receipt	
	half	

4   **3 07** Play the recording for them to listen and repeat the sentences in Exercise 2.

«Activity» Who am I?

Use the sentences given in the boxes on the next page, or make up some others about famous living people your students will know (see Preparation).

Divide the class into groups. Tell the students you are a famous person and they have to guess who you are.

You go into one corner. All the groups send one person to ask you for a clue. You say a sentence.

The students go back to their groups and report what you said. Each group sends a different student for another clue.

If they think they know who you are, they can write the name on a piece of paper and show it to you. If they are wrong, they must miss a turn of hearing the clues.

If you think they will not use reported speech forms without supervision, ask them to write the reported version and send it back to you for checking before you say the next clue.

Note: you may need to check these facts as time goes by. This activity is adapted from an idea in *Activity Box* by Jean Greenwood, Cambridge University Press.

> I live in the USA.
> I'm a woman.
> I have a daughter and two sons.
> My ex-husband is a film director.
> I had a house in London but I sold it.
> I've sold millions of records.
> I've appeared in several films.
> (Answer: Madonna)

> I'm a man.
> I have lived in Britain, Spain, the United States and Italy.
> My wife was a singer in a very successful girl band.
> We have three sons.
> I often change my hairstyle.
> I've played in lots of international football matches.
> (Answer: David Beckham)

Corpus spot   *Said or told?*

Ask students to correct the mistakes. Elicit/Supply the forms:
*We say something **to** somebody.* but *We tell somebody something.*
We say (that) something is true. but *We tell **somebody** (that) something is true.*
You may wish to remind them also: *We tell somebody to do something.* (= give a command, see Unit 21)

Answers
a told **b** said **c** told **d** said **e** told

≪Activity≫ UFO Survey

1 *Conducting a survey*

Check that students understand the statements.

Remind them that they should say the statements, not merely show them to people. They should work in pairs, taking turns to speak or to note the responses. Discuss with them how they do this. Spend some time eliciting and practising language they need to approach people when doing a survey, e.g. *Excuse me, we're doing a survey. Do you have a few minutes to answer some questions?* and a suitable way of ending the interview, such as *Thank you for your help.*

2 *Presenting results*

Ask the pairs to write up their reports as indicated. Some students may enjoy producing graphics to illustrate their findings, such as pie charts or bar charts.

Exam folder 22

SB pages 146–147

Listening Part 4

Read the information in the Summary box with the class.

1 This exercise can be extended by asking students if they know of any other words which mean the same as the ones in the box, e.g. *worried = anxious, surprised = astonished, sure = certain, happy = cheerful, annoyed = cross, thankful = grateful, uncertain = unsure.* There is no word which means the same as *embarrassed*.

Draw students' attention to the negative prefix *un-*. Check which of these adjectives can take it (*unsure, uncertain, unhappy, ungrateful, unembarrassed*).

Answers
b anxious **c** astonished **d** unsure **e** cheerful
f embarrassed **g** grateful **h** cross

2 Ask students to work in pairs. Check their answers.

Extend the exercise by drawing students' attention to the prepositions following *approve, disagree* and *intend*.

Ask them what preposition to use after *apologise* (*to* someone *for doing* something) and ask them for examples (e.g. *I apologise for being late*).

Answers
b 2 **c** 6 **d** 1 **e** 7 **f** 4 **g** 8 **h** 3

3 Discuss the questions with the class.

4 **3 08** Look at the Exam Advice box with the class.

Play the recording twice without stopping to let students experience exam conditions, then check the answers.

Recording script

Look at the six sentences for this part.
You will hear a conversation between a girl, Dina, and a boy, Jason, about Dina's sister, Jessica.
Decide if each sentence is correct or incorrect.
If it is correct, put a tick (✓) in the box under A for YES. If it is not correct, put a tick (✓) in the box under B for NO.

Dina: Hi, Jason. How are you?
Jason: Hey, Dina. It's good to see you. I've got a job just near here. But what are you doing in this part of town? I thought you worked in the city centre.
Dina: Yes, I do. And it's really hard work.
Jason: Yeah?
Dina: Yeah. It's a hotel and we're in the middle of the holiday season, so I'm always busy. But I work on Sundays so it's my day off today. I'm going to see Jessica. You know she has a flat just up the road from here?
Jason: Your sister? What's she doing these days? Is she still sitting at home waiting for the perfect job?
Dina: Well – that's not quite fair.

Jason: Why's that, then?
Dina: She studied really hard at school.
Jason: We all did, in my opinion.
Dina: She's been very unlucky. She has to ask my parents for money, but she hates doing it.
Jason: Perhaps.
Dina: Yeah, it's true. Anyway, she told me something strange on the phone.
Jason: What?
Dina: Well, she said she'd seen a ghost in the road near her flat.
Jason: And you think she did?
Dina: She saw it three times. It was a woman in a long skirt. She walked along the road about seven o'clock and then disappeared near the park gates. I hope I'm going to see her too. I think it's exciting.
Jason: Well, I think you're both mad. Seven o'clock? That's exactly when it begins to get dark at this time of year.
Dina: So?
Jason: You can't see clearly. It's probably someone going home from work in a long coat.
Dina: No, she said she was quite sure it wasn't a real person. What about coming to Jessica's place with me? Then we can all watch.
Jason: Thanks for asking me, but actually, I prefer watching TV to waiting for ghosts.
Dina: OK.
Jason: Let's meet next week. We can go to a film or something. We can have a laugh about your ghost.
Dina: OK, let's meet. But you'll be embarrassed when I tell you I've seen the ghost.
Jason: I doubt it. See you next week. Say hello to Jessica from me.
Dina: Yeah. See you.
Jason: Bye.

Writing folder

Writing Part 1

In the exam, there are only five sentences plus an example. These sentences give students practice in a range of structures.

Go through the instructions and the Exam Advice box and ask students to do the questions.

Draw their attention to the sample exam answer sheet.

TOPIC: Friendship

In this unit:	
Grammar	Defining relative clauses (*which/who/that/whose/where* clauses); adjectives + prepositions
Functions and vocabulary	Friendship; introducing people
Pronunciation	Linking words ending in a consonant
PET skills	Listening for opinions and specific information (Listening Part 4); describing people and objects (Speaking Part 3)
Revision	Personality adjectives (Units 2 and 6)
Exam folder	Reading Part 1; Speaking Part 2

Preparation

Listening, Exercise 2 You may want to hand out copies of the recording script (from CD-ROM or webpage) if students find the listening difficult.
Activity *Relative clauses* Photocopy the lists of nouns (on page 185) and cut them up.

SB pages 148–151

Introduction

1 Check the meaning of *best friend* and look at the list of qualities a best friend should have. Check students understand the meaning of *should* here (*I think it's important that ...*).

   Ask students to work individually to rate the list items 1–10. (You could ask them to consider only friends of the same sex and then compare the answers of boys and girls.)

2 Put students into small groups and get them to compare their lists. Ask each group what most people put as 1 and 10. If students are interested, let some of them explain to the class why they made their choices.

3 Give each group a few minutes to add other things to the list and report back to the class.

4 Look at the photographs together and talk about what kinds of personality the people might have and what they might be interested in. Revise *to get on with someone, sensitive, serious, lively, hard-working, confident, cheerful, friendly,* etc. (from Units 2 and 6).

Give students a minute to decide which person in the photographs they would most like to be friends with and ask some students who they chose and why. In a large class, you may prefer students to tell each other in groups so everyone has a chance to express their opinions.

Look at the Vocabulary spot together.

 Corpus spot *Meet* and *make*

Answers
a In the first lesson I <u>met</u> a girl from Valencia and now she's my best friend.
b I <u>made</u> many new friends but I missed my old ones.
c The film begins at seven, so <u>meet</u> me at ten to seven outside the cinema.

Listening

1 **3 09** Look at the table and check students understand what they will listen for. Make sure they remember the difference between *will* and *might*.

   Play the recording.

Suggested answers
There are no right or wrong answers but discuss what seems most likely and why.
Pair 1 might become friends; Pair 2 will probably become friends; Pair 3 probably won't get on with each other.

Recording script

Conversation 1
Samantha: Alex, I'd like you to meet Monica. Alex, meet Monica. Monica loves rock climbing like you. I'm sure you're going to get on really well.
Monica: Hi, Alex. You don't go to this college, do you?
Alex: No, I don't – Samantha's my cousin. She often invites me to parties here. But actually I'm not very keen on the music. In fact, they usually play the kind of music that I hate.
Monica: Oh, I love this music. I'll never get tired of listening to it. Anyway, even if you don't like the music you can talk to people.
Alex: I've never met anyone here who I'm really interested in talking to.
Monica: What about that girl I saw you with just now?

Alex: She's not my type.

Monica: But this room is full of interesting people. Come on, I'll introduce you to some people that you'll like.

Alex: I'd rather not.

Monica: OK. Have a good evening then. I'm going to enjoy myself.

Alex: Wait a minute. I'm sorry I was rude about everyone here. You see – the truth is, I'm just a bit nervous of people I don't know.

Monica: I see. Why didn't you say that? Well, let's go over there where it's less crowded. We can have a chat about climbing. Where do you usually go?

Conversation 2

Neil: Hi, I'm Neil. This is my first day here.

Francis: Hi, I'm Francis. I've been here for a week. It's not a bad place to work, this restaurant.

Neil: Yeah?

Francis: It's very different from the job I had last summer on a building site. That was really heavy work. At least here we only have to carry a few plates.

Neil: Is everybody friendly here?

Francis: Well, the older waiters aren't really interested in the same kind of things as students doing a holiday job like us.

Neil: Oh.

Francis: But they'll chat to you when they have time. That waiter over there used to play football for Arsenal when he was young.

Neil: Did he?

Francis: Well, he played for them a few times. He's got a friend who sometimes gets free tickets. I'm an Arsenal supporter.

Neil: Really? Me too. There's a match on Wednesday evening which will be really good. I'm quite excited about it because I haven't been to a match this season yet.

Francis: They're playing Chelsea, aren't they?

Neil: That's right.

Francis: I'm not sure if I can go. What time does it start? Oh, there are some customers over there who are waiting for a table. Come on, we'd better start work.

Conversation 3

Peter: Ah, there you are, Kate. Carla wants to meet you. Carla, this is Kate. Kate, this is Carla.

Carla: Hi, Kate.

Kate: Hi, Carla.

Carla: Peter says you're looking for someone to share your flat with.

Kate: That's right. I am actually.

Carla: Well, I'm going to come to university here and it's too far for me to travel to my parents' house every day. Anyway I'm fed up with living there. So could I share your flat?

Kate: Why not?

Carla: Oh, that's great. Does anyone else live there or will it be just the two of us?

Kate: There's one other person who is studying biology.

Carla: Great. It'll be really good to live with people my own age. I want to find a place where I can have parties and my friends can come and stay. My parents don't like me making any noise, but you won't mind, will you?

Kate: What kind of noise? Music is fine. I always have a CD on when I'm in the flat.

Carla: Good, because I play in a band. I play the guitar and I also play the violin, but not in the band.

Kate: Oh, well I do need to study.

Carla: Oh, don't worry. I play an electric guitar which has a volume control and I'm quite good at it.

Kate: That's good news!

Carla: I saw a flat which is very near the university. But it was so tidy I decided I couldn't live there. My parents are always getting angry with me because I'm untidy but I don't expect you're tidy either, are you?

Kate: Well, I do prefer to keep the flat tidy ...

Carla: Oh, we're going to be such good friends. Thank you for inviting me to live with you.

PET Listening Part 4

2 Ask students to read the four questions for Conversation 1 and remind them that Monica is a girl and Alex is a boy.

Point out that in Listening Part 4 candidates are told which speaker is which in the instructions and it is very important that they take this information in so they can answer the questions. In Listening Part 4, they will always hear the answer – a statement is only incorrect according to what the speakers say, not what they haven't said or what the listener might think they mean.

3 09 ◀ Play Conversation 1 again and give students a minute or so to think about their answers before doing the same with Conversations 2 and 3.

Answers
b false   c true   d false   e true   f false   g true
h false   i true   j true   k true   l false

If students have struggled with the questions, you may like to photocopy the scripts (see Preparation) and play the conversations again while they read them.

3 Ask students what Peter says when he introduces Kate and Carla. **3 09** ◀ Play the beginning of the third conversation again if necessary.

Ask students round the class to introduce two students to each other, practising both registers.

Language focus

Relative clauses

Students learn about defining relative clauses in this unit. They will also come across non-defining relative clauses. They are not expected to be able to understand the subtle differences between the two types for PET.

1   Look at the two example sentences together and ask when we use *who* (for people) and when we use *which* (for things).

   Either let students write the other sentences on their own and then talk about the answers or go through them together.

Language presentation

Write question **f** and its answer on the board:
I saw a flat. It's very near the university.
I saw a flat which is very near the university.
Then write: *I saw a flat. I liked it.*
Ask students how they will join these two sentences:
I saw a flat which I liked.
Ask them why you don't need to repeat *it* (because *it* refers to *the flat*).
Elicit or point out the difference between *I saw a flat which is very near the university* and *I saw a flat which I liked.*
In the first sentence, the verb *is* belongs to *a flat* (the word *which* is the subject of the relative clause) but in the second sentence the verb *liked* belongs to *I* (the word *which* is the object of the relative clause).

2   Ask students to do the exercise and check the answers together.

Check that students have understood the difference between the sentences in Exercise 1 and the sentences in Exercise 2. (In Exercise 1, the relative pronouns are the subject of the clauses (no new subject) and in Exercise 2, the relative pronouns are the object of the clauses.)

3   In informal speech, *that* is used more often than *who* or *which*.

4   Look at the examples and discuss when *whose* (= *of who/which*) and *where* (= place) are used.

   Ask students to do the exercise.

↴ Grammar spot   Relative clauses

Answer
Subject relative clauses
a which
b who

Object relative clauses
c which
d who

Relative clauses with *where* and *whose*
e where
f whose

5   The poem leads to an exercise which practises relative pronouns in context. Read the poem together and discuss any new vocabulary. Talk about what a *sea* means here (*a lot*).

   Discuss what the poem is about and, if appropriate, students can say whether it is relevant to their own experiences.

6, 7   Ask students to complete the exercises alone or in pairs and check the answers, making sure they understand when they can put *that* and when they can omit the relative pronoun.

8 Students make up some sentences of their own. They could read their sentences to each other in groups, correcting each other where they can. If appropriate, ask students to read some aloud to the whole class for you to check.

⟪Activity⟫ Relative clauses   PET Speaking Part 3

You need to have photocopies of the sheet of nouns (see Preparation).

Tell students they are going to describe people, places and things to each other without using the word themselves. Each group will have a list of words all starting with the same letter. Look at the example together.

Divide students into groups. Each group writes a definition for each of the nouns on a piece of paper, using the structures in the examples. Then the pieces of paper are exchanged between groups. Each group must identify the original nouns from the definitions they have been given and decide which letter was common to all the nouns in the list. They can then check back with the group that wrote them.

Adjectives + prepositions

1 Some adjectives and prepositions were introduced in Unit 19 (*good at, bad at, fed up with, interested in* and *afraid of*). This exercise practises these and others.

Students can complete the exercise alone or in pairs. You could ask students to learn these expressions for a test in another lesson.

Point out that lots of adjectives are followed by *about* + *-ing*, e.g. *pleased, happy*, etc.

Some adjectives can also be followed by a preposition and the infinitive. These are not practised here (to avoid confusion) but students will already know some of

them anyway, for example they have met *I'm pleased to meet you* in this unit.

2 Do some sentences from the table orally around the class. Ask students to write some sentences (this could be homework, if time is short).

3 Ask students to prepare their questions individually, using the words in the table, and then put them in pairs to ask their questions to a partner.

⟪Activity⟫ Friendship

Use this exercise to summarise the unit topic.

1 Students work in groups and decide which quotations they agree with.

2 Ask students to write their own quotations and read them out.

⟪Pronunciation⟫

This practises linking words ending in a consonant.

1 We join a word to the word which follows if the second word begins with a vowel. Practise saying some of the expressions together.

Ask students if they remember that there are two ways of pronouncing *of* and *at* (see Unit 5 for the weak form of *of* and Unit 16 for the weak form of *at*).

Practise saying the weak forms *of* /əv/ and *at* /ət/ in a couple of the expressions and also practise *about* /əbaʊt/.

2 **3 10** Play the recording and ask students to repeat.

Recording script

kind of you
full of people
nervous of people
tired of school
good at football
bad at history
fed up with school
keen on music
interested in people

---

3 Look at the expressions in their complete sentences and ask students to join all the words which begin with a vowel to the end of the word before.

4 **3 11** Play the sentences and ask students to repeat them. If you feel it is necessary, ask students to work in pairs, reading alternate sentences to each other and correcting each other when they forget to make the elisions.

Recording script

a It's kind of Samantha.
b This room is full of interesting people.
c I'm quite good at it.
d She's bad at playing the guitar.
e I'm not very keen on this kind of music.
f I'll never get tired of this song.
g I'm not interested in talking.

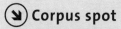 Corpus spot

Adjectives + prepositions

Answers

a I began to run because I was afraid <u>of missing</u> the bus.
b I was very worried <u>about</u> the weather before I came to England.
c He was disappointed <u>with</u> his car.
d I am very happy <u>with/about</u> your idea.
e He is very bad <u>at</u> explaining things.
f I am very pleased <u>with</u> the present you sent.

Exam folder 23

SB pages 152–153

Reading Part 1

Look at the Summary box together, then answer the questions in the Check! box.

> **Answers**
> a signs, notices, labels, phone messages, emails, postcards, Post-it notes, text messages
> b *a/the/some*, verbs
> c guess

Look at the instructions and the Exam Advice box together. Remind students that the correct answer may not be the one which has the same words as the text.

Time students while they do the task. Give them five minutes. If they need more time, give them another two minutes. In the exam they should allow 45 minutes for the Reading test (an average of nine minutes per part). Some of the other parts have a greater reading load than Part 1, so if they can practise working quickly at the beginning of the exam, they should not run out of time.

> **Answers**
> 1 C   2 C   3 A   4 B   5 A

> ### Corpus spot   *Stay* and *live*
>
> Look at the use of *stay* in question 5 of the exam task they have just done and point out that students often use *live* where they should use *stay*.
>
> > **Answers**
> > a ✓   b staying   c ✓   d stayed   e stayed

Speaking Part 2

Look at the Summary box about this part of the exam.

1 Look at the pictures together and make sure students are clear what they represent and what the situation is.

2 Ask students to think about the questions and then discuss them together – they must decide what shops they need to visit, if they will need to buy heavy items at the end, go to the bank at the beginning, etc. They may think of other points to consider.

3 Ask them to think about the expressions they learnt in Exam folder 9. Look back if necessary or write them on the board with students prompting. If your students are confident, rub the expressions off before they do the task so they are encouraged to remember them.

> **Answers**
> a making suggestions:
>   *We'd better do X because ...*
>   *Why don't we do X?*
> b agreeing and disagreeing:
>   *I (don't) agree (that) ...*
>   *That's (not) a good idea.*
> c giving your opinion:
>   *I think ...*
>   *In my opinion ...*

4 Put students in pairs to do the task. Tell them they should try to reach agreement. Look at the Exam Advice box. Say you will give them three minutes. In the exam, they will be expected to speak for two or three minutes. Have a class discussion comparing plans.

Reassure students that if they really can't think of anything to say, the examiner will ask a question to prompt them.

24 I've got an idea

In this unit:

Grammar	Past simple passive; future passive
Functions and vocabulary	Talking about shapes, materials and objects; talking about things you don't know the name of; guessing vocabulary
Pronunciation	Linking words ending in *r* and *re*
PET skills	Describing objects (Speaking Part 3); sentence transformations (Writing Part 1); reading and listening for gist
Revision	*it could/might/must/can't be* (Unit 13); *a kind of* (Unit 1); present simple passive (Unit 11); dates (years) (Units 6 and 14)
Exam folder	Listening Part 3
Writing folder	Writing Part 3

Preparation

Introduction, Exercise 3 Make copies of the recording script (from CD-ROM or webpage) so students can use it as a model.

Activity *Past passive* Photocopy the activity (on page 185), i.e. the two lists of inventions and the two sets of answers (enough so everyone in each group can see one – the class will be divided into two if there are twelve students or under; into four if there are more students).

Activity *Describing objects* Photocopy the pictures (on page 186) and cut them up (one picture for each group of three or four).

Exam folder 24 Make copies of the recording script (from CD-ROM or webpage) for students. Photocopy the sample answer (on page 173).

SB pages 154–157

Introduction
PET Speaking Part 3

1   Students practise describing objects they don't know the name of. Ask them to look at the pictures and guess what the inventions are.

Revise *It might/could/must/can't be* (Unit 13) and *a kind of …* (Unit 1).

Answers
a the first dishwasher   b a bicycle you can inflate
c the first digital computer   d the first camera
e an electric serving train at a dinner table
f a Sinclair C5 car (a single seat electric car with pedals)   g a wheelchair which people can sit or lie in and which helps them to stand up   h a velocipede (a form of transport for land and water – it rolled over the land and floated on the water)

2   **3** 🔊12 Play the recording.

Answers
1 h velocipede   2 e an electric serving train

Recording script

1   It's round and it's made of plastic, or it might be made of glass. It's like a ball but there's a man inside. He's holding something and turning it. It's used for moving across water but it also works on land.
2   It's a kind of railway line which is on a dinner table. It's made of metal. It's used for carrying food around the table.

3   Give students the photocopied recording scripts from Exercise 2 so they can use them as a model (see Preparation). Students work in pairs to write a brief description of one of the other objects. They use the present passive here in fixed expressions.

Ask some students to read their descriptions aloud and the others can guess.

4

Answers
The first camera, the first dishwasher and the first computer were successful. The electric serving train was not successful. The C5 electric car was not successful because it might be dangerous on busy roads and was very slow. The wheelchair is a new invention. The inflatable bicycle is unlikely to be successful!

5   Have a brief discussion.

Reading

1   Tell students they are going to read about three different inventions. Read the first paragraph of *Ben and Jerry's invention* together and help with difficult words like *delicious, flavour, crunch* and *parlour*.

2   Tell students you are going to give them two minutes to scan the other two paragraphs and say what they think the inventions are. Scanning texts quickly before beginning a detailed reading is useful for PET Reading Parts 3, 4 and 5. If they don't know the names of the inventions, they can use the expressions they practised at the beginning of the unit.

There will probably be vocabulary which students do not know, e.g. *dust*, *blow(er)*, *dirt*, and *chain*. Go through the texts encouraging them to guess what the words mean.

Answers
Charles D. Seeberger: escalators (moving stairs);
Hubert Cecil Booth: vacuum cleaner

3   Put students into three groups – Ben and Jerry, Charles D. Seeberger and Hubert Cecil Booth. They work as individuals to scan the paragraphs to find the three which finish their text and then put them in the correct order. The vacuum cleaner text is the easiest, so you could give that to weaker students. Give a time limit, e.g. five minutes.

4   They compare their answers with the rest of their group. They underline any unknown vocabulary and together try to work out what it means.

5   Get a student from each group to tell you what their text was about and what order they chose. Write the order on the board and then get everyone to read the two texts they haven't yet read and check the order.

Answers
Ben and Jerry: **g, b, e**
Charles D. Seeberger: **i, c, a**
Hubert Cecil Booth: **d, h, f**

6   Go over new vocabulary and talk about guessing the meanings from the context. Check students know what all the words mean and get them to work in pairs to put them under the correct headings. Students can add other words from the texts if they wish.

Answers

ice cream	escalator	vacuum cleaner
a flavour	a public building	dust
a cone	to transport	to clean
a factory	moving stairs	a machine
a customer	an underground station	dirt
a product	to step on/off	a spot
		a handkerchief

Language focus
Past passive

1   PET Writing Part 1

Language presentation

Revise the present passive.

Look at the sentence in Exercise 1 and underline *are sold*. Elicit that this is the present passive. Point out that this passive sentence doesn't include a *by* clause. Ask students why – we could put *by shops or restaurants* but this is understood and isn't really important. Remind them that we only say *by* in a passive sentence if it is important to know who the agent is. Ask them to give you the sentence in the active voice and write it on the board: *Shops sell Ben and Jerry's famous products in delicious flavours.*

Ask students if there are any other passive verbs in the Ben and Jerry text – *The Homemade Ice Cream Parlour was opened by Ben and Jerry in May 1978.* Write this sentence on the board. Ask them how this is different from the other passive sentence (it is in the past). Get one student to come and write it in the active voice on the board (*Ben and Jerry opened The Homemade Ice Cream Parlour in May 1978*).

Write on the board: *Ben Cohen and Jerry Greenfield started the company* and ask students to put it into the passive – *The company was started by Ben Cohen and Jerry Greenfield.*

Discuss the formation of the passive voice in the simple past (the simple past of the verb *to be* + a past participle).

2   Students look back at the first paragraphs about Charles D. Seeberger and Hubert Cecil Booth and find five verbs in the past passive. They check with a partner.

Answers
were used   were invented   was placed
was put   was pushed (up)

Language presentation

Write the passive sentences from the Hubert Cecil Booth paragraph on the board and ask two students to come and rewrite them in the active voice.

Moving chains *were used* by people in ancient Egypt.
The people in ancient Egypt used moving chains.

Moving stairs *were invented* by Charles D. Seeberger.
Charles D. Seeberger invented moving stairs.

Time students while they look for more passive verbs in the rest of the texts. See who finds the most. There are 13 (all past passive except 'is tested' and 'is sold').

Answers
a were put   **b** was held   weren't charged
c was opened   were displayed   **d** was sucked
e is tested   is sold   **f** none   **g** was given
h was built   was named   was needed   **i** were built

Students complete the Grammar spot as a summary.

 Grammar spot Passive (past simple)

Answers
\+ was invented
\– weren't charged
? was invented

3 In Writing Part 1, students are often tested on the passive. Look at question **a** together and ask why the passive sentence doesn't say *by the pilot* (because this is understood).

Answers
b showed the passengers
c served lunch
d didn't tell the passengers
e didn't stamp
f ordered one man to open

4 Look at the two examples together and refer students back to the Grammar spot. Remind students about learning irregular past participles.

Answers
c was hired by the station manager.
d are held by the company.
e were frightened by 'The Puffing Billy'.
f weren't built by the British.
g was invited to Buckingham Palace by the King and Queen.
h were replaced by clean electric trains.
i are produced by the company all the time.

 Corpus spot *Do* and *make*

Answers
a do **b** make **c** made **d** did **e** do **f** do

«Activity» Past passive

First, practise saying dates (years). Students sometimes have to write the year in Listening Part 3.

Language presentation

Read these dates and ask students to write them down: 1942, 1998, 1911, 1765, 1804, 2003, 2014.

Point out that we read dates in pairs – *nineteen forty-two* – except for the years of this century when we say *two thousand and fourteen*, etc. Remind them to say the *oh* in *eighteen oh four*. Ask them how they would talk about the years between 1990 and 1999 (*the nineteen nineties*).

Practise asking questions in the passive by writing some sentences on the board and asking students to make questions, e.g. Picasso was born in 1881. *When was Picasso born?* Coffee is grown in Brazil. *Where is coffee grown?*

1 Look at the pictures and talk about what they are. Divide the class into two teams (Group A and Group B). Give Group A their list of inventions and Group B theirs (see Preparation).

Each team works together to try to match the date and place to the inventions on their sheet.

2 Give out the answers, but give Group B's answers to Group A and vice versa. Practise a couple of questions in the passive, e.g. *When were matches invented?* The groups check their guesses by asking questions of the other group. Each group asks the other group a question in turn (they can only ask about *when* or *where* in one question, not both). They get a point for each year and a point for each country they get right. The winning team is the one that gets the most points.

Note: if your class has more than twelve students, you may want to divide it into more groups so the groups are no bigger than six. If so, you can still do the question session as a whole-class activity, but each group will ask fewer questions and use the questions from other groups to help them.

Future passive

1 Read the text together and talk about how realistic the idea is. Underline the first verb together and then get students to underline the others. Use the Grammar spot to talk about the formation of the future passive.

Answers
I think a special car <u>will be invented</u> which <u>will be driven</u> by a computer so a human driver <u>won't be needed</u>. It <u>will be made</u> of plastic and it <u>will be programmed</u> to go on the road or fly through the air. A fee <u>will be paid</u> by car owners at the end of the year to the government. They <u>will be charged</u> according to how many kilometres they have travelled by air and on the road.

 Grammar spot Future passive

Answer
\+ will be driven
\– won't be needed
? will be paid

2 If students can't think of anything to write about, discuss some of these ideas together: a vacuum cleaner with a computer which cleans the house on its own; a lipstick which lasts for 24 hours; a plane/car which can change size; clothes which don't need washing; a chair which changes size and shape for different people.

≪Pronunciation≫

1 This exercise practises linking words ending in *r* and *re*. We don't usually pronounce the *r* at the end of words, but if a word ending in *r* or *re* is followed by a word beginning with a vowel then we often join them with a /r/ sound. Ask students to mark the words which will be joined by a /r/ sound.

> **Answers and recording script**
> a Sugar‿and salt are‿added.
> b Shops asked them to deliver‿ice cream.
> c The mixture‿is frozen.
> d There‿are four‿escalators in the station near my house.
> e He had a better‿idea.
> f Where‿is Ben and Jerry's ice cream sold?

2 **3 13** Play the sentences and students repeat them.

3 This exercise practises linking words ending in any consonant sounds with the word following if it begins with a vowel.

> **Answers and recording script**
> a Television was‿invented‿in the 1920s.
> b Where‿are‿escalators‿used?
> c Ben‿and Jerry's‿ice cream‿is‿sold‿in many places.
> d Many shops have‿escalators.
> e Some‿inventions‿aren't successful.
> f I met him‿at four‿o'clock.
> g Some people went‿up‿and down‿all day.
> h I've lost your‿address.

4 **3 14** Play the recording and ask students to repeat.

≪Activity≫ Describing objects

1 Ask students to read the description and call out what it is (*umbrella*).

2 Give one of the photocopied cards to each group (see Preparation) or let students think of their own ideas.

   In small groups they should write their descriptions using the questions in their books to help them.

3 Each group reads out their description(s). The first person to guess can call out the answer.

Exam folder 24

SB pages 158–159

Listening Part 3

Ask students to look at the Summary box and answer the questions in the Check! box.

> **Answers**
> a what kind of recording it is, e.g. a recorded message, radio broadcast; what it is about; what you have to do
> b read the questions and think about what kind of words can go in each space (there are 20 seconds for reading)
> c yes, but the words around the space may be different
> d twice

1 Read the instructions together. The man is going to talk about a museum.

2 Ask students to look at the questions.

> **Answers**
> a The Weston Museum of Science
> b 1 a year 2 a day of the week 3 a noun (an exhibition) 4 a noun (an activity children would enjoy) 5 an ordinal number 6 a place

3 **3 15** Play the recording and ask students to fill in the answers. Look at the Exam Advice box.

4 **3 15 ◄I** Play the recording again.

5 **3 15 ◄I** Give students a photocopy of the recording script (see Preparation). Say you are going to play the recording again, but this time they are going to shout *Stop* when they expect to hear the answer. This gives them practice in listening for the cues in the questions. Demonstrate what you are going to do with the first question. Stop the recording at the marks // and discuss how what is said matches the cues on the question paper. As you discuss the cues, get the students to mark them (marked in bold in the recording script) with a wavy line.

6 Ask students to underline the answers on their scripts.

> **Answers**
> 1 1859 2 Friday(s) 3 planets
> 4 photography/photograph(s) 5 third 6 car park

Recording script

You will hear a man talking on the radio about a museum.

For each question, fill in the missing information in the numbered space.

Radio presenter: And today we are looking at things to do in the Weston area. One of the big attractions is, of course, the Museum of Science.

It's in South Avenue – it's been there since 1951 but before that it was in a smaller building in **Market Square** for nearly 100 years. // Weston's had a Museum of Science since 1859. So that's something to be proud of. The museum is open from Saturday to Thursday from **9 am until 5 pm**. // It has longer opening hours on a Friday, when it stays open until 9 pm. The museum shop is open from 10 until 5 every day except Monday, when it closes early.

There's plenty to see in the museum. You can cross a desert or travel through the human body. And there's a new gallery opening this week with a new exhibition. // Go there to find out more about the planets – imagine landing somewhere a million miles away from Earth. What would it feel like?

Every week there's a different **children's activity – this week** // the subject is photography. Children can take their own photographs. That's for children between the ages of eight and fourteen.

The museum is on four floors. On the ground floor are the shop and the cloakrooms. The permanent exhibitions are on the first and second floors. By the time you've visited those you'll be thirsty, so carry on to **the café** // on the third floor, which is open all day for drinks and snacks.

One important piece of information. If you visit the museum before **24 July** // you won't be able to use the car park. It's closed for repairs. But you are allowed to park in the hotel car park opposite.

Now the phone ...

Writing folder

Writing Part 3

1 This exercise practises using linking words and adjectives. Do it together, revising the language as necessary as you go through the answers.

> **Answers**
> a 8 b 3 c 7 d 1 e 6 f 5 g 2 h 4
>
> a I really like that band
> b I was listening to music
> c While I was watching the band
> d Although I like music
> e The music was so loud
> f I used to like folk music
> g I enjoy listening to music
> h You can have this CD
>
> 1 I don't own many CDs.
> 2 but I don't play an instrument.
> 3 when I fell asleep.
> 4 because I don't like it.
> 5 but now I prefer rock music.
> 6 that we couldn't talk.
> 7 my phone was stolen.
> 8 so get me a ticket too.

2 Read the beginning of the letter Alessia wrote. Ask students to try to join the sentences.

> **Suggested answer**
> Dear Sophie,
> I went to a concert last week. My friend bought the tickets *but* she couldn't go *because* she was ill *so* my brother came instead. The band was *so* good *that* I didn't want the music to stop. *Although* my brother doesn't like listening to their CDs, he enjoyed the concert (or My brother doesn't like listening to their CDs *but* he enjoyed the concert). *When* the concert finished at 11 o'clock, we went backstage to meet the band.

3 Ask students to do the exercise.

> **Answers**
> **good:** enjoyable, excellent, exciting, fantastic, great, wonderful
> **bad:** awful, hopeless, terrible, useless
> **big:** enormous, large
> **small:** tiny
> **unusual:** extraordinary, strange, unexpected
> **famous:** well-known

4 For possible answers, see the lists in Exercise 3.

5 Discuss what kind of things students will say in the letter. Draw attention to the Exam Advice box. See page 173 for a photocopiable sample answer.

EXTRA

If appropriate, when students have finished their letters, they could pass them to another student. They can then work on someone else's letter using a different colour and try to make it more interesting by joining some of the sentences and adding adverbs and adjectives. If they then give them to you, you can see what both students have done.

Units 19–24 Revision

Speaking

1 Follow the procedure outlined on page 42 of the Teacher's Book.

Exercises 2–7 could be set for homework and discussed afterwards in class.

Telephoning

2

Answers
b May I have your name?
c Can you hang on a minute?
d I'm afraid he's not available at the moment.
e Can you call back in about an hour?
f This is Regina.
g I can't speak to you just now.
h I'll call you back in twenty minutes.
i Can you give me their number?

Vocabulary

3

Answers
1 g 2 i 3 d 4 b 5 h 6 f 7 a 8 e 9 c

Grammar

4

Answers
2 B 3 C 4 A 5 A

5

Answers
2 A 3 B 4 B 5 C

6

Answers
b invented these machines c phone me d will open
e Don't play football f give my brothers
g rang you but you didn't answer h was examined
i is fed by our neighbours j she had won
k 'll/will be given a lift

7

Answers
b who c which d whose e who f who
g where h which/– i which

Progress Test 4 Key

1 B 2 A 3 A 4 C 5 B 6 A 7 B 8 C 9 C

10 B 11 B 12 A 13 A 14 B 15 A 16 B 17 C

18 B 19 A 20 A 21 C 22 C 23 B 24 B 25 A

26 daughter 27 novelist 28 announce 29 neighbours

30 approached

Progress Test 4

Choose the correct answer, A, B or C.

1 We've arranged .... our niece at half past six.
   A meet   B to meet   C meeting

2 Dave .... to take us to the station in his car.
   A offered   B finished   C didn't mind

3 Does the school let students .... parties in the hall?
   A have   B to have   C having

4 I'm not afraid .... saying what I believe.
   A to   B from   C of

5 Mary has found the purse that .... yesterday.
   A lost it   B she lost   C she lost it

6 The lead singer danced .... than the other members of the group.
   A worse   B worst   C badly

7 The doctor told me .... the hospital.
   A that I phone   B to phone   C phone

8 It was really bad .... that you had a cold at the weekend.
   A chance   B time   C luck

9 It was .... a good party that no one wanted to leave.
   A so   B as   C such

10 I'm ringing .... about the exam results.
   A for ask   B to ask   C for asking

11 A cousin of .... has bought a house in this road.
   A us   B ours   C our

12 We asked the mechanic .... the motorbike for us.
   A to mend   B he mended   C did he mend

13 I want to .... my hair cut before my holiday.
   A have   B make   C do

14 I want to .... a phone call before I go out.
   A do   B make   C speak

15 Gilda told us that the party .... at about ten o'clock.
   A began   B begun   C to begin

16 Did you make .... with anyone in your evening class?
   A friend   B friends   C friendly

17 This is the person .... gave me your address.
   A which   B where   C who

18 At midnight, the club was full .... teenagers.
   A with   B of   C by

19 These pictures .... painted by a friend of Picasso's.
   A were   B had   C have

20 I'm not very keen .... loud music.
   A on   B for   C to

21 The next match will be .... in Manchester.
   A play   B to play   C played

22 This room is used .... dancing and acting.
   A to   B by   C for

23 Alice is the girl .... guitar I borrowed for the concert.
   A that   B whose   C her

24 Be careful when you step .... the bus.
   A out   B off   C down

25 We used to live next .... to my grandparents.
   A door   B house   C place

Find one spelling mistake in each sentence. Write the correction in the space.

26 That man's doughter is a well-known singer.
   ....

27 The novelest was very angry when he read the reviews.
   ....

28 Who is going to anounce the winner of the competition?
   ....

29 Our nieghbours are building a beautiful swimming pool.

30 My stepfather aproached the boys who supported my team. ....

Shop till you drop

In this unit:	
Grammar	Reported questions; *too much / too many / not enough* + noun; verbs with two objects
Functions and vocabulary	Shops and shopping; asking for things; trying on clothes
Pronunciation	Stress: correcting what people say
PET skills	Describing a picture (Speaking Part 3); discussing advantages and disadvantages (Speaking Part 4); listening for detail and attitude (Listening Part 4); sentence transformation (Writing Part 1)
Revision	Reported speech (Unit 22); clothes (Unit 14)
Exam folder	Reading Part 3

Preparation

Activity *A new jacket* Photocopy and cut out cards A–D (on page 186) for half the class, one card per student. Photocopy and cut out cards 1–4 (on page 186) for the other half of the class, one card per student.

SB pages 162–165

Introduction

PET Speaking Part 3

1 This exercise practises describing a photograph.

Give students a few moments to study the photographs, then elicit brief descriptions of the kind of shopping environments they show:
a shopping in a market b in a supermarket
c in a shopping mall d online shopping
e shopping by catalogue.
Supply vocabulary as necessary.

PET Speaking Part 4

2 This exercise practises discussing advantages and disadvantages.

Allocate the photographs to different pairs and ask students to mark the advantages and disadvantages of shopping in that way.

3 Ask each pair to work with another pair who looked at a different photograph and compare their conclusions.

4 Discuss the question with the class, asking them to support their ideas.

Listening

PET Listening Part 4

3 **16** This task practises listening for detail and attitude.

Ask students to read the rubric and sentences (a–h) and discuss with them what they already know before they start listening.

Play the recording.

Answers
b false **c** false **d** true **e** true
f false **g** true **h** false

Recording script

Darren: Hello?
Andy: Hi, Darren?
Darren: Yeah.
Andy: Look, it's Andy. I'm in town. Can you come and drive me home?
Darren: Where are you?
Andy: In the city centre. You know, Dad gave me some money last week and I wanted to buy a pullover ...
Darren: Well, it's a bit late. I want to eat.
Andy: Oh, come on. I've just had a really bad experience.
Darren: What? What's going on?
Andy: It's, like, I was just nearly arrested.
Darren: What for? You only went to buy some clothes! What have you done now?
Andy: Well, first I went into Tempo, you know, the big clothes store?
Darren: Yeah.
Andy: And I looked at the pullovers, and I got one. And then I decided to get a shirt too, but after I'd looked at them I wasn't sure, so I went to a couple of other places to see what they had. A friend told me they were selling some quite cool ones in the market. But when I asked about them, the man who runs the stall said he'd sold them all already. And I bought some shoes and went to the burger bar because it was time for lunch.
Darren: OK.
Andy: Then I went back to Tempo and found some shirts I liked and I said to the assistant I wanted to try them on and he said that was OK. But they weren't any good, so I told the assistant they didn't fit and he put them back on the shelf. They didn't have any

other sizes in stock. Then, when I was going out of the shop, this woman came up to me. She asked me if I was leaving the shop. I said I was. She asked me if I'd paid for everything in my bag. I said I had because I knew I'd only got the pullover I bought earlier, and the shoes.

Darren: Right.

Andy: She said she was the store detective and then she asked me if I would come to the manager's office with her and I agreed, although I added that I wasn't very happy about it. Everyone was looking at me. It was really bad.

Darren: I believe you!

Andy: In the manager's office, the store detective showed the manager the pullover and the manager asked me how long I'd been in the shop and how many things I had bought. So I told him I'd bought a pullover at about 9.30 but I hadn't bought anything else. I was getting a bit angry and I asked what was going on. Then he asked me whether I had a receipt for the pullover. And of course I couldn't find it. And I tried to explain I'd thrown away the Tempo bag and had put the pullover in the shoe shop bag.

Darren: Oh, Andy.

Andy: Well, I didn't know. But anyway they didn't believe me. They asked me a lot more questions.

Darren: Like what?

Andy: They asked which assistant had served me. I said I didn't remember who had served me. It had been early in the morning. Then the store detective asked the manager if he wanted her to call the police and he said yes.

Darren: Oh, no.

Andy: But then my luck changed. One of the assistants came into the room and I recognised her. She was the one that served me in the morning. I asked her if she remembered me and she did. I've never felt so happy in my life.

Darren: Yeah, I'm sure. OK. So where are you now?

Andy: I'm in the manager's office. He said he was sorry for troubling me and he told me I was welcome to use his phone. Can you come and give me a lift home? There are too many people at the bus stop at this time. I'm really tired and I haven't got enough money for a taxi.

Darren: Sure. I'll be ten minutes. See you outside Tempo.

Andy: Thanks, Darren.

Language focus

PET Writing Part 1

Reported speech

Exercises 1 and 2 revise reported speech in preparation for reported questions.

1   Remind students that they have already studied reported speech (Unit 22), then ask them to do the exercise in pairs.

Draw attention to the change from *are selling* to *were selling*.

Answers
b he'd / he had sold them all already.
c (that) I wanted to try them on.
d that was OK.
e they didn't fit.
f I was.

2   Do the exercise together, writing the answers on the board.

Answers
b OK / All right, *etc.* but I'm not very happy about it.
c I bought a pullover at about 9.30.
d I threw away the Tempo bag and put the pullover in the shoe shop bag.
e I don't remember who served me.
f I'm sorry for troubling you. You're welcome to use my phone.

3   Work through the exercise with the class, writing the answers on the board.

Answers
b Have you paid for everything in your bag?
c Will/Would you come to the manager's office with me?
d How long have you been in the shop and how many things have you bought?
e What's going on?
f Do you have / Have you got a receipt for the pullover?
g Which assistant served you?
h Do you want me to call the police?
i Do you remember me?

Language presentation

Elicit/Supply the rules for changing direct questions into reported questions using Exercise 3 answers as guidance, i.e. verbs change as they do from direct statements (present becomes past, past simple or present perfect becomes past perfect) and pronouns change as necessary.

Point out that *Yes/No* questions use *if/whether*; *Wh-* questions use the question words.

Draw attention to the word order in reported *Yes/No* questions. This is the aspect which most students find difficult to remember.

Grammar spot   Reported questions

Complete the examples with the class to summarise the rules.

> **Answers**
> I asked her if she *liked* it.
> He asked me whether I *had* a laptop.
> She asked me if I *would come* shopping with her.
> I asked what *was happening*.
> They asked which assistant *had spoken* to me.

4   Ask students to write the answers in pairs and check them together.

> **Answers**
> **b** I spoke   **c** I'd ever worked
> **d** why I wanted to work in that shop
> **e** how I would travel   **f** I could start

5   Allow a few minutes for students to offer their opinions and give reasons for them.

6   This exercise could be homework, if time is short.

> **Answers**
> **b** what time I had found it
> **c** if/whether I had been alone
> **d** where I lived
> **e** how long I had lived there
> **f** if/whether I would be at that address for the next month
> **g** if/whether I had an email address

Too much, too many, not enough

Language presentation

Revise the meaning of *too*, if necessary (*more than enough*). (See Unit 14 for *too* + adjectives.)

Ask students to complete the rules in the Grammar spot and check them by writing them on the board. Point out that *enough* goes before a noun but after an adjective.

Grammar spot   *Too much, too many, not enough*

> **Answers**
> **a** too many   **b** too much   **c** enough

Students use the Grammar spot to help them complete the exercise, either in class or for homework.

> **Answers**
> **a** too much   **b** enough   **c** too much
> **d** too many; enough   **e** enough   **f** too much
> **g** too many

⟪Pronunciation⟫

This practises contrastive sentence stress.

1   **3 17** Play the recording and stop after the first answer. Draw attention to the underlined word and ask why the speaker stressed it (because she was correcting the questioner).

Ask students to listen to the other exchanges and underline the stressed word in each answer.

> **Answers and recording script**
> **1 A** Did you say ten o'clock?
>   **B** No, I said <u>two</u> o'clock.
> **2 A** Did you say there were five guests?
>   **B** No, I said there were <u>nine</u> guests.
> **3 A** Did you say we had a spelling test?
>   **B** No, I said we had a <u>reading</u> test.
> **4 A** Did you say you came by air?
>   **B** No, I said I came by <u>car</u>.
> **5 A** Did you say she was a doctor?
>   **B** No, I said she was a <u>teacher</u>.
> **6 A** Did you say you came from France?
>   **B** No, I said I came from <u>Greece</u>.

2   **3 17** ◀ Play the recording again, pausing it for students to repeat the exchanges. Remind students to stress the underlined word.

3   Do the example to demonstrate to the class. Then ask the class to practise in pairs.

> **Answers**
> **b** Did you say there were fifteen students?
>   No, I said there were <u>sixteen</u> students.
> **c** Did you say we wanted ham sandwiches?
>   No, I said we wanted <u>jam</u> sandwiches.
> **d** Did you say she was a model?
>   No, I said she was an <u>actress</u>.
> **e** Did you say it was quarter to eleven?
>   No, I said it was quarter to <u>seven</u>.

⟪Activity⟫ Whispers

Students play the game in groups of three.

Verbs with two objects   PET Writing Part 1

This transformation may come up in the exam.

> ### Language presentation
>
> Study the examples with the class. Draw their attention to the word order. If this is a tricky area for your students, demonstrate with an object in the classroom, e.g. say: *Matea, give Imran your book.* (She does so.) Say: *Matea gave Imran her book. Matea gave her book to Imran.* Repeat with other objects/students and ask the class to tell you what they did, using both structures.

1   Do the first two sentences of the exercise with the whole class, then let them finish it individually.

> **Answers**
> b I sent my parents a postcard from London.
> c Will you send my boss the bill?
> d He wrote me a long letter when he arrived in India.
> e On my birthday, the children brought me my breakfast in bed.
> f Can you bring us some more bread, please?

2   Check Exercise 1 before asking students to do this exercise.

> **Answers**
> a Take this note to the headteacher, please.
> b Show your passport to the immigration officer.
> c We took some fruit to our classmate when he was ill.

⟪Activity⟫ A new jacket

Direct students to the pictures in their books and elicit suggestions about where the people are and what they are saying.

Divide the class into two halves and distribute cards A–D to one half of the class, and cards 1–4 to the other half (see Preparation).

Tell students to find a person with the other half of their conversation and then to practise saying it together. When all students have found a partner, ask four different pairs to read their conversations.

> **Answers**
> A 2   B 4   C 1   D 3

Ask four pairs to write the conversations up on the board and let students copy them down for reference, noting which conversation belongs with which picture.

Exam folder 25

SB pages 166–167

Reading Part 3

Look together at the Summary box about this part of the test. Ask students to do the Check! questions in pairs.

> **Answers**
> a A (Remind students to look at the instructions, which will help them. Look at the photograph together – sometimes there is an accompanying picture in the exam.)
> b A
> c B (some parts of the text are not tested)

Ask students to do the task as if they were in an exam. Allow nine minutes. In the exam, they should allow no more than this per part – they can go back if they have time at the end.

Give them the answers and go through each one, getting them to highlight the relevant part of the text.

> **Answers**
> 1 B 2 B 3 A 4 B 5 A 6 A 7 A 8 B 9 A 10 B

> ### ⬎ Corpus spot   Shopping
> These errors mainly revise points that arose in earlier units.
>
> > **Answers**
> > a do   b malls   c high   d go   e shop

In this unit:	
Grammar	First conditional; *unless* ; *if* and *when*
Functions and vocabulary	Advertising; persuading and reporting verbs
Pronunciation	Stress in common short phrases
PET skills	Reading for gist and detailed meaning; understanding verbs used in Reading Part 4; sentence transformation (Writing Part 1)
Revision	Agreeing and disagreeing (Unit 19); telling a story (Unit 12)
Exam folder	Speaking Parts 1 and 2
Writing folder	Writing Part 3

Preparation

Activity *Adverts* If possible, it would be useful to bring some English language advertisements to class.

SB pages 168–171

Introduction

1   At the top of the page are parts of famous logos. Students work in groups to identify as many as they can.

> **Answers**
> **a** McDonalds   **b** Google   **c** Virgin   **d** Mercedes-Benz
> **e** Coca-Cola

2   See how many logos there are in the classroom. Direct students' attention to their clothes, bags, shoes, etc. and discuss the importance of logos in students' lives. Ask questions like *Why do you like wearing logos? Do you look for clothes with special logos? Do you ever look for clothes without logos? Do you spend extra on trainers because of their logo or do you buy a cheaper pair without a logo?*, etc. If there aren't many logos in your classroom, talk about where you might find them outside the classroom – on buildings, on cars, etc.

3   Ask students to look at the adverts and suggest what they are trying to sell. Talk about whether they are successful/effective or not. Point out that *adverts* and *ads* are short for *advertisements*. Ask students which adverts they think are the most and least successful.

> **Answers**
> They are advertising tissues, washing powder and an airline.

4   Discuss the importance of adverts. Do students feel they are influenced by what they see on television, in magazines, in the streets, etc. or are they influenced more by their peers? What is their favourite advert? Why? Where does it appear?

Reading

1   Ask students to read the photo story and think about the questions, which check general understanding. Go over the answers and check any vocabulary as necessary, e.g. *strict, lonely, mess, none of your business* (point out that this is not a very polite expression), etc.

> **Answers**
> **a** play computer games
> **b** on Friday at home and on Saturday with his parents
> **c** a surprise party for Robert
> **d** no
> **e** she heard the boys talking about it
> **f** no
> **g** they will make a mess in the house
> **h** nothing

PET Reading Part 4

2   Check that students understand the exact meaning of the underlined verbs. Ask them to work individually to answer the questions.

> **Answers**
> **1** D   **2** A   **3** D   **4** C

Look at the Vocabulary spot together. The next exercise practises some of these verbs.

3   This could be homework. These verbs are being taught for recognition purposes in Reading Part 4.

> **Suggested answers**
> **b** encourages/encouraged   **c** influence
> **d** recommends/recommended   **e** warned / is warning
> **f** prevented / are preventing   **g** apologise

⬂ Corpus spot

> **Answers**
> **a** I want to warn you <u>about</u> the cold weather here.
> **b** This will encourage me <u>to</u> study harder.
> **c** I explained <u>to</u> her how it was made.
> **d** My illness prevented me <u>from going</u> out.

Language focus
First conditional

Language presentation

Look at the sentences in the Grammar spot together and talk about what they mean. (We use this kind of conditional sentence when there is a possibility of something happening in the future.)

Look at the tenses of the verbs and discuss the fact that the verb in the *if* clause is in the present tense although it refers to the future. Point out that the *if* clause can go first or second. Elicit that we use a comma at the end of the *if* clause if it comes first.

Students complete the Grammar spot.

 Grammar spot   First conditional

Answers

condition	result
IF + ...**present tense**...... ,	............**will**........... .

If only a few people **go** *to the party, it* **won't be** *a problem.*

result	condition
............**will**..............	IF + ...**present tense**..........

*He'***ll have** *a really good time* **if** *the boys* **organise** *a party for him.*

Look at the example **a**. Students do the other sentences.

Answers
b will be   **c** will get   **d** won't happen   **e** will stay
f feels   **g** won't have   **h** will be

Unless

PET Writing Part 1

Language presentation

Look at the *if* sentence in the Grammar spot. Ask students what verb they will write so that the sentence means the same.

 Grammar spot   *Unless*

Answer
Unless Robert **goes** *to his granny's house, he will be at home.*

1   Do the first one or two questions together and then students work on their own. They may be asked to do a transformation from *if not* to *unless* or vice versa in Writing Part 1.

Suggested answers
a Unless the meeting is cancelled, Robert's parents will be away.
b Unless Carolina tells Robert about the party, it will be a surprise.
c Robert will enjoy the party unless the boys ask too many people.
d Unless the boys organise a party for Robert, he won't have one.
e Robert's parents won't know about the party unless Carolina tells them.

2   This exercise mixes *if* and *unless*.

Suggested answers (Accept other answers as long as they make sense and *if* and *unless* are used correctly.)
b I can come shopping with you if you lend me some money.
c I won't tell anyone if you tell me the secret.
d I won't pass my exam unless you help me with my revision.
e The letter will get there tomorrow if you post it by five o'clock.

EXTRA

You could ask students to write sentences about themselves using *if* and *unless*.

If and *when*

Language presentation

Look together at the two pairs of sentences in the Grammar spot and discuss the fact that *when* makes something definite and *if* makes it uncertain.

⬆ **Grammar spot**   *If* and *when*

Answers
1   In sentence A the speaker knows that Robert's parents will come home. (*when* = they will definitely come home)
In sentence B the speaker is not sure where Robert's parents are. (*if* = they may be at home or they may not)
2   In sentence B Robert will definitely answer the door. (*when* = the speaker is sure)
In sentence A Robert will possibly answer the door. (*if* = the speaker isn't sure)

Ask students to do the exercise.

Answers
b if   **c** if / when   **d** If   **e** When   **f** if   **g** when
h If / When   **i** if

«Activity» Finishing a story

Ask students to look back at the photo story in Reading. Give students a different role each in the three conversations and get them to look at their parts and then act out the conversation, without their books if they can.

Ask students to write the fourth conversation about what happened next and act it out for the class.

«Pronunciation»

This practises stress in common short phrases.

1 **3 18** Read the first line of the conversation yourself to demonstrate the task. Then play the rest of the conversation and ask students to underline the stressed syllables.

Check the answers. The speakers stress the words which are important to what they are saying. One way to demonstrate this is to read out only the stressed words and ask students if they would still be able to follow the conversation. Then read out the unstressed words and ask the same.

> **Answers and recording script**
> **Joanna:**   What's *the* time?
> **Michael:**   Five *to* nine.
> **Joanna:**   Oh dear.
> **Michael:**   What's *the* problem?
> **Joanna:**   It doesn't matter.
> **Michael:**   Tell me.
> **Joanna:**   I'm late *for* college. *Can* you give me *a* lift?
> **Michael:**   *Of* course I can.
> **Joanna:**   Thank you.
> **Michael:**   You're welcome.

2 **3 18** Play the conversation again and get students to repeat it. Make sure they are using the weak sound /ə/ in the places marked in italics above (see also Unit 29). You could then ask students to read the conversation with a partner.

«Activity» Adverts

Talk about slogans (see Preparation). Ask your students to think of some – they may know some in English or you could tell them some.

If you have a monolingual class, you could talk in English about two or three popular slogans in the students' own language – how effective they are, why they use certain words, etc.

Then ask students to work in groups to write simple slogans for the adverts in their books using *if*, *when* and *unless*. Give them a couple of examples.

> **Suggested answers**
> If you buy this fridge, your food will stay fresher. / When you use this fridge, your food will taste good.
> If you travel with this airline, you'll be very comfortable. / Unless you fly with this airline, you'll feel tired.

«Activity» Superstitions

1 Look at the pictures of superstitions and teach any unfamiliar words, if necessary. Ask students if they believe in superstitions. Ask them to work individually or in pairs to write some sentences about the pictures. Whether something is good luck or bad luck tends to vary from one culture to another. If most of these have no meaning for your students, get them to add some different ones.

> **Answers for British culture**
> If a black cat crosses your path, you will have good luck.
> If you break a mirror, you will have seven years' bad luck.
> If you see a ladybird, you will have good luck.
> If you pick up a horseshoe, you will have good luck.
> If you see a rainbow, you will have good luck.
> If you walk under a ladder, you will have bad luck.
> If you open an umbrella indoors, you will have bad luck.

2 Students discuss their answers in groups and add more superstitions if they haven't already done so.

Exam folder 26

SB pages 172–173

Speaking Part 1

Look at the Summary box together and go through the Check! questions.

> **Answers**
> a four – two examiners (one doesn't speak) and two candidates
> b the examiner
> c some of these: where you live / come from, what job you do / what you are studying, why you're learning English, your interests, your daily life
> d Could you speak more slowly, please?
>   Could you repeat that, please?
> e two or three minutes, therefore only a minute or so for each candidate

1 Ask students round the room to spell different words, e.g. the street where they live, their surname, their brother's/sister's name or the name of their school.

2 Give students a couple of minutes to think of things they could say and then pool ideas.

3 Students ask and answer. If appropriate, ask a few students to ask and answer in front of the class so you end up covering a range of questions and answers. Look at the Exam Advice box.

Speaking Part 2

Look at the Summary box and then answer the Check! questions together.

Answers
a some pictures to look at
b the other candidate
c Could you speak more slowly, please?
   Could you repeat that, please?
d about two or three minutes
e the examiner will ask a question

1 Ask students to work in pairs to look at the pictures on page 201 in the Student's Book. They should think about what they like to do in their town and what they would like to be able to do. Ask for ideas round the class.

2 In their pairs, students put the facilities in order of importance for them. Ask round the class to compare answers.

3 Start with the most popular facility and talk about whether it is a good thing to spend money on.

4 If necessary, look back at Exam Folder 9 for useful expressions and remind students that they should learn these. Students change pairs and have a discussion. Time them for three minutes.

Writing folder

Writing Part 3

1 Ask students to do the exercise and go through it together.

Answers
a after   b Next   c While   d when

Point out that *Next* is used in a similar way to *Then*, but usually connects actions which are part of a sequence, and often follows *First*. Remind them that *While* emphasises the fact that the past continuous action was interrupted by the past simple event.

2 Ask students to work in pairs to put the sentences in order.

When they have finished, ask different students to come up and write each sentence on the board in the correct order. As they do so, discuss how they decided. Draw attention to the time markers (*when, at the same time, then, After, In the evening* and *ever since*).

Answers
1 g 2 e 3 d 4 a 5 c 6 j 7 f 8 h 9 b 10 i

3 If you wish, spend a few minutes brainstorming ideas for possible storylines. Remind students of the Exam Advice in Writing folder 20 about choosing a story that does not need vocabulary they do not know.

The writing can be done for homework. Suggest that students give themselves fifteen minutes, or time them in class. If you wish, ask students to compete to see who can use the greatest number of words from the box, but tell them they do not have to use them all. Remind them they must also use the correct tenses.

Draw students' attention to the Exam Advice box. Provided they answer the task with appropriate language, the examiner will not award or deduct marks for an imaginative storyline, or lack of it. The story students have just worked on is about a mistake over a hotel room – it is not necessary for them to think up a complicated or exciting plot.

27 Travellers' tales

TOPIC: Travel experiences

In this unit:	
Grammar	Adverbs at the beginning of a sentence; reflexive pronouns (*myself, yourself*, etc.); *each, every, all*
Functions and vocabulary	Travel; saying why people do things; word building
Pronunciation	/eə/ as in *there*, /ɪə/ as in *here*
PET skills	Predicting missing words and listening for specific detail (Listening Part 3); giving an opinion (Speaking Part 4)
Revision	Guessing unknown words; present and past simple passive (Units 11 and 24); giving advice (Units 9 and 19)
Exam folder	Reading Part 2

Preparation

Introduction, Exercise 3 Make an OHT of the song words, with spaces, or write it up on the board before the lesson, to use when going through the answers. Alternatively project it from the CD-ROM or webpage onto the whiteboard.
Language focus *Adverbs at the beginning of sentences*
Exercise 2 Make copies of the recording script (from CD-ROM or webpage) for students.
Activity *Word-building Snap* Photocopy and cut up the cards (on page 187), one sheet (set 1 and set 2) per pair or group. If necessary and possible, provide one English–English dictionary per group.

SB pages 174–177

Introduction   PET Listening Part 3

In this task students practise predicting missing words and listening for specific detail.

1   **3 19** Give students a few moments to study the photographs, then play them the song, emphasising that they need not understand every word, but should try to get the singer's general idea. Discuss which photograph matches it best and why.

2   This is a modern folk song by John Tams, recorded in 2000 and not specially written for EFL students. Explain *strand* (beach) and *glade* (small clear area in a wood) and tell students that these are poetic words, not used in everyday English. Invite suggestions about parts of speech which will fit the spaces. Some students may remember the correct words. Ask for possible alternatives.

> **Answers**
> **a** shining **b** sky **c** silver **d** shining **e** road
> **f** hard **g** high **h** out **i** never **j** gold **k** land

3   **3 19** Play the song again for them to write the words in the spaces (see Preparation). Teach the proverb *Every cloud has a silver lining* and discuss the meaning. If students wish, play the song again. Some classes might enjoy singing along with the recording or writing a further verse of their own.

4, 5 Discuss with the class the singer's reason(s) for travelling, then ask them to discuss the questions in Exercise 5 in pairs or small groups for a few minutes.

Go round the class asking for their ideas and use the opportunity to revise/teach relevant expressions with prepositions, e.g. *on holiday, on business, for pleasure,* etc. and the use of the infinitive for purpose, e.g. *to study, to learn a new language, to meet new people, to see new places, to go to work, to find work, to escape from problems at home,* etc.

Refer students to the Vocabulary spot.

6   Ask students their opinions on the best way to travel and use the opportunity to revise/teach relevant expressions, e.g. *by air, on foot, by bike, by car, by train, alone, with friends, with your family,* etc. (see also Unit 5).

Listening

1   This exercise brings together the guessing skills students have acquired. Go through the four points **a–d**, checking that students remember/understand them. You could do the following:

   a elicit/offer examples of words in the students' mother tongue(s) which are similar to their English counterparts, e.g. *taxi* (and where applicable warn against false friends)

   b revise suffixes for occupations (*-er, -ist*): see Unit 20

c elicit/offer examples of compound words,
e.g. *raincoat, notebook, classroom,* etc.

d refer back to the gapped song.

2 Ask students to think about the words and write down their guesses, if any, but do not discuss them at this point. Emphasise that they are not expected to know these words.

3 **3 20** Tell students that they may not understand everything they are going to hear, but they should listen out for the words in Exercise 2 and use the contexts to help them guess or to confirm their guesses about meanings. Play the recording.

Note: It is common for UK school-leavers to have a break after they leave school and before starting further education or employment; this is often referred to as a gap year. Others may travel and work during their university vacations or between university and starting full-time work.

4 Discuss the meaning of each word in Exercise 2 and ask students to say how they guessed them. Reassure them that the exact meaning of some words cannot easily be guessed, although a general idea is possible (e.g. *basement* is probably a room, exactly what kind of room is more difficult to guess).

Answers
a a musical instrument
b someone who looks after children in their home
c someone who works for no money
d a wooden path
e someone who studies buildings and objects which are very old
f a fire that people build when they are camping
g part of a house which is underground

Recording script

Host: Hi, everyone, and welcome to International Chat, our phone-in programme for students everywhere. Today's subject is working abroad and we'd like to hear from anyone who's done this. Many employers and universities say that before you start a course or a job at home, it's a good idea to spend some time travelling in other countries. Some students are helped by their parents, others have to find a job. We'd like to hear about your experiences.
And our first caller is Joe. Joe, tell us about your experience.

Joe: Well, I had a great time in Ireland. I stayed on a traditional farm where I picked potatoes and looked after the cows. I did repairs to the farmhouse too. I was given a room and my food and every evening the old farmer played his accordion and sang Irish songs and told stories. His wife was a wonderful cook. <u>Her home-made bread</u> was out of this world.

Host: Well done Joe, you obviously enjoyed yourself there. And now we go to Natasha. Where did you work, Natasha?

Natasha: I'd reached Finland, and I was in Helsinki. <u>I earned about £110 each week</u> for five days' work. I was employed as a nanny. I helped the older children get ready for school in the morning and then looked after the little one all day.

Host: And did you find the job by yourself?

Natasha: Well, <u>luckily</u>, <u>a Finnish friend helped me to write a little notice</u> about myself in Finnish and we put it in some playgroups. Lots of families like to have some help with the children and they prefer someone who can speak English, but you need to advertise in Finnish.

Host: Thanks for that tip, Natasha. And now we go to Owen from Lancashire. Did you earn money abroad too?

Owen: No. I wasn't paid, I was a volunteer. I wanted to do something to help the environment. I was <u>in Canada</u> and I helped to build boardwalks on Vancouver Island. These allow more people to walk in the forest.

Host: Is that good for the environment?

Owen: Yes, it'll help prevent the forest from being destroyed by people who want to cut down the trees.

Host: And did you have a good time?

Owen: <u>Obviously</u>, I liked helping to save the forest. <u>It was fairly wet there, it rained</u> nearly **every** day, and it was hard work, but it was fun. I liked **all** the people there and the forest was wonderful – the big trees, the wild fruit and the mushrooms and the mist.

Host: Well, that sounds magic, doesn't it? And let's hear from Jennifer, who worked in very different weather, I think.

Jennifer: That's right. I was in the desert, in the Middle East, helping archaeologists. <u>Of course</u>, the sun was really hot during the day, but it was very cold at night. Some people might think it's very romantic to dig up old buildings which were buried for hundreds or thousands of years, but <u>unfortunately</u> digging is very hard work. <u>Actually</u>, we needed to be quite fit and know how to look after ourselves. You quickly get sore hands and <u>backache</u>.

Host: And what about the accommodation?

Jennifer: Oh, the camp was great. **Each of** the workers had a small tent. There were people from every part of the world and after we finished working, there was normally a campfire and a couple of musicians. But most of all, it was wonderful to spend time in the desert which was so beautiful and <u>empty</u>. Very different from Manchester, where I'm studying now.

Host: Yeah, I can believe that. Thank you, Jennifer. And we have time for one more caller. And it's Martin, who found ways of earning money in Los Angeles, in the USA.

Martin: Hello. Yes, I was staying with my <u>uncle</u>. He knew an old man who wanted some help in his house and arranged for us to meet. He gave me free food and I was paid $12 an hour. I painted some rooms for him, which I hadn't done before. <u>Surprisingly</u>, his <u>landlady</u> was so satisfied with the job I did that she asked me to paint her basement and then a friend asked me as well. I was employed by lots of people. **Each** person told their friends about me. I had a wonderful time and earned quite a lot of money. <u>In fact</u>, I had an email from someone last week offering me work there next summer.

Host: Well, that's great. And that's all we have time for. But I hope our listeners will be encouraged by those stories and start making their own plans for travelling and working abroad.

PET Listening Part 3

5 **3** **20** ◀ This task practises listening for specific information.

Briefly discuss the theme (students working abroad) and structure of the radio programme (phone-in with people describing their experiences).

Direct students to sentences a–j and ask them to discuss in pairs the kind of word needed for each space.

Play the recording again for students to write their answers.

Let students compare their answers in pairs, then go through them with the whole class, playing and stopping the recording again as appropriate and checking any vocabulary as necessary.

> **Answers**
> **b** (home-made) bread   **c** 110   **d** a (little) notice
> **e** Canada   **f** (fairly) wet/rainy   **g** back   **h** empty
> **i** his uncle   **j** landlady

6 Let students discuss the questions for a few minutes in pairs or small groups and then invite them to share their opinions round the class.

Older classes may have a discussion based on their own experiences of travelling, working abroad or volunteering.

《Activity》 Word-building Snap

The game is played in small groups (or pairs) of students. Pair work will probably require more teacher monitoring and arbitration. Play one round with a group to demonstrate what they have to do.

Photocopy, cut up and give out the sets of cards and the dictionaries (see Preparation). One student (Student A) has Set 1 face down and the others have Set 2, divided as equally as possible among the group, also face down.

Student A turns over the first card of Set 1. Each of the other students turns over one card in turn. If anyone thinks the two words combine to make a new word, they say *Snap* and then say a sentence with the word in it. If the others accept this as correct, the student scores a point and the group writes down the word. Disputed words can be checked in a dictionary, or with you. If the word does not exist, or if someone says *Snap* but cannot produce a sentence, they do not get a point.

If there is no combination possible, students with the cards in Set 2 continue to turn over their cards until a word can be made. Then Student A turns over the next card and the process is repeated.

When the group reaches the last card in Set 2, those cards are shuffled and redistributed. This can be done as often as time allows, or until the group reaches the end of Set 1. The winner is the student who scores the most points.

Later, when the game is over, each group adds up the number of words they wrote down to see which group found the most.

Language focus

Adverbs at the beginning of sentences

1 Explain that the adverbs in these sentences apply to the meaning of the whole sentence rather than just the verb and that they express the speaker's attitude.

Do this exercise orally with the whole class, drawing attention to the stress patterns. *Luckily, fortunately, actually* and *obviously* are all stressed on the first syllable; *unfortunately, unluckily* and *surprisingly* are all stressed on the second syllable; *of course* and *in fact* are stressed on the last syllable.

> **Answers**
> **b** Obviously   **c** Of course   **d** Unfortunately
> **e** Actually   **f** Surprisingly   **g** In fact

2 Check that students understand all the adverbs, especially those which are false friends in some languages (e.g. *actually*). Draw attention to the adverbs which mean the same (*luckily = fortunately; in fact = actually; obviously = of course; unluckily = unfortunately*).

Point out that when writing, we separate the adverb from the sentence by a comma.

You may like to give out photocopies of the recording script (see Preparation) for students to find and underline the sentences with the adverbs in.

3 Ask students to write the answers individually (for homework if preferred) and then to compare answers in pairs, correcting any errors they spot.

4 Ask students to choose two adverbs from Exercise 1 and write a pair of sentences for each one like the sentences in Exercise 3.

Reflexive pronouns

Language presentation

Students keep their books closed. Write on the board:

You obviously enjoyed you.

We needed to know how to look after us.

She helped me to write a little notice about me.

Ask the students if these sentences are correct English.

Elicit/Supply *yourself/ourselves/myself* and correct the sentences on the board. Explain that when the object of the verb is the same as the subject we must use this kind of pronoun, called a reflexive pronoun.

Elicit/Supply the reflexive forms for *I (myself), you* (singular) *(yourself), he (himself), she (herself), it (itself), we (ourselves), you* (plural) *(yourselves)* and *they (themselves).*

1 Do the first three sentences with the whole class, then let them finish it individually. Go through the answers.

Answers
b talking to yourself **c** hurt herself **d** help yourselves
e didn't enjoy ourselves **f** ask myself
g look after themselves

2 This exercise could be done in pairs or could be homework, if time is short.

 Grammar spot *Each other / themselves*

Answers
a Picture 1 **b** Picture 2

3 Ask students to use their own ideas to illustrate the difference between *hurt themselves* (e.g. two people falling over) and *hurt each other* (e.g. fighting) by drawing (or describing) cartoons.

Each, every, all

Language presentation

Point out that *every* and *each* are often used interchangeably.

If appropriate, students could be taught the semantic difference between *every* (means *all members of a set*) and *each* (emphasises that members of a set are viewed separately), e.g.

The sun shone every day last week.

The guide gave us some information about each city when we arrived in it.

All can of course also be followed by *of*; this is omitted here as it is not essential at this level, but could be mentioned if appropriate.

Discuss the difference between *every day* (a series of days) and *all day* (a whole day). This is revision from Unit 16.

 Grammar spot *Every, each, all*

Look at the Grammar spot examples with the class and ask them to complete the notes with you.

Answers
a
We use *each* and *every* + a *singular* countable noun.
We use *each of* + a *plural* countable noun.
We use *all* + a *plural* noun or an uncountable noun.

b
All day means *a complete day*.
Every day means *more than one day*.

The following exercise can be done for homework.

Answers
b each **c** every **d** All **e** all **f** each
g all **h** each

«Pronunciation»

This practises making and distinguishing between the sounds /eə/ and /ɪə/.

1 Model the sounds /eə/ (as in *pair*) and /ɪə/ (as in *near*). Practise them round the class. Ask students to identify them in the sentence in their books.

Answers
/eə/: chair /ɪə/: Here

2 **3** 21 Play the recording for students to repeat, pausing as necessary. Then ask them to mark the words containing the two sounds in different colours. ◀◀ You may need to play the recording again. Go through the answers and ask them to put the words into the correct columns. Draw attention to the fact that /ɪə/ is almost

always spelt *ear* or *eer* (*here* being the main exception) and /eə/ is usually spelt *air* or *are*, but there are important exceptions (*ere* and *eir* are also possible). If students confuse *there* and *their*, teach them that *there* is spelt like *here* and *where* and it belongs in the same group of words about place.

Answers

/eə/	/ɪə/
rarely	*fear*
fair	beard
hair	dear
care	near
stairs	appear
There	volunteers
pears	engineer
Where	steered
pairs	
carefully	

Recording script

a   He rarely feels fear.
b   He's got fair hair and a beard.
c   Take care on the stairs, dear.
d   There's a box of pears near the door.
e   Where did they appear from?
f   The volunteers worked in pairs.
g   The engineer steered the old car carefully.

3   When students have finished, ask them to work in pairs and take turns to say the sentences and listen to each other's pronunciation.

Using the passive

1   Look together at the two pairs of sentences and remind students as necessary of the passive forms and the use of *by* for the agent (see Unit 24).

Do the exercise round the class, discussing any problems as they arise.

Answers
b paid me.   c buried the buildings for hundreds of years.
d employed me.   e will encourage our listeners.

2   Read the email with the class.

Answer
Chris feels he was doing something useful.

3   Let students do the exercise in pairs or for homework and correct it round the class. If appropriate, you may wish to mention briefly the fact that the passive is often used in more formal English.

Answers
b are started (by tourists)
c was cleaned (by volunteers)
d were collected
e will be employed (by the government)
f are damaged (by pollution)
g will not / won't be spoiled

《Activity》 Eco-questionnaire   PET Speaking Part 4

1   Begin by discussing the meaning of the title of the questionnaire (on page 203 in the Student's Book). Read the questionnaire with the class, discussing the meaning of each question.

2   If possible, let students use the questionnaire with another class or people such as their families. If they are doing it themselves, have them work in pairs, interviewing each other, and remind them to be strict about truthfulness. The people who score the highest marks are the people who care most about the environment; the people with the lowest marks are the people who care least about the environment. There may be some comment about the way the Key is scored. Ask the class to discuss its fairness.

Write the scores on the board and ask the class to suggest advice for people with low scores. Use the opportunity to revise giving advice (Unit 9).

3   Have a short discussion about the three kinds of people students are asked to write about. Ask some questions to give them ideas, if necessary. For example, for question **a** you could ask: *Is this the kind of person who buys lots of new clothes every week? Does this kind of person own a large, fast car? Does this kind of person love walking in the country?* You may wish to teach/revise words such as *environment, pollution, ecology* and *recycle* at this point, depending on the level of interest in the class.

Ask students to draft sentences in pairs and then invite them to compare what they have written with each other.

Exam folder 27

SB pages 178–179

Reading Part 2

Look at the Summary box and the Check! questions and answer them together.

> **Answers**
> a five
> b eight
> c three (students do not need to understand every word of every text but they need to read each text carefully)
> d no
> e underline the important information
> f that the answer contains everything that the person wants

Ask students to do the task in nine minutes. They may feel they need more time than this as there is a heavy reading load in this part but they should be encouraged not to spend too much time on it.

Look at the Exam Advice box together.

> **Answers**
> 1 C   2 A   3 E   4 F   5 D

When you have checked the answers, you may like to go through the questions together if students have made mistakes, underlining the information in the answer texts and discussing why other texts are wrong.

> **Corpus spot**   *Travel, trip* and *journey*
>
> These words are frequently misused by PET students. *Travel* and *journey* may also be false friends. Looking them up in a good English–English dictionary and discussing some of the examples may be helpful.
>
> > **Answers**
> > a trip   b journey   c travel

28 What would you do?

In this unit:

Grammar	Second conditional
Functions and vocabulary	Celebrity jobs; expressions with prepositions
Pronunciation	Auxiliaries
PET skills	Giving opinions (Speaking test); understanding vocabulary in context; scanning (Reading Part 2)
Revision	*It could be*, etc. (Units 13 and 24); giving opinions, agreeing and disagreeing (Unit 19); *if* and *when* and first conditional (Unit 26)
Exam folder	Listening Part 2
Writing folder	Writing Part 1

Preparation

Activity *A desert island* Provide pieces of paper for students to write on and give in to you.
Exam folder 28 Make copies of the recording script (from CD-ROM or webpage) for students.

SB pages 180–183

Introduction

1   Look at the photographs of famous people and discuss who they are and why they are famous.

2   Ask students to work in groups to match the adults to the photographs of them when they were children.

Remind students of how to agree and disagree and say what they think. Look at the expressions in their books.

Answers
a 3 David Beckham   b 1 Kate Winslet   c 5 Madonna
d 2 Barack Obama   e 4 Prince Harry

3   Each group reports back and compares answers.

4   Look at the skeleton sentences in the book and discuss which sentences students will make with *when* (*grow up* – there's no question about this!) and which with *if* (all the others, unless they are absolutely sure, e.g. a prince could say *When I become king ...*). This is revision from Unit 26. Choose one of the photographs and say some sentences using first conditional structures, e.g. someone might say *When I grow up, I'll be a famous Hollywood actor. If I earn lots of money, I'll have three houses in different countries.*

Now ask students to choose one of the people in the photographs and write some sentences using the first conditional. Ask a few students to read theirs out and see if other students can guess who they are talking about.

EXTRA
If students are interested, they (and you) could bring in photographs of themselves as babies / small children. You could pin them up and get the other students to guess who they are.

Reading

PET Reading Part 2

Ask students if they can guess what a celebrity is (a famous person) – some of the people in the photographs on page 180 are celebrities. Students need to know this word before they start reading. Ask them to look at the names of the jobs at the top of the article and guess what they mean. If they can't guess, they should be able to after they have read the texts.

1   Students read the paragraphs to themselves and try to match them to the jobs in the box. They are scanning, so they don't need to understand every word.

Answers
A celebrity chef   B stylist   C fashion designer
D personal assistant   E personal trainer
F bodyguard

2   Put students into small groups to discuss the follow-up questions and any words or expressions they don't know.

Answers
Job A
1   to do the cooking themselves (not literally to get their hands dirty)
2   I take care of
Job B
3   choose clothes for the celebrity
4   because a celebrity has to look wonderful at all times
Job C
5   everyone wants to see him/her
6   new and modern
7   celebrities might not want his/her clothes any more
Job D
8   all the jobs the celebrity doesn't want to do
9   when the celebrity is angry about something

Job E
10 because the celebrity wants to look good
11 the celebrity might fall in love with the trainer
Job F
12 because he/she has to make sure the celebrity is safe and always be ready for a problem
13 he/she sometimes has to work long hours

Go through the answers and vocabulary.

Look at the Vocabulary spot. Ask students if this expression exists in their own languages. Students may be able to think of other expressions like this that they have come across in English.

3 Students work in groups to think of the advantages and disadvantages of being famous. Some are mentioned in the texts. Have a brief discussion about whether students would like to be famous.

Suggested answers
Possible advantages
Having lots of money
Not having to do boring jobs, e.g. cleaning
Travel
Being on TV
Having expensive clothes

Possible disadvantages
Photographers following you
People writing things about you that aren't true
Not having a normal life
Not being able to trust people
Having to stay famous

Language focus
Second conditional

Language presentation

Look at these sentences together.
A: If I work in the restaurant every evening, I'll save enough money for a holiday.
B: If I worked for a pop star, I would go to exciting places.

Ask students which speaker is talking about something which will probably happen (Speaker **A**). Ask how likely the situation is for **B** (unlikely or imaginary: he/she doesn't work for a pop star and doesn't think he/she ever will).

Check students know that *would* can become *'d*.

Write the second sentence the other way round: *I'd go to exciting places if I worked for a pop star* and ask if it still has the same meaning (yes). Ask what is different (the comma is omitted when the *if* clause comes second).

Ask students to complete the Grammar spot.

 Grammar spot   Second conditional
Students complete the Grammar spot.

> If I *had* a stylist, I *would look* good all the time.
> I *would look* good all the time if I *had* a stylist.

1 Together, think of any other jobs that involve working with famous people, e.g. football/tennis coach, chauffeur, gardener, nanny, hairdresser, secretary, pilot, accountant, housekeeper, manager, etc. Choose one job and make some sentences together using the second conditional. Look at the example and point out that after *if*, either *was* or *were* can be used with *I*, *he*, *she* and *it*.

Give students a minute to think and then ask students around the class to make some similar sentences. Write some of them on the board.

2 This exercise checks that students have understood which verb forms to use.

Answers
b If I *didn't have* so much homework to do, I *'d go* out with my friends.
c I *'d buy* a new computer if I *had* plenty of money.
d If I *owned* a plane, I *'d fly* in it every day.
e If Andrea *got up* earlier, she *wouldn't be* late every day.
f If my neighbours *were* friendly, I *'d invite* them to my party.
g If Suzi *was/were* old enough, she *'d learn* to drive.
h My brother *would teach* you the guitar if he *had* time.

3 This exercise could be homework, if time is short. Warn students that they are first and second conditionals mixed.

Suggested answers
c I would fly it to school every day.
d you wouldn't come to this class.
e I'll be very tired tomorrow.
f I'll never finish it.
g everyone would fall in love with you.
h I'd have more free time.

Expressions with prepositions

1 Ask students to try and remember the expressions from the texts in the Reading exercise.

Answers
b by **c** in **d** at on **e** in **f** in **g** at **h** in **i** at
j on **k** in **l** At **m** in

When they have finished, they can go back to the texts to check.

2 Students add the words to the circles. They are all from earlier units.

Look at the Vocabulary spot together.

«Pronunciation»

This practises recognising and deducing auxiliaries in speech. Auxiliaries often carry the meaning of a verb but they can be difficult to hear, so the meaning has to come from the rest of the sentence. In addition, some auxiliaries are represented by the same contraction.

1 Ask students to complete the exercise.

Answers

b 've have **c** 'll will **d** 'd had **e** 'd would
f 're are **g** 's has **h** 'll will **i** 's is

2 **3 22** Play the recording. Check the answers.

Recording script

a If I had a car, I'd lend it to you.
b Wait for me – I've almost finished watching this programme.
c They'll be late if they don't hurry.
d They'd already arrived when I got there.
e If she lived near her friends, she'd be happier.
f You're not listening to me, are you?
g This is the first time he's played the trumpet in public.
h We'll ring you if we go swimming next weekend.
i She's coming home late tonight.

Discuss which auxiliaries are represented by the same contraction – *'d* is short for *had* and *would*, and *'s* is short for *is* and *has*.

3 **3 23** Students listen and repeat parts of the sentences.

Recording script

a I'd lend it to you
b I've almost finished
c They'll be late
d They'd already arrived
e She'd be happier
f You're not listening
g He's played the trumpet in public
h We'll ring you
i She's coming home

4 **3 24** Students listen to the recording and try to hear the differences.

Answers and recording script

a They'd already left.
b He'll help you.
c The pop star's leaving. ✓
d It'd be too dark to see anything. ✓
e I'd seen the programme before.
f She's got plenty of money.

«Activity» A desert island

This continues practice of the second conditional.

1 Check students remember *desert*. Ask different students to read aloud what each person says. Ask why the people don't say *If I go to a desert island, I will …* (because it is an imaginary situation).

2 Ask each student to write two sentences on a piece of paper (see Preparation). Warn them that the sentences will be read by other people in the class later, so that they don't write anything too personal which might be embarrassing. Give an example yourself and write it on the board.

If I went to a desert island, I'd take my TV and a very long book to read. I'd miss my friends and my family.

Collect the pieces of paper in.

3 Put students in groups and give each group some of the pieces of paper. They should try to guess who each piece of paper belongs to.

Bring the whole class together. One person from a group identifies the owner of one of their pieces of paper and asks about some of the things on the paper, e.g. *Mario, if you went to a desert island, would you take a football? Would you miss your computer?* to try to determine if they have chosen the right person. After asking the questions, they can decide if they have chosen the right person or not. Do as many as you have time for.

4 Each student should think of a favourite star and write down what they would say. Make several students reporters who go round the class interviewing the stars. The stars should say what they would take if they went to a desert island and what they would miss. Alternatively, get students to work with a partner. They should each think of a star but should not tell their partner who they have chosen. Each student writes the sentences for his/her star, then reads them out to his/her partner, who guesses who the star is.

This continues practice of the second conditional.

1 Check students understand the questions and options, then ask them to answer for themselves.

2 They exchange their answers with a partner and mark each other's quizzes using the scores on page 184. Find out if students agree with the summary about themselves.

EXTRAS

Students could work in pairs. One student shuts their book and the other student asks them Questions 1–3 from the quiz. They give their answer without having the book in front of them. They then swap roles for Questions 4–6.

If there is time, students could write some more questions to add to the questionnaire, working out the scores, then they could give it to some other students in another class to try.

Exam folder 28

SB pages 184–185

Listening Part 2

Look at the Summary box about this part of the exam. Ask students to answer the Check! questions in pairs.

Answers
a what you will hear / who will speak
b choose A, B or C
c read the questions (candidates are given 45 seconds to do this)
d they give you some idea about what you will hear
e twice
f wait till the second time you hear it, and if you still don't know, guess

Look at the Exam Advice box. Students should learn to leave a question and move on. They will have a second chance.

1 **3 25** Play the recording twice and then check the answers.

Answers
1 B 2 C 3 A 4 C 5 B 6 A

2 **3 25** ◁ Give each student a photocopied script (see Preparation) and play the recording again. Even if they have got all the answers right, it is useful for them to see what was actually said and how it compares with the question. Ask them to underline the words in the script which give them the answer to each question. **Note:** These are underlined in the recording script.

3 By circling the words that show the other options are wrong, students will see that they can arrive at the correct answer by eliminating the other two. **Note:** These are circled in the recording script.

Recording script

You will hear a radio interview with a young actor called Paul.

For each question, put a tick (✓) in the correct box.

Interviewer: This week we're interviewing Paul Mason, who became famous for playing the good-looking teenage son called Frank in the soap opera, *Along our street*. Paul, when did you first join the soap opera?

Paul: I started playing Frank (in the soap opera in 2007. I was just 15 years old). I'd been on TV a couple of times before. I was in a children's drama series when I was about ten years old but I didn't actually say anything and (I appeared on a quiz show, again for children's TV,) (when I was about 13).

Interviewer: So, did you enjoy acting in the soap opera?

Paul: I did – the boy I played, Frank, was very much like me – he had a (nicer personality than me), though. But I played Frank for four years and I really needed to get experience and have the chance to play (lots of different) (parts). After two or three years it was time to move on. But Frank was such a big part in the soap opera, it was difficult for me to leave.

Interviewer: You became very popular, especially with teenage girls.

Paul: I had lots of girlfriends, yes. And (I loved people) (coming up to me in the street), wanting my autograph. I was always busy, (never tired) – I didn't need much sleep. Everyone wanted to be my friend but it was only because I was rich and famous. They weren't real friends. I didn't know who I could trust and I wasn't ready for that. I was too young.

Interviewer: So what did you do next?

Paul: I was in a play in a London theatre and because I'd spent so long in front of a TV camera I did everything wrong on the stage – I'd never acted in front of an audience before and (it frightened me). I got better but it was (much more difficult for me than TV).

Interviewer: And what about the future?

Paul: (I'm giving TV a break. I've made a film) called *The Last Journey*, which will be in the cinemas in two months. But I'm hoping to do more plays in theatres. I intend to be one of the actors people will remember – not just on TV but for playing serious parts on the stage too.

Interviewer: How do your parents feel about your success?

Paul: Neither of them are actors but they knew that was what I wanted to do and (they've always supported me.) (They're very proud of me.) They're anxious, though, that suddenly one day I won't have any work or it will change me – it's not like working in an office which is what they both do.

Writing folder

Writing Part 1

This practises sentence transformations. In the exam, there are only five sentences plus an example. The sentences in this folder give students practice in a range of structures.

Look at the Exam Advice box and then ask students to do the questions.

> **Answers**
> 2 remember to (tests *forget = didn't remember*)
> 3 do you have / have you got (tests reported to direct speech)
> 4 lent (tests *borrow something from someone / lend something to someone*)
> 5 are (tests *X has got = there are*)
> 6 whose (tests relative pronoun *whose*)
> 7 too expensive (tests *can't afford = too expensive (for us)*)
> 8 buy anything (tests irregular past tense; *nothing = not anything*)
> 9 owns (tests passive to active)
> 10 but (tests conjunctions *although* and *but*)
> 11 we hurry (tests *if* + negative = *unless* + positive)
> 12 tired (that) (tests *so* + adjective and *such a* + noun)

Corpus spot   *Borrow* and *lend*

This practises the transformation in Question 4 above.

> **Answers**
> a Could you <u>lend</u> me that book for two weeks?
> b ✓
> c I <u>lent</u> Tom my bicycle.
> d ✓
> e When I got home, I didn't have the beautiful scarf my mother had <u>lent</u> me.

Corpus spot   *There is/are*

This practises the transformation in Question 5 above.

> **Answers**
> a There <u>are</u> a lot of interesting historic buildings.
> b There <u>are</u> three films to choose from.
> c In the centre there <u>is</u> a new club.
> d There <u>are</u> a lot of things to do in my town.
> e You could go to the National Museum where <u>there</u> is a painting by Michelangelo.
> f Sometimes there <u>is</u> a special guest on the show.
> g There <u>are</u> two cupboards in my room.
> h We will go to a big park where <u>there</u> is a roller coaster.

29 What's on the menu?

TOPIC: Food and restaurants

In this unit:	
Grammar	*So do I; nor/neither do I*; polite question forms
Functions and vocabulary	Asking politely; food; restaurants; apologising
Pronunciation	Unstressed words
PET skills	Negotiating, agreeing and disagreeing (Speaking Part 2)
Revision	Reported questions (Unit 25); making decisions together
Exam folder	Reading Part 4; Speaking Parts 3 and 4

Preparation

Introduction, Exercise 2 If possible, provide poster-size pieces of paper and marker pens so that lists can be made large enough to be displayed, instead of just passed round the class.

Activity *Agreeing and disagreeing* Photocopy and cut up the pictures (on page 188).

SB pages 186–189

Introduction

1 This can be a race against time, if appropriate. About five minutes should be long enough. Ask students to work alone to find as many things as they can in the photograph which begin with the letters at the top of the table. If necessary, let them use dictionaries.

Ask the student who has the most items to come up and write the answers on the board. Let another student take over if he or she makes a mistake or spells a word incorrectly. Repeat with the other letters.

Suggested answers (other answers also possible)
B bananas, bread, bowl, basket
C cucumber, cheese, chicken, cups, crisps, cola, cake, chocolate
E, F, G egg, fizzy drink, fruit, fruit juice, fork, glass, grape
K, L knife, lemon, lemonade, lettuce
O, T oil, onion, orange, tart, tomato
P pear, pepper, pie, plate, pizza
S sausage, strawberry, spoon, salad, salt

Ask if there are any things in the photograph that are not written up (e.g. *apples*, *meat*). They could also suggest names for types of meat, e.g. *beef*, *salami*, etc. if they wish. Call out some of the words and ask individual students to point to them in their books to check they know what they mean.

PET Speaking Part 2

2 This exercise practises choosing and negotiating.

Check that students understand *picnic* and offer a context if appropriate, e.g. *You are going to a pop concert in a park and you plan to eat before it starts.*

Students negotiate planning a picnic using the food in the photograph and write their list of food on a piece of paper (poster-size if available: see Preparation) with quantities.

This may be a good point to teach/revise *loaf*, *slice* and *packet* and to check students know measurements in English, e.g. *grams* and *kilograms*. Give each group a number to identify them, which they write at the top of their list.

3 Display the poster lists or pass the lists from one group to another so the whole class sees every list. They should discuss the questions in their book. Have a class discussion about their conclusions.

4 Ask students to unravel the anagrams. Check they understand all the words.

Answers
b oil **c** chips **d** coffee **e** cream **f** fish
g hotdog **h** jam **i** milk **j** sugar **k** cabbage
l peanut **m** salt **n** spinach **o** mushroom

5 Students work in groups to divide food into *healthy* and *unhealthy*. Some of the answers are debatable, so encourage students to discuss their answers, e.g. *milk*, *peanut*, *oil* and *salt*.

One group writes their answers on the board and the rest of the students say whether they agree or not.

Look at the Vocabulary spot together. Other adjectives which take *un-* include *comfortable*, *pleasant*, *friendly*, *kind*.

If students are interested, have a brief discussion about healthy eating, and about fast food compared to traditional meals, etc.

This could be homework. These are common PET mistakes which can lose marks.

Answers
a We decided to <u>have</u> our dinner in a pizzeria.
b What about <u>having</u> a cup of coffee together?
c That restaurant is the best place to <u>have</u> a romantic meal.
d After the film we'll <u>have</u> a drink in the bar.
e We went to the beach and <u>had</u> an ice cream there.

Listening

1 Tell students to look at the pictures. Discuss briefly where the people are and where students would prefer to eat.

2 **3 26** Ask students to listen to the five conversations and write the number of the conversation next to the appropriate picture, **a**, **b**, **c**, **d** or **e**. Play the five conversations.

Answers
a 4   b 5   c 3   d 2   e 1

Recording script

Conversation 1
Alison: So, let's go and eat. I'm hungry.
Daniel: So <u>am I</u>. Where shall we go?
Alison: There are plenty of restaurants round here. Do you like Mexican food? Or what about Thai?
Beata: Can you tell me what Thai food tastes like? I've never tried it.
Daniel: No, nor <u>have I</u>.
Alison: Well, I love it. It's quite spicy.
Beata: Oh, is it? I'm not very keen on hot spices.
Daniel: No, neither <u>am I</u>.
Alison: OK. Er, so not Thai or Mexican. There's a good Italian restaurant further up the road.
Daniel: Oh, I love Italian food.
Beata: Really? So <u>do I</u>.
Alison: Right, let's go there then.

Conversation 2
Graham: Good evening. Table for two?
Greta: For three, please. We're meeting a friend.
Graham: Certainly. Inside or outside?
Greta: I don't like sitting outside.
Brigitte: Neither <u>do I</u>, so inside, please.
Graham: Thank you. There's a table just there, near the window.
Brigitte: That'll be all right.

Greta: Yes, it's fine.
Graham: Would you like to order any drinks before your friend arrives?
Brigitte: Er, yes. I'm really thirsty. I can't wait.
Greta: Neither <u>can I</u>.
Brigitte: I'd like an orange juice, please.
Tina: Hi! Sorry I'm late. I got lost.
Brigitte: So <u>did I</u>. It's hard to find, isn't it? Never mind. Come and sit down. We're just getting some drinks.
Tina: I'll have a mineral water, I think.
Greta: So <u>will I</u>.
Graham: Still or sparkling?
Tina: Still, please.
Graham: Thank you. I'll bring the menu in a moment.
Greta: Thank you.

Conversation 3
Bob: Now, what are we going to have?
Carl: What do you recommend?
Bob: They do home-made soup, that's usually very nice. And there's always a hot dish.
Carl: Oh, yeah. I see. 'Today's special', it says on the board. <u>Can you explain what that is?</u>
Bob: It says underneath, look. Lancashire Hotpot.
Carl: It sounds a bit funny. <u>I'd like to know if it's got meat in it.</u>
Bob: It's made of lamb with potatoes and onions, cooked for a long time. A traditional dish from the north of England. Very good on a cold day like today.
Carl: Oh, right. I'm a vegetarian so I won't have that.
Bob: OK. We'll ask for a menu. Would you like a starter?
Carl: No, thanks. I'll just have a main course. I don't want to fall asleep this afternoon.
Bob: No, neither do I. OK, now, where's the waiter?

Conversation 4
Gary: Yes?
Tammy: One burger, one milkshake, one vegeburger and one cappuccino, please.
Gary: What flavour milkshake?
Tammy: Oh, sorry. Rosie, <u>do you know what flavour milkshake your friend wants?</u>
Rosie: Oh, she didn't say.
Tammy: Oh, typical.
Rosie: <u>Can you tell us what flavours you've got?</u>
Gary: Chocolate, strawberry, banana and vanilla.
Rosie: She'd like strawberry, I think.
Gary: OK. Now do you want to eat in or take away?
Tammy: Take away. Oh, and one portion of chips.
Gary: OK. That's thirteen pounds twenty.
Tammy: Here you are.
Gary: Enjoy your meal.
Rosie: Thank you.

Conversation 5

Nigel: Excuse me!

Marco: Yes? Can I help you?

Nigel: I hope so. You see, we ordered a tuna salad and a baked potato with cheese fifteen minutes ago! <u>Can you find out if there's a problem?</u>

Marco: I'm sorry, we are very busy, as you see.

Nigel: But we said we were in a hurry and the waitress promised to be quick.

Laura: <u>Can you find out if we're going to get our food soon?</u> We have to catch a train at one fifty-five.

Marco: OK. <u>Can you remember what your waitress looked like?</u>

Nigel: Oh, here she comes now.

Anna: I'm ever so sorry. Someone else took your order by mistake.

Nigel: All right. Thank you. Now we can eat.

Laura: This potato isn't properly cooked. Part of it is almost raw!

Nigel: Oh, no. Well, that's it. I'm going to see the manager.

Language focus

So do I and *neither/nor do I*

1 Students read through Conversations 1 and 2 and try to fill the spaces.

> **Answers**
> **Conversation 1 b** have I   **c** am I   **d** do I
> **Conversation 2 e** do I   **f** can I   **g** did I   **h** will I

2 **3 26** ◄) Play the recording for the first two conversations again for students to see if they were correct.

Check vocabulary as necessary, e.g. *spicy, hot spices, What does X taste like, mineral water, still, sparkling,* etc.

> ### ⬇ Corpus spot   👁
>
> ***To be thirsty, lucky,* etc. + verb**
>
> > **Answers**
> > We <u>were</u> hungry so we stopped for a meal.
> > We use *to be* before adjectives such as *thirsty, hot, cold, lucky, sad, afraid*.
> >
> > **a** At first, I <u>was</u> afraid, but then I saw my family.
> > **b** We <u>were</u> lucky because the weather was very nice.
> > **c** I <u>was</u> very surprised when she told me.
> > **d** I'll <u>be</u> cold if I don't wear my scarf.
> > **e** When I read it I <u>was</u> shocked.
> > **f** I <u>am</u> hot and I want to go for a swim.

Language presentation

Ask students when we use *So* (to agree when the previous statement is positive) and when we use *Neither* or *Nor* (to agree when the previous statement is negative – there is no difference in meaning between *neither* and *nor*).

Point out that the verb and subject are inverted.

Build up a list on the board of the different auxiliaries used in the conversations.

It may be useful to revise briefly a few short answers (Unit 9). Draw attention to the parallel with these forms.

⬇ Grammar spot   *So/nor/neither*

Complete the Grammar spot orally round the class and then ask students to write the answers.

> **Answers**
>
> | | |
> |---|---|
> | I've really enjoyed this evening. | So have I. |
> | I've never tried this before. | Neither/Nor have I. |
> | They enjoyed the main course. | So did I/we. |
> | We didn't want a big meal. | Neither/Nor did I. |
> | I'll come here again. | So will I. |
> | I won't finish all this. | Neither/Nor will I. |
> | He's going to give the waiter a tip. | So am I. |
> | I can't eat any more. | Neither/Nor can I. |
> | We'd like to come here again. | So would I. |

PET Speaking Part 2

≪Activity≫ Agreeing and disagreeing

Photocopy the pictures and cut them up (see Preparation). Make extra sets for large classes. There must be enough for each student to have a card.

Offer statements for students to agree with or not, e.g. *I haven't got a computer. (Really? I have!); I like getting up early. (Really? I don't.); I'm not interested in pop music. (Really? I am.),* etc. Look at the instructions and examples in the Student's Book.

Go through a few of the cards to show that they can say whatever they like as long as it makes sense (albeit humorously, if they wish).

Give each student a card and tell them to circulate (in groups for classes of more than 20), making statements about themselves and the picture on the card. Whenever they meet someone and agree with each other's statements, they swap cards and start again.

If students cannot easily move about, they can work in pairs, taking turns to agree and disagree, then passing the cards on to the pair next to them.

Polite question forms

1 **3 26** ◀ Play Conversations 3, 4 and 5 again. Students underline anything in their books which is different from the recording (they read direct questions, but the recording has embedded questions).

Check vocabulary as necessary, e.g. *dish, traditional, lamb, potatoes, onions, starter, main course, milkshake, portion, tuna, raw* and *cooked.*

🔄 Grammar spot   Polite question forms

Students write the (direct) questions they have underlined in Conversations 3, 4 and 5 on the left-hand side of a sheet of paper.

3 26 ◀ Play the recording again and stop it when you come to each embedded question and ask students to tell you what they heard.

They write each embedded question next to the direct question.

Language presentation

Discuss when *if* is used (in *yes/no* questions). Make sure students notice the word order (like a statement). Point out that these are reported questions, and refer back to Unit 25 as necessary.

Ask why some sentences have question marks at the end (because they are introduced by direct questions).

Ask students why the embedded questions were used in the conversations (they are more polite).

2 Do this exercise orally round the class first. The writing could be done for homework.

≪Pronunciation≫

These exercises build on work done in Units 5, 18, 24 and 26.

1 **3 27** Ask students to listen to the recording and underline the sound /ə/. ◀ Check what they have underlined and replay the recording for them to repeat the phrase.

2 **3 28** Do the same with the next two phrases, replaying for students to repeat after you have checked what they have underlined. Draw attention to the pronunciation of *and, some, but* and *burgers.* Remind them about word stress (Unit 26).

3 **3 29** Ask students to work in pairs, reading the sentences and underlining where they think the sound /ə/ occurs in the sentences. Write the sentences on the board while they are working.

Play the recording for them to check what they have underlined, then ask individuals to come and underline the sound /ə/ on the board. The class can correct any mistakes or omissions. ◀ Unless they produce the sound /ə/ very easily, play the recording again for them to repeat while looking at the board.

Clean the board and ask them to shut their books. Play the recording again for them to repeat, pausing as necessary.

«Activity» Eating out

In small classes this can be a whole class activity. Check students understand the difference between eating *out* (not at home, but in a restaurant etc.) and eating *outside/outdoors* (in a garden or on a pavement etc.).

1 Help students to plan menus. Encourage them to include a variety of dishes from different countries if they can. Monolingual groups may get ideas from the picture on page 186 and from the conversations they have listened to. Allow L1 names of dishes where appropriate.

2, 3 Draw attention to the language in the table before students begin their role plays. The apologetic forms are formally polite.

If appropriate, act out the role of a tourist with one waiter for the class to see how you ask and order.

Make sure students change the role of waiter so that everyone gets a chance to practise asking, ordering and apologising.

Exam folder 29

SB pages 190–191

Reading Part 4

Look at the Summary box about this part of the exam together.
Ask students to think about the questions in the Check! box for a moment and discuss their answers.

Answers

a no (Questions 1 and 5 test information from the whole text. The others are in the order of information in the text.)

b yes (One or two words may give the answer to one of the detail questions.)

Ask students to do the task as if they were in the exam. Allow them nine minutes.

Answers

1 B   2 B   3 C   4 D   5 A

Speaking Part 3

Look at the Summary box about this part of the exam together.

1 Ask students in pairs each to choose one of the photographs (on page 204 in the Student's Book) and think about the questions.

Remind them of the questions they learnt in Exam folder 3. Look at the Exam Advice box. They should remember to describe the place as well as the people in the photograph.

Remind them of the expressions they learnt for when they don't know the name of something: *I don't know the word in English. It's a kind of X.*

2 Students work in pairs and take turns to describe one of the photographs. Tell them the first student must continue talking until you tell them to stop.

Stop the first student in each pair after one and a half minutes and point out that this is about the amount of time they will need to speak for in this part of the exam. Time the second student in the same way.

When they have finished, build up a description of each photograph with the whole class to get an overview of all the things they could talk about.

Speaking Part 4

Look at the Summary box about this part of the exam together.

1 Ask students to do this in pairs, then brainstorm with the whole class (see Exam folder 9).

2 Look at the Exam Advice box. It is important that students express themselves clearly and accurately in English, but everything they say need not be true.

Students can work in pairs to discuss the questions in their book. Tell the class that you will give them about three minutes, as in the exam.

Ask a few students to report back to the class.

TOPIC: Boys and girls

In this unit:	
Grammar	*hardly*; *before/after* + *-ing*
Functions and vocabulary	Informal language; saying goodbye
Pronunciation	Revision of /ʌ/, /ae/, /ɒ/, /ɑː/, /aʊ/, /ɔː/, /e/, /eɪ/, /ɪ/, /iː/, /ʊ/, /uː/, /ɜː/, /aɪ/, /əʊ/
PET skills	Sentence transformation (Writing Part 1); saying goodbye at the end of a Speaking test
Revision	Tenses (present simple, present continuous, *going to*, *will* future, past simple, past continuous, past perfect, passive); vocabulary of clothes, countries, musical instruments, colours, jobs, the body, furniture, school subjects, places, food, travel, sports, animals
Exam folder	Listening Part 4, Speaking Parts 3 and 4
Writing folder	Writing Parts 1, 2 and 3

Preparation

Activity *After doing that* ... Photocopy the cards (on page 189) – one set for a class of 15 students or fewer; otherwise two sets.

Pronunciation Photocopy the caller's cards (on page 190) and cut them up so that there is one set for each caller. Photocopy sufficient students' cards (also on page 190) for each student or pair to have a different card and cut them up. Have about ten plain 'counters' per student or pair.

Activity *Different topics* Photocopy and cut up the cards (on page 188) (letters of the alphabet cards and topic cards). Students will also need some blank pieces of paper.

Exam folder 30 Make copies of the recording script (from CD-ROM or webpage) for students.

Writing folder Photocopy the sample answers (on page 173).

SB pages 192–195

Introduction

Look at the photographs together and talk about what the people are doing.

---

1 Students write down individually which things they (would) like or wouldn't/don't like to do. Write the activities in a column on the left-hand side then make four more columns – two for boys (one for *like* and one for *don't like*) and two for girls (one for *like* and one for *don't like*). Do a hand count and note on the board how many people liked or didn't like any particular activity. See if any pattern emerges and discuss why some activities are more popular among boys, etc. If no pattern emerges, discuss if this is what was expected. If the class is single sex, follow the same procedure, then discuss what the missing sex would choose.

2 Revise school subjects and add any that students want to know. Students write down their three favourite subjects. In a mixed sex class, put students into groups of the same sex to compare their lists and see which subjects are the most popular. Compare the results as a class. Are they as expected – do boys tend to favour different subjects from girls? Are the results different from ten years ago, twenty years ago, etc.?

In a single sex class, make a list of the subjects in order of popularity and discuss what a list for the opposite sex would have on it.

3 Read through the statements together. Check vocabulary as necessary, e.g. *salary*, *physically*, *government*, *mixed* and *brave*.

Either discuss the statements as a class or give different groups a few statements to discuss before they report their discussion to the class.

Discuss the title of the unit. In many countries, little boys and girls are dressed in different colours. Should boy and girl babies be treated differently?

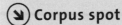

↘ Corpus spot   *Like* and *would like*

Answers
a I <u>would</u> like to hear from you soon.
b ✓
c I <u>would</u> like you to join me and my friends on Saturday.
d ✓
e Would you like <u>to</u> go to the cinema with me?
f ✓

Reading and Language focus

Revision of tenses

This revises the present simple, present continuous, *going to*, *will* future, past simple, past continuous, past perfect, passive, verbs and expressions followed by infinitive and *-ing*.

1 If you have a mixed sex class, get the boys to read Jake's diary entry for Monday and the girls to read Lucy's. If not, divide the class into two halves. They choose the correct verbs. They discuss in pairs what they have read about Jake and Lucy.

> **Answers**
> Jake really likes Lucy but he doesn't think she likes him. Lucy thinks Jake is a nice boy compared to the others but she doesn't know if he likes her.
> **Jake:** sit   speaks   notices   am going to ask   will say   was chosen   playing
> **Lucy:** whistle   think   smile   see   doesn't like   was picked   'll go

2 Students continue reading Jake or Lucy's diary entries, filling in the correct verbs and putting the entries in order. Do not correct them at this stage.

> **Answers**
> See Exercise 5.

3 Put students into groups or pairs with people who have read the same diary entries. They compare their answers and the order they have chosen. Do not try to correct answers at this stage – students get a chance to do this when they listen to the recording.

4 Students now work in pairs – one person who has read Jake's diaries and one person who has read Lucy's. They ask each other the questions to get an overall picture of what has happened. They can ask other questions if they want.

5 **3 30** Play the recording of Jake and Lucy reading their diaries. Students should now check their answers (the correct order) and the correct form of the verbs. Check vocabulary as necessary, e.g. *muscles, cool, your thing, fed up with, whistle, embarrassing, support, to bump into, my type, courage, make-up, mate.* ◼ You may need to play the recording more than once.

> **Answers**
> Jake   Tuesday C   Wednesday D   Thursday B   Friday E
> Lucy   Tuesday I   Wednesday J   Thursday H   Friday G
> **Jake**
> B: was looking   saw   had   ran
> C: came   scored   chatted   to ask   saying   'll write
> D: saw   laughed   were changing   like
> E: wants   thinks   'll ask
> **Lucy**
> G: didn't seem   to help   're meeting / going to meet
> H: ask   'll have   bumped   had just had   put
> I: watched   scored   chatted   had never played   will I do   isn't   going   'll be
> J: was talking   walked   to laugh/laughing

Recording script

Jake: Monday. I'm ordinary, I suppose – nothing special. Most important of all, not special enough for Lucy. Lucy is great – really pretty and always smiling. In class I <u>sit</u> as close to her as I can but she never <u>speaks</u> to me. I will sit there until she <u>notices</u> me. This term I <u>am going to ask</u> Lucy to go out with me, but I expect she <u>will say</u> no. I'm pleased I <u>was chosen</u> for the school football team. I'm looking forward to <u>playing</u> tomorrow.

Lucy: Monday. I'm fed up with boys. Honestly, when they <u>whistle</u> at you, they <u>think</u> they're really cool but they're just embarrassing. The only nice boy in our class is Jake, but I hardly know him. I always <u>smile</u> at him when I <u>see</u> him but I'm worried that he <u>doesn't like</u> me. Anyway, my mate, Sophie, told me that Jake <u>was picked</u> for the school football team last week, so maybe I'<u>ll go</u> and support the team tomorrow.

Jake: Tuesday. What a surprise! Lucy and her mate, Sophie, <u>came</u> to watch tonight's game! I <u>scored</u> a goal but Lucy hardly noticed me. I think she was just there to see Gary Smart. I <u>chatted</u> to Lucy and Sophie after the match. I still want <u>to ask</u> her to go out with me but I'm afraid of <u>saying</u> the wrong thing, so maybe I'<u>ll write</u> her a note instead.

Lucy: Tuesday night. Sophie and I <u>watched</u> Jake play football tonight and he <u>scored</u> a goal. Before going home we <u>chatted</u> to him. He said he <u>had never played</u> for the team before. I told Sophie I might ask Jake to go out with me. But what <u>will I do</u> if he <u>isn't</u> interested in <u>going</u> out with me? I'<u>ll be</u> so embarrassed.

Jake: Wednesday. Changed my mind about writing to Lucy. I <u>saw</u> her with her friends this morning, and they all <u>laughed</u> when I went past. I must be one big joke to them. I heard Gary Smart talking about Lucy while we <u>were changing</u> for football training. Lots of girls <u>like</u> him. I can't see why myself – unless muscles, cool clothes and a great haircut are your thing.

Lucy: Wednesday. I <u>was talking</u> about Jake with Sophie and the others today at school when he <u>walked</u> past. We all started <u>to laugh</u> because we were embarrassed. I hope Jake isn't mad with me.

Jake: Thursday. This morning, after coming out of the English class, I <u>was looking</u> for Lucy, when I <u>saw</u> her with Gary Smart. He was really close to her and he <u>had</u> his hand on her arm, so I was right. I'm sure they're going out together. I just <u>ran</u> out of the building.

Lucy: Thursday. I'm sorry we laughed at Jake yesterday. If I <u>ask</u> him for his help with the maths homework, I<u>'ll have</u> a chance to spend more time with him. I <u>bumped</u> into Gary Smart. He <u>had just had</u> a swim and he looked really pleased with himself. He even <u>put</u> his hand on my arm. He's really not my type.

Lucy: Friday. Finally found the courage to ask Jake about the maths homework. He <u>didn't seem</u> too pleased but he agreed <u>to help</u> me. We<u>'re meeting</u> in the library on Monday night, so I'll ask Sophie to do my hair and make-up.

Jake: Friday. Great. She's going out with Gary Smart, but she <u>wants</u> me to do her homework for her. I must be the class idiot. But perhaps if she <u>thinks</u> I'm clever, she<u>'ll ask</u> me for help again and we can become friends.

6 Ask students to predict what happens next.

3 **31** Play the recording of the rest of the diaries and ask students to answer the questions.

Answers
a because he talked about Gary Smart a lot
b because he was afraid she didn't like him
c in her maths book
d excited
e yes
f This is a story from a teenage magazine rather than true life.

Recording script

Lucy: Monday. Met Jake in the library and he was so sweet and funny and shy and clever and gorgeous! He talked a lot about Gary Smart. I thought maybe he was missing a football practice with him or something but then I realised that he thought Gary was my boyfriend! I told him that wasn't true and we had a great time after that talking and laughing. We did hardly any maths and then we walked home together.

Jake: Monday. I didn't ask Lucy to go out with me after we finished working in the library because I didn't want to spoil things. She said she likes smart, funny guys, so that means I'm not the one for her. But I can't forget her. Maybe a short note would be best …

Lucy: Tuesday. Wow! I got a letter from Jake!! After handing back my maths book at school, he walked away. When I opened it, there was a letter from him, saying he liked me and inviting me to go bowling. We're meeting after school tonight. I don't know what to wear or say, but I can't wait!

Jake: Wednesday. We went bowling and we had a drink in the café afterwards. I really think she likes me and wants to go out with me. I can't believe it. Life is great.

Lucy: Wednesday. We went bowling and then sat in the café talking. When we sat down I told him that I had been so pleased to get his note and that I felt the same as him. We both laughed. I'm meeting him tomorrow too.

Check vocabulary as necessary, e.g. *gorgeous* (used especially by girls talking about boys), *to spoil, bowling.*

(↘) Vocabulary spot

Look at the Vocabulary spot together. With a monolingual class, you could talk about expressions used mainly by young people in that language and then go on to look at these ones in English. There are a couple of others in the text: 'unless cool clothes and a great haircut are *your thing*' (if something is 'your thing' it's something you are specially interested in) and 'he was so sweet' (kind and thoughtful). Point out that these words are not normally used in written English except in diaries and magazines.

Answers
mad = angry   guy = boy/man*   smart = clever
mate = friend   cool = good
my type = the kind of boy/girl I like
*NB When *guys* refers to a group of people, it can sometimes include women too.

Hardly

Language presentation

Hardly + verb
Write this sentence on the board and ask students what *hardly* means (*almost not / only just*).

I hardly know him. (= I know him a little)

Point out that we don't use *not* with *hardly*. Ask about the position of *hardly* – it goes before the verb.

Write *I have spoken to her* and ask where *hardly* would go (between the auxiliary and the participle).

Hardly + noun
Write these sentences on the board and ask students what they mean.

I have hardly any time. (= almost no time)
We saw hardly anything. (= almost nothing)

Grammar spot *Hardly*

Students complete the Grammar spot.

> **Answers**
> *Hardly* + **verb**
> *Hardly* goes before the verb.
>
> *Hardly* + **noun**
> *Any* goes after *hardly* and before the noun.
> (also *anybody*, etc.)

1 Do the exercise together. It practises *hardly* + verb.

> **Answers**
> **b** I hardly (ever) see her   **c** I hardly slept
> **d** she hardly danced   **e** I hardly remember it

2 This exercise practises *hardly* + noun/pronoun. Look at sentence **a** together and then ask students to do sentences **b–f**.

> **Answers**
> **b** Hardly anybody/anyone   **c** hardly any
> **d** Hardly anybody/anyone   **e** hardly anything
> **f** hardly any

3 Students can write these and read them out or do them orally.

Before and *after -ing*

 Grammar spot   *Before* and *after -ing*

Look at the Grammar spot together.

> **Answers**
> The *-ing* form follows *after* and *before*.

PET Writing Part 1

1 Ask students to do the exercise, then check the answers.

> **Suggested answers**
> **b** After playing in the match, Jake talked to Lucy.
> **c** Before meeting Jake in the library, Lucy asked him for help with her maths.
> **d** After seeing Lucy with Gary, Jake felt sad.
> **e** Before going out with Jake, Lucy asked Sophie to do her hair.
> **f** After meeting Lucy in the library, Jake decided to write her a letter.
> **g** After getting a letter from Jake, Lucy told him she liked him.

2 Discuss a few ideas with the class before asking them to write their own sentences.

≪Activity≫ After doing that . . .

The whole class does this together (see Preparation). In a large class, it will be better to split students into groups of no more than 15 so the game doesn't become too difficult. The first student is given a pile of cards face down. He/She turns the top card over, e.g. *ride an elephant* and says *Yesterday, I rode an elephant*. He/She puts the card at the bottom of the pile and passes the pile to the next person, who says *After riding an elephant, I ate a burger* (activity on the next card). He/She puts the card at the bottom of the pile and passes it to the next person, who says *After riding an elephant and eating a burger, I fell asleep* (activity on the next card) and so on. By the time the pile gets to the fifteenth person, they will have to remember fifteen different activities. If someone forgets, move on to the next person. Keep going as long as the students can remember – you can go round a second time in a small class.

If students enjoy the game, you could play again and they could make up their own activities. It could also be done using *before* as an alternative.

≪Pronunciation≫

Play Rhyming Bingo to revise vowel sounds covered in the course: /ʌ/, /æ/, /ɒ/, /ɑː/, /aʊ/, /ɔː/, /e/, /eɪ/, /ɪ/, /iː/, /ʊ/, /uː/, /ɜː/, /aɪ/, /əʊ/

Students can play in pairs or groups. (Each student has a card, or the students can share one.) There must be one 'caller' for every six students (or pairs) so that each student (or pair) has a different student's card (see Preparation). Thus the game can be played by the whole class (with the teacher as caller), or in groups (with students taking turns to be caller). The caller has their cards in a shuffled pile face down, or in a bag.

To play Each student, or pair, has one student's card, face up, and access to the counters. The caller takes out one card at a time and reads it. Students check their cards, and if they find a word which has the same vowel sound as the called word, they cover it with a counter. The caller puts their cards aside in order. The winner is the first person to cover a horizontal row. The student reads out each word and the caller checks that it has the same sound as one of the words they have called. The caller's cards are then re-shuffled, the students exchange cards and the game is repeated as time allows.

⟪Activity⟫ Different topics

This activity revises vocabulary of clothes, countries, musical instruments, colours, jobs, the body, furniture, school subjects, places, food, travel, feelings, sports, animals, families.

Photocopy the cards (see Preparation) and put them into two piles – letters of the alphabet in one pile and topics in the other pile.

Put students into teams of four or five. Each team takes a sheet of paper.

Have a practice first. Hold up one letter and one topic and say they will have twenty seconds to write down as many words as they can which fit the topic and begin with the letter.

Carry on as long as appropriate, then go through the answers. Students can take turns to write on the board the words the teams call out and another student can take the scores. Students only get a point if the words are spelled correctly. They get two points if they have a word that no other team has.

Saying goodbye　　　　　　PET Speaking Part 4

This is the last exercise in the book, so it is appropriate to check students can say goodbye! Look at the different expressions and match them to the situations.

Answers
1 g　2 b　3 a　4 e　5 f　6 c　7 d

Exam folder 30

SB pages 196–197

Listening Part 4

Look at the Summary box about this part of the exam. Ask students to do the Check! questions in pairs.

Answers
a two
b read the questions

3 🔲32 Play the recording twice. Then, if it is helpful, give out the photocopied scripts (see Preparation) and get students to underline where the answers are.

Answers
1 B　2 A　3 A　4 B　5 B　6 B

Recording script

Look at the six sentences for this part.
You will hear a conversation between a boy, Andy, and a girl, Sarah, about dancing.
Decide if each sentence is correct or incorrect.
If it is correct, put a tick in the box under **A** for **YES**. If it is not correct, put a tick in the box under **B** for **NO**.

Sarah: Hi, Andy. Are you coming to the drama class?
Andy: Sorry, I'm busy.
Sarah: Not another computer class. You ought to do something different occasionally.
Andy: I only do that class on Thursdays now. I'm going to a dance class today.
Sarah: Really? I didn't know you were interested in dancing. Why haven't you ever said anything?
Andy: Well, nobody knows really, except my parents. My friends would think it was a huge joke. They prefer playing football.
Sarah: But there's nothing wrong with boys dancing, you know. I read somewhere that dancers are often fitter and stronger than footballers. It would be good for your friends to know – why not invite them to watch you dance one day, then they might understand.
Andy: I'm not sure.
Sarah: When did you start dancing?
Andy: When I was seven. My auntie, who's a ballet teacher, used to look after me, so she had to take me to her classes. I had to sit and watch. Then one day I persuaded her to let me join in. She wasn't very keen on the idea but I loved it.
Sarah: So, you've done classes ever since?

Andy: I stopped when I was about eleven. But three years ago I decided to join another class. Usually I'm the only boy but there are two other boys who sometimes go.

Sarah: That's nice for you.

Andy: I actually prefer it when they're not there because they're not really serious about it and I can't concentrate.

Sarah: So, you're really serious about it.

Andy: I want to go to the Dance Academy in London next year.

Sarah: Wow! And what do your parents think?

Andy: They're not keen. They don't think it's a good career. It only lasts a few years and it's difficult to get jobs. But I want to do it.

Sarah: Well, you must persuade them. If that's what you really want to do, you'll never forgive yourself if you don't try.

Andy: Thanks. I'll let you know what happens.

Speaking Part 3

Look at the Check! box and answer the questions together. Refer students to the Summary box.

Answers
a Remind them of the questions they have learnt to help them think of things to say (Exam folders 3, 8 and 29).
b Check they remember the expressions *a kind of* and *I don't know the word in English*.
c Each student will speak for about one and a half minutes.

Ask students in pairs to choose one photograph each (on page 205 in the Student's Book) and describe it to each other. Time them – about a minute each. Get some students to tell the class what they said so everyone has a chance to develop a bank of ideas of the kind of things they can talk about.

Look at the Exam Advice box together. They may not know much about dancing but they can still describe what the people look like, what clothes they are wearing, etc.

Speaking Part 4

Look at the Check! box and answer the questions together. Refer students to the Summary box.

Answers
a the other student   **b** invent some
c the conversation will last about three minutes

Ask students to work in pairs and discuss as many of the questions as they can. Time them for three minutes.

Look at the Exam Advice box together.

Writing folder

Writing Parts 1, 2 and 3

Ask students to work through the three tasks under exam conditions. Draw their attention to the Summary boxes. Allow 45 minutes for the three tasks.

Answers
Writing Part 1
1 such a   **2** as/so crowded   **3** we chose
4 were/was   **5** didn't include

Writing Part 2
Answers must cover the three points in the question. Structures and vocabulary must be appropriate and accurate. See page 173 for a photocopiable sample answer.

Writing Part 3
Deduct marks for serious errors of basic grammar (e.g. tenses, pronouns, spelling), for answers which are less than 90 words long and for serious irrelevancy. Award marks for accurate language, variety of structure and vocabulary and generally effective communication. See page 173 for photocopiable sample answers.

Units 25–30 | Revision

Speaking

1 Follow the procedure outlined on page 42 of the Teacher's Book.

Exercises 2–7 could be set for homework and discussed afterwards in class.

Vocabulary

2

Answers
b peanut **c** dessert **d** egg **e** pepper **f** glass
g bread **h** orange

Grammar

3

Answers
c I wanted to know when he had decided to be a football manager.
d I asked him what other jobs he had done.
e I asked him if/whether he would always work as a football manager.
f I wanted to know which countries he had visited.
g I asked him if he worked hard.
h I wanted to know how much money he earned.
i I asked him if he had any hobbies.
j I asked him what would happen to his job if the team lost again.

4

Answers
b all **c** too much **d** too many **e** When **f** hardly
g every **h** unless **i** enough **j** If if

5

Answers
b had **c** was/were **d** 'd/would stay **e** is
f 'll/will have **g** 'll/will catch **h** was/were
i 'd/would go **j** visit **k** 'll/will buy **l** spoke
m 'd/would be **n** get **o** 'll/will show

Vocabulary

6

Answers
b afford **c** store **d** size **e** try **f** fitting **g** matches
h fit **i** stock **j** bring **k** change **l** refund **m** receipt

Common mistakes

7

Answers
Dear Lizzie,
Thanks for the <u>beautiful</u> scarf. <u>It's</u> perfect. I had a great birthday with Emily <u>and</u> Paul. <u>At</u> lunchtime <u>we tried</u> the Mexican <u>restaurant</u> in the <u>shopping</u> mall. Have you ever <u>been</u> <u>there</u>? The food <u>was</u> <u>delicious</u> but it was <u>terribly</u> crowded.
I look forward to <u>hearing</u> from you.
<u>Love,</u>
Cornelia

Progress Test 5 | Key

1 B **2** C **3** C **4** A **5** A **6** B **7** A **8** B **9** A
10 C **11** C **12** B **13** B **14** A **15** B **16** B **17** C
18 B **19** C **20** A **21** B **22** B **23** B **24** C **25** A
26 receipt **27** destroy **28** environment **29** sausages
30 milkshake

Progress Test 5

Choose the correct answer, A, B or C.

1 Adrian wanted to know where .... the DVD player.
   A did you buy   B I had bought   C was bought

2 I'm afraid there aren't .... cups for everyone to have some coffee.
   A many   B much   C enough

3 May I .... on these shirts to see if they suit me, please?
   A pull   B wear   C try

4 If you buy the tickets, ... for the meal after the show.
   A we'll pay   B we'd pay   C we paid

5 The shop didn't have any black jeans .... stock.
   A in   B of   C on

6 No one will know my story .... you tell them.
   A if   B unless   C although

7 My boss .... this language course to me.
   A recommended   B influenced   C persuaded

8 The interviewer asked the singer if he .... always lived in California.
   A did   B had   C would

9 Can you send ...., please?
   A me an application form
   B to me an application form
   C an application form me

10 Luckily none of my friends hurt .... when our tent fell down.
   A ourselves   B himself   C themselves

11 If you .... near the sea, you'd probably swim more often.
   A live   B would live   C lived

12 I lost my father's favourite CD last week. .... I found it before he realised.
   A Actually   B Luckily   C Unfortunately

13 He'll certainly send us an email unless he .... our address.
   A would forget   B forgets   C will forget

14 The students were never .... danger while they were climbing the mountain.
   A in   B at   C on

15 What .... if we invited you to our party?
   A did you say   B would you say   C had you said

16 The archaeologists found the old city .... accident.
   A in   B by   C with

17 'I really enjoy learning folk songs.' 'So .... I.'
   A am   B have   C do

18 Can you .... me where the waiter put our coats?
   A say   B tell   C explain

19 Michaela hasn't phoned her parents. Nor .... I.
   A has   B had   C have

20 Which girl is responsible .... the actors' make-up?
   A for   B on   C to

21 I asked .... the students in the class to look for my notebook.
   A each   B all   C every

22 Would you like sparkling or .... mineral water?
   A flat   B still   C soft

23 After .... the email, he left the room.
   A read   B reading   C had read

24 Do you know how much ....?
   A cost these postcards   B do these postcards cost
   C these postcards cost

25 Goodbye and .... a safe journey!
   A have   B make   C go

Find one spelling mistake in each sentence. Write the correction in the space.

26 Obviously, you need the recept if you ask for a refund.
....

27 It's essential that we don't distroy any more forests.
....

28 Is the environment important to young people?
....

29 We can have mushrooms, sasauges or chicken.
....

30 It doesn't take many minutes to make a chocolate milkchake. ....

   © CAMBRIDGE UNIVERSITY PRESS 2010

Photocopiable sample answers

Sample answers for Writing folder Unit 8

Dear Emily.

Thank you for inviting me to the concert with you next Saturday. I'm sorry but I can't come with you because I'm going to the seaside for the weekend with my family.

I hope you enjoy it.

Best wishes,

Hans

Dear Tim,

I went to the city centre last Saturday. A friend gave me a lift on his motorbike. We went to the cinema and then to a café. Would you like to come with us next weekend?

All the best,

Jakub

Sample answer for Writing folder Unit 14

Dear Jenny,

I go shopping on Saturdays with my friends. There's one shop which is our favourite because it has fashionable clothes, but they aren't too expensive. I like buying T-shirts in bright colours. Last week I bought a red one and a yellow one. I usually wear jeans and trainers. I have three pairs of trainers and I'm saving my money to buy another pair. When I go out I sometimes wear a skirt and shoes with high heels. I don't usually wear a coat. I have a short blue jacket which I put on when it's very cold. Write to me soon.

Love,

Rose

Sample answers for Writing folder Unit 12

a

It was a key with the name of a bank on it. I took it to the bank. A man was talking to the manager. 'I must have my money!' he shouted.

'We need the key,' said the manager.

'Is this the key?' I asked.

They were very surprised. I explained where I found it.

b

I explored the shops and then walked home. I was happy until I reached Oxford Road. Suddenly I felt worried.

I couldn't remember the number of our house. All the houses were new. Which was our house? I didn't know. I got out my mobile.

c

We ran down the hill to the road. We wanted to catch a bus, but it didn't arrive.

It was very cold and almost dark. We walked to the village.

We wanted a lift to the city, but we couldn't find one. We walked for a long time.

d

Suddenly, the phone rang.

'Hi, John. Can you meet me at the club?' said Lee.

John walked sadly to the club. 'Lee doesn't remember it's my birthday,' he thought. When he went in, all his friends were waiting for him.

'Happy birthday, John!' they shouted.

Everything was ready for a party. John was very surprised. At the end, he thanked his friends.

e

'It's a secret,' he answered. 'But I can tell you that it's dangerous. A journalist went to meet this man last year. We haven't seen him since he got into the man's car. I'm meeting him in a park. My friends are already hiding behind the trees. I must go now.'

f

One night last week she caught a mouse. When I opened the back door she was sitting on the step with the mouse in her mouth. She dropped it at my feet. I didn't know what to do. I didn't want to touch it.

Sheba went into the house and fell asleep on my chair. I put on some gloves and picked up the mouse.

Sample answers for Writing folder Unit 20

When I reached the station, the train had left. I looked at the station clock and then I looked at my watch and I realised it was slow. My friend had caught the train to Manchester and I had missed it. I dialled her number but she had switched it off. So I decided to go to the bus station and catch a bus to Manchester. I was running down the road towards the bus station when I saw someone running towards me. It was my friend. She was very late. So we caught the next train together.

I found the book on my way home from school. I noticed it in a rubbish bin. It looked very old. I sat on the grass and looked at the pictures, which were of African animals. They were very beautiful. When I got home, I put it in my bedroom and forgot about it. A few months later my mother was looking for something in my room and she found the book. 'Where did you get this?' she asked, and I explained. She recognised the artist – it was my great-grandfather who lived in Africa. So now I own a very special book.

We took the wrong turning off the main road. The road climbed up the mountain and became very narrow. We decided to go back but then we saw something yellow a few metres from the road. We stopped the car and got out. It was a climber. He had broken his leg and couldn't move. It was very cold and lonely on the mountain. We carried him to our car and took him to the hospital in the next town. We went to visit him the next day. He asked us for our address and he sent us some flowers.

When we arrived at the hotel, the owner looked very worried. 'The room you booked isn't available, so you have to go to the hotel next door.' We were annoyed because the hotel next door didn't have a good view of the sea. We carried our bags next door. We noticed there were lots of people with cameras and microphones in the hotel. They were making a film in the hotel. They needed some people to be hotel guests in the film, so we are now film actors. We were pleased we had to change to a different hotel.

Sample answer for Writing folder Unit 24

Dear Alessia,

I went to a concert last week. My friend Ivana invited me to go with her. I like listening to her CDs, so I know we like the same kind of music.

The band was called *Red Boots*. I hadn't heard of them before but they were amazing. They all wore really fantastic clothes and red boots with high heels. They had extraordinary hair, too.

The singer was a tiny woman with a very unusual voice. The band played electric violins and drums. It was a strange sound, but exciting. Some of the songs were well known and others were written by the band.

It was an excellent evening.

See you soon,
Mia

Sample answers for Writing folder Unit 30 (Part 2)

Dear Jerry,

My friends and I are going to the cinema next Friday to see an adventure film called Danger Country. Would you like to come with us? We're meeting at 6.15 in the café next to the cinema.

Hope you can come.
Daniel

Sample answer for Writing folder Unit 30 (Part 3)

Dear Kim,

Thank you for your letter. You're very lucky because you can choose your holiday. Both places are good, I think, but in different ways.

If I had your choice, I would go to the seaside with your friend's family. You will be with your friend, so that will be fun. Also, you will see a new place. It would be great to be at the seaside in the summer weather.

On the other hand, if you don't go away with your family, perhaps you will miss them. Have you talked to your parents? What do they say?

Love,
Nancy

Sample answer for Writing folder Unit 30 (Part 3)

When we set out, the sky was blue and the sun was shining. My friends owned the boat and they went sailing every weekend. At first, I enjoyed it. The water was calm and the sun was hot, but suddenly the sun was covered by clouds and it started to rain. It also became windy. I was very frightened but my friends were pleased because sailing was boring without the wind. After two hours, we could see the beach again. I decided that I didn't really like sailing but my friends went again the next day.

Photocopiable activities

Unit 4 Activity *Time expressions*

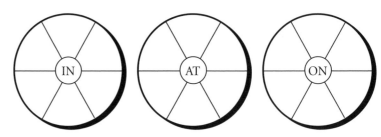

MY BIRTHDAY	THE MORNING	SUNDAY	THE WINTER	✱	FOUR O'CLOCK	JUNE
✱			5TH JUNE		?	THE WEEKEND
LUNCHTIME			1999			FRIDAY
2014			TUESDAYS	AUGUST	THE SPRING	✱
THE EVENING			✱	?	?	MONDAY MORNING
✱			THE END OF THE WEEK			2.30
THURSDAY EVENING	THE MOMENT	MIDNIGHT	✱	24TH APRIL	NIGHT	**START**

© CAMBRIDGE UNIVERSITY PRESS 2010

Unit 5 Activity *What do I need?*

make a cup of coffee	play tennis	sing a song	go for a walk	play a computer game
write a letter	have a shower	cook a meal	have a party	paint a picture
do your homework	have a swim	walk in the mountains	take a photograph	buy a jacket

Unit 5 Activity *Compound nouns*

Card A

boarding	sleeping	departure	address	adventure
lorry	computer	traffic	mobile	shop
flight	film	night	carrier	town
driving	police	rock	business	home

Card B

game	phone	pass	film	driver
book	lounge	bag	lights	assistant
student	town	club	test	hall
festival	attendant	star	officer	bag

Unit 6 Activity *Past simple Bingo*

Caller's cards

arrive	be	become	begin	check	come	feel	fly
find	get	give	go	grow	hear	kiss	like
look	make	meet	mend	need	run	sing	see
show	shut	start	stop	take	tell	walk	work

Student's cards

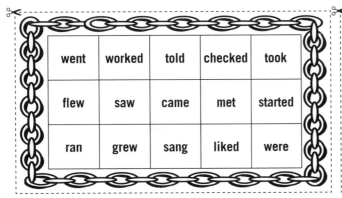

went	worked	told	checked	took
flew	saw	came	met	started
ran	grew	sang	liked	were

made	checked	liked	told	needed
walked	went	ran	were	took
sang	became	saw	got	started

stopped	shut	were	sang	heard
met	felt	went	kissed	grew
told	looked	became	took	needed

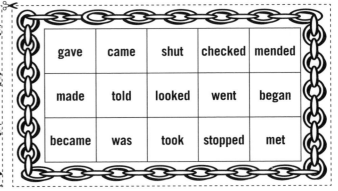

gave	came	shut	checked	mended
made	told	looked	went	began
became	was	took	stopped	met

began	took	worked	found	sang
ran	was	shut	gave	showed
saw	kissed	met	arrived	went

told	walked	shut	was	arrived
kissed	heard	began	saw	got
found	showed	ran	mended	felt

PHOTOCOPIABLE ACTIVITIES

Unit 7 Activity *Comparatives Snap*

nice	wide	safe	cheap	short
long	tall	friendly	busy	tidy
pretty	happy	slim	hot	sad
wet	serious	expensive	intelligent	interesting

er	er	er	er	er
r	r	r	r	r
y ier	y ier	y ier	y ier	y ier
more	more	more	more	more
mer	mer	mer	ter	ter
ter	ter	der	der	der

© CAMBRIDGE UNIVERSITY PRESS 2010

Unit 7 Activity _Mazes_

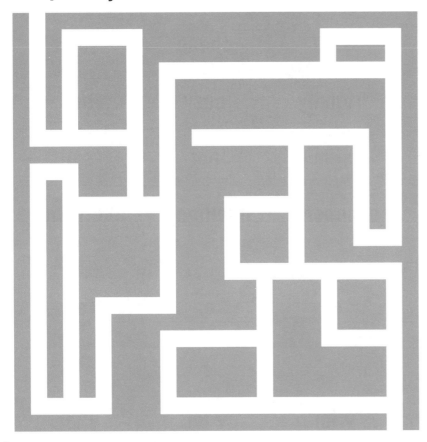

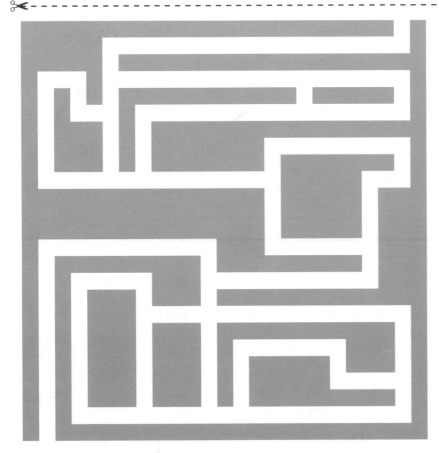

Unit 9 Activity *Illnesses*

You've hurt your knee.	Your shoulder hurts.
You've cut your hand.	You've got a pain in your foot.
You've got a headache.	You've got a sore elbow.
You feel sick.	You've got a cough.
You've got toothache.	You've got a cold.
You've got stomach ache.	You've got a temperature.
You've got a sore throat.	You've got a pain in your ankle.
You've got earache.	You've got a sore thumb.
You've got a sore finger.	You've broken your leg.
Your neck hurts.	You've broken your arm.

Unit 9 Activity *Giving and receiving advice*

Problem: When I play tennis with my friend, I always lose. Advice: Why don't you advertise in the newspaper?	**Problem: When I go cycling I'm very slow because my bicycle is very old.** Advice: You shouldn't lend him any money again.	**Problem: I fell off my bicycle and hurt my head.** Advice: Why don't you have some extra lessons? I know a really good maths teacher.
Problem: I like playing computer games but after a few hours I always have a headache. Advice: You shouldn't ride without a helmet.	**Problem: I want to be an engineer but I got a bad mark in my maths exam.** Advice: Why don't you have some lessons at the sports club before you play another game?	**Problem: Every time I lend my friend some money, he forgets to give it back to me.** Advice: You'd better apologise to her.
Problem: My car makes a strange noise when I drive fast. Advice: You shouldn't play for hours.	**Problem: I've got earache but I want to go swimming this afternoon.** Advice: Why don't you buy a new one and give the old one away?	**Problem: When I visit my grandmother she always cooks the same food. She thinks I like it.** Advice: You'd better invite them too.
Problem: I'm having a party next week but my neighbours always complain about the noise. Advice: You'd better take it to a mechanic. I know a really good one.	**Problem: I forgot to meet my friend last week and she refuses to speak to me.** Advice: You'd better buy her a new recipe book.	**Problem: I want to join a rock group but I don't know any other musicians.** Advice: You shouldn't go swimming. You'd better go to see the doctor.

How healthy are you?

100	← 99	← 98	← 97	← 96	← 95	← 94		← 93	← 92	← 91
Well done!	Do you exercise three times a week? 100←YES NO→77					Do you sleep at least seven hours every night? 96←YES NO→86				

81	→ 82	→ 83	→ 84	85	→ 86	→ 87	→ 88	→ 89	→ 90
			Do you eat fresh fruit every day? 47←NO YES→93						

80	← 79	← 78	← 77	← 76	75	← 74	← 73	← 72	← 71
				Did you eat two or more burgers last week? 82←NO YES→30					

61	→ 62	63	→ 64	→ 65	→ 66	→ 67	→ 68	→ 69	→ 70
	Did you eat any vegetables yesterday? 37←NO YES→83								Have you got a car? 45←YES NO→79

60	← 59	← 58	← 57	56	← 55	← 54	← 53	← 52	← 51
			Do you put extra salt on your food? 69←NO YES→42						

41	→ 42	→ 43	→ 44	→ 45	→ 46	47	→ 48	→ 49	→ 50
					Have you got more than one TV in your house? 33←YES NO→58			Do you and your family go for walks together? 36←NO YES→59	

40	← 39	38	← 37	← 36	← 35	← 34	← 33	← 32	← 31
	Are you a member of a sports club? 65←YES NO→22								

21	→ 22	→ 23	→ 24	→ 25	→ 26	→ 27	→ 28	→ 29	→ 30
					Have you got a bicycle? 7←NO YES→72				

20	← 19	18	← 17	← 16	← 15	← 14	← 13	← 12	← 11
		Do you love chocolate? 24←NO YES→8							Are you keen on computer games? 52←NO YES→3

1	→ 2	→ 3	→ 4	→ 5	6	→ 7	→ 8	→ 9	→ 10
					Do you and your friends enjoy dancing? 1←NO YES→21				

Start here

Unit 11 Activity *Numbers*

453	120,986	45,703	5,609	4,987,000	65,000,000
46,760	8,964	475	542	129,843	11,376
34	12	145,900	3,000,000,000	990,802	32,600,000
5,431	1,298	65,780	346,120	4,760	316

Unit 13 Activity *Comparing pictures*

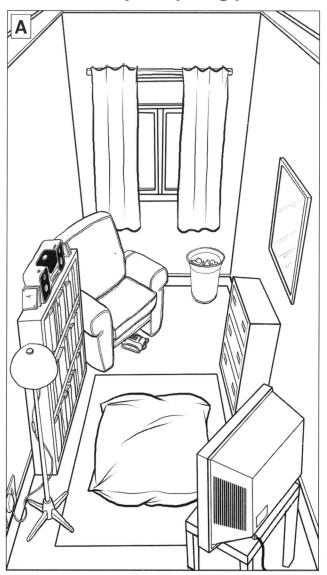

Unit 15 Activity *Jobs*

postman/woman	actor/actress	taxi driver
website designer	hairdresser	clown
manager of a pop group	model	pilot
salesperson	mechanic	musician
flight attendant	detective	teacher
politician	dentist	spy

Unit 15 Activity *Adverbs*

angrily	lazily	shyly	quickly	happily
slowly	quietly	urgently	loudly	nervously
secretly	sleepily	miserably	seriously	excitedly

Unit 16 Activity *I'm going to ...*

You're going to go to a party.	You're going to have a long, relaxing bath.
You're going to swim twenty kilometres.	You're going to ride a motorbike.
You're going to go skiing.	You're going to paint a picture of someone.
You're going to make a cake.	You're going to have a barbecue.
You're going to dance in a ballet.	You're going to take a photo of a large group of people.
You're going to show your car to someone who is interested in buying it.	You're going to go camping.
You're going to get married.	You're going to take part in a television show.
You're going to cut down a large tree.	You're going to go sky-diving.

Unit 18 Activity *Telling a story*

Unit 18 Activity *Films*

1 In which film is the post delivered by owls?
2 Which film hero is known as *007*?
3 What kind of films did Charlie Chaplin star in?
4 Which film tells the story of a disaster that happened in the Atlantic Ocean in 1912?
5 A scientist made a monster from dead bodies. It starred in more than 100 films. What was the name of the scientist?

6 What was the name of the first full-length Disney cartoon film?
7 Where was *Lord of the Rings* filmed?
8 Which animal appears at the beginning of MGM films?
9 When was the first film produced with sound?
10 Which country makes the most films in a year?

Unit 19 Activity *Families*

Your name is Jack. You have two brothers. You are the youngest. You aren't married.

Your name is Ben. You have two brothers. You are the middle one. You aren't married.

Your name is Sam. You have two brothers. You are the eldest. You aren't married.

Your name is Julia. You are married and you have three sons. Your sons aren't married.

Your name is Paul. You are married and you have three sons. Your sons aren't married.

Youe name is Simon. You aren't married and you have two sisters – one older and one younger than you.

Your name is Robert. You are married and you have one son and one daughter.

Your name is Emma. You are married and you have one son and one daughter.

Your name is Tom. You have one younger sister and no brothers.

Your name is Rosa. You have one older brother and no sisters.

Your name is John. You are married and you have two daughters and one son.
Your daughters are married but your son isn't.

Your name is Jane. You are married and you have two daughters and one son.
Your daughters are married but your son isn't.

Unit 23 Activity *Relative clauses*

a motorbike	Thailand	a doctor
a mother	a tomato	a door
a map	tennis	a daughter
milk	a taxi driver	a dancer
money	a ticket	a drum
Mexico	a tooth	a director
a millionaire	a trumpet	a dishwasher
a metre	trainers	a desert
coffee	Spain	a post office
a cinema	a soldier	a pen
a cloud	a sister	a police officer
a concert	a shower	a planet
a cousin	shorts	a photograph
a comedy	a soap opera	a poem
Chile	shampoo	Poland
a city	a station	a present

Unit 24 Activity *Past passive*

Group A: List of inventions

Matches	the first century	USA
The microwave oven	1800	Italy
The shopping trolley	1876	China
The telephone	1936	USA
The electric battery	1945	Scotland

Group B: List of inventions

The zip	1456	France
The bicycle	1565	USA
Printing	1913	USA
The electric guitar	1869	Germany
The pencil	1936	Switzerland

Answers to Group A's questions: to be given to Group B

Matches were invented in the first century in China.

The microwave oven was invented in 1945 in the USA.

The shopping trolley was invented in 1936 in the USA.

The telephone was invented in 1876 in Scotland.

The electric battery was invented in 1800 in Italy.

Answers to Group B's questions: to be given to Group A

The zip was invented in 1913 in the USA.

The bicycle was invented in 1869 in France.

Printing was invented in 1456 in Germany.

The electric guitar was invented in 1936 in the USA.

The pencil was invented in 1565 in Switzerland.

Unit 24 Activity *Describing objects*

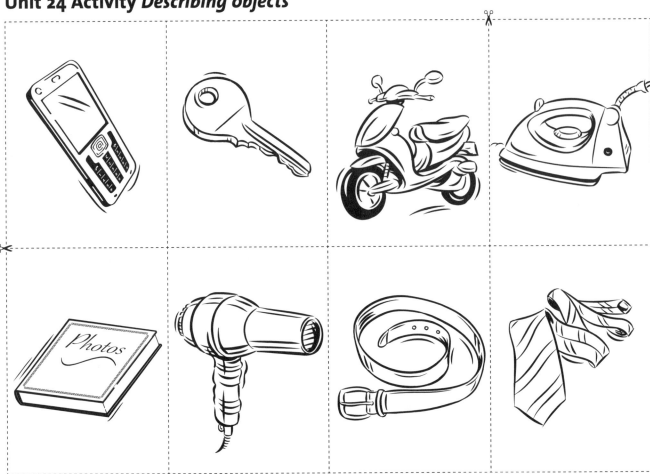

Unit 25 Activity *A new jacket*

A Hello. Can I help you? Yes, we do. They're over there by the shirts.	**1** It's too tight. Do you have a larger size?
B Would you like to try on some of these? What size are you? Of course, the fitting room is in the corner.	**2** Oh, yes please. Do you have any cotton jackets?
C How does that feel? I'm not certain, but I'll go and have a look for you.	**3** But I want to wear it with another pair too. Can I bring it back if I change my mind?
D That fits you perfectly. And the colour matches your trousers. Yes, if you keep the receipt we can give you a refund.	**4** 38, I think. Or perhaps 40. Can I try both?

PHOTOCOPIABLE ACTIVITIES

Unit 27 Activity *Word-building Snap*

Set 1

after	air	arm	base	basket	bed
business	boy	card	class	cross	cup
ear	foot	girl	handle	hair	head
home	house	in	key	motor	news
note	notice	out	over	pass	police
post	pull	rail	round	sales	sea
sign	snow	sun	thunder	time	to
tooth	under	week	wheel	wind	

Set 2

about	ache	ball	bars	bike	board
book	brush	card	chair	cut	day
doors	dresser	dryer	end	friend	glasses
ground	light	line	man	mail	night
noon	over	pants	paper	paste	port
post	ring	rise	roads	room	screen
shade	side	storm	surfing	table	take
way	wife	woman	work		

Unit 29 Activity *Agreeing and disagreeing*

Unit 30 Activity *Different topics*

CLOTHES	COUNTRIES	MUSICAL INSTRUMENTS	COLOURS	JOBS
THE BODY	FURNITURE	SCHOOL SUBJECTS	PLACES	FOOD
TRAVEL	FEELINGS	SPORTS	ANIMALS	FAMILIES

A	B	C	D	H
L	M	N	P	P
R	S	S	T	T

Unit 30 Activity *After doing that ...*

© CAMBRIDGE UNIVERSITY PRESS 2010

PHOTOCOPIABLE ACTIVITIES

Unit 30 *Pronunciation*

Caller's cards

cut *(rhyming words: much / some / lunch / dull / sun / fun)*	**cost** *(rhyming words: sock / want / watch / wash / clock)*	**bag** *(rhyming words: sat / black / man / bad / hat)*	**March** *(rhyming words: card / large / heart / can't / park)*	**town** *(rhyming words: round / down / how / house / found)*
sport *(rhyming words: walk / board / ball / warm / tall / bought)*	**tell** *(rhyming words: send / leg / left / ten / red)*	**day** *(rhyming words: take / great / train / pain / break)*	**hill** *(rhyming words: in / milk / sit / will / fish / film)*	**eat** *(rhyming words: please / street / leave / feet / sea)*
book *(rhyming words: look / foot / pull / cook / full)*	**shoe** *(rhyming words: choose / blue / pool/ roof / food / fruit)*	**bird** *(rhyming words: heard / shirt / earth / work / nurse / purse)*	**boat** *(rhyming words: throat / phone / show / slow / snow)*	**say** *(rhyming words: take / great / train / pain / break)*
like *(rhyming words: fine / line / fly / try / night / mine)*	**goal** *(rhyming words: throat / phone / show / slow / snow)*	**cheese** *(rhyming words: please / street / leave / feet / sea)*	**chip** *(rhyming words: in / milk / sit / will / fish / film)*	**hall** *(rhyming words: walk / board / ball / warm / tall / bought)*
wet *(rhyming words: send / leg / left / ten / red)*	**come** *(rhyming words: much / some / lunch / dull / sun / fun)*	**map** *(rhyming words: sat / black / man / bad / hat)*	**out** *(rhyming words: round / down / how / house / found)*	**girl** *(rhyming words: heard / shirt / earth / work / nurse / purse)*
long *(rhyming words: sock / want / watch / wash / clock)*	**car** *(rhyming words: card / large / heart / laugh / park)*	**cry** *(rhyming words: fine / line / fly / try / night / mine)*	**good** *(rhyming words: look / foot / pull / cook / full)*	**school** *(rhyming words: choose / blue / pool / roof / food / fruit)*

Students' cards

some	how	ball	send	sit
feet	sock	sat	large	train
blue	look	throat	work	night

slow	milk	bad	card	round
fun	tall	cook	want	left
foot	pain	shirt	line	street

snow	fruit	break	can't	pool
red	pull	try	leave	warm
wash	dull	down	in	heard

film	full	choose	please	phone
nurse	mine	ten	take	heart
man	much	house	board	clock

sea	bought	watch	hat	leg
clock	fly	park	great	roof
phone	fish	earth	found	sun

lunch	walk	sock	round	leg
train	large	black	look	food
show	fine	purse	will	feet

Acknowledgements

The authors and publishers acknowledge the following sources of copyright material and are grateful for the permissions granted. While every effort has been made, it has not always been possible to identify the sources of all the material used, or to trace all copyright holders. If any omissions are brought to our notice, we will be happy to include the appropriate acknowledgements on reprinting.

p 124: activity adapted from an idea in *Activity Box* by Jean Greenwood, Cambridge University Press; p 174 (and also p 28): activity adapted from an idea in *The Grammar Activity Book* by Bob Obee, Cambridge University Press.

Illustrations by Tom Croft, Mark Duffin, Julian Mosedale, Martin Sanders, Nigel Sanderson